THE TAMBURITZA TRADITION

Languages and Folklore of the Upper Midwest

JOSEPH SALMONS *and* JAMES P. LEARY, *Series Editors*

Published in collaboration with the Center for the Study of Upper
Midwestern Cultures at the University of Wisconsin–Madison

The Tamburitza Tradition: From the Balkans to the American Midwest
RICHARD MARCH

Wisconsin Talk: Linguistic Diversity in the Badger State
Edited by THOMAS PURNELL, ERIC RAIMY,
and JOSEPH SALMONS

THE TAMBURITZA TRADITION

From the Balkans to the American Midwest

RICHARD MARCH

THE UNIVERSITY OF WISCONSIN PRESS

The University of Wisconsin Press
1930 Monroe Street, 3rd Floor
Madison, Wisconsin 53711-2059
uwpress.wisc.edu

3 Henrietta Street
London WC2E 8LU, England
eurospanbookstore.com

Printed in the United States of America

Library of Congress Cataloging-in-Publication Data

March, Richard, 1946–
The tamburitza tradition : from the Balkans to the American Midwest /
Richard March.
p.   cm — (Languages and folklore of the Upper Midwest)
Includes bibliographical references and index.
ISBN 978-0-299-29604-9 (pbk. : alk. paper) — ISBN 978-0-299-29603-2 (e-book)
1. Tambura (Fretted lute)—History. 2. Tambura (Fretted lute)—Balkan Peninsula.
3. Tambura (Fretted lute)—United States. 4. Tambura (Fretted lute) music—
History and criticism. 5. Folk music—Balkan Peninsula—History and criticism.
6. Folk music—Middle West—History and criticism. I. Title. II. Series:
Languages and folklore of the Upper Midwest.
ML1015.T3M37   2013
787.8′21629181—dc23
2013015067

Živjeli tamburaši

Contents

Illustrations

Preface

This book was a long time in coming, which is responsible for some of its peculiarities. My formal research for this work began in 1975 when Dr. Richard M. Dorson, my professor at the Folklore Department of Indiana University, received funding from the National Endowment for the Humanities to conduct research on the urban folklore of the Calumet Region of northwest Indiana. He assembled a team of several researchers drawn from his graduate students, nicknamed the "Gary Gang" after the steel-mill town where we did much of our research. At that time, team research was a virtually unknown practice among the corps of highly individualistic American folklorists. Dr. Dorson was a scholar of folk narrative with a historical orientation. He selected folklorists for the research team with other specializations (i.e., music, material culture, visual ethnography) to augment his own strengths.

From preliminary research Dr. Dorson was aware of and interested in the large Serbian American and Croatian American communities of the Calumet Region. He recruited me because I can speak Croatian and already had familiarity with Croatian American and Serbian American traditional culture. I am Croatian American and I have cousins who are Serbian American. My mother was a Croatian immigrant; my maternal grandmother lived in our household. From them I learned basic "kitchen language" in the local dialect in which my mother and grandmother chatted daily. We were active participants in the Croatian

Fraternal Union, an ethnic lodge. We frequently attended their dinners, dances, concerts, and summertime picnics at which Croatian music, especially tamburitza music, was ever present.

Listening to my grandmother's reminiscences about her life and the daily work routines in Nerezine, her home village on an Adriatic island, aroused my interest in Croatian folk culture. I heard tamburitza music at the ethnic events we attended, and family members told me that my late uncles used to have a tamburitza ensemble. My Aunt Agnes was a singer in Croatian operettas and the on-air hostess of a Croatian radio program that emphasized tamburitza. My mother, Jane March, was a singer in the Slavulj Croatian Choir in Los Angeles. I always felt a personal connection to the tradition.

I became a musician, but tamburitza was not my emphasis. As a boy I played violin in the school orchestra and also played *domra*, a Russian instrument, in a balalaika orchestra that rehearsed in my neighborhood. From my teenage years on I played guitar and other stringed instruments in the folk, blues, and rock scenes of the 1960s and 1970s.

As an undergraduate at the University of California at Berkeley, I studied the literary Croatian language to improve upon my rudimentary knowledge of the family dialect. The language knowledge I attained in college prepared me to enroll in the ethnology program at Zagreb University from 1971 to 1973. There, I learned much from the renowned professors Dr. Milovan Gavazzi, Dr. Branimir Bratanić, and then-*Asistent* Aleksandra Muraj. I became acquainted with numerous fellow students, several of whom became professional ethnologists, my lifetime friends, and colleagues. In Zagreb I enlisted some Croatian sidemen and started a band, playing American blues and country music. We were reasonably successful, getting frequent gigs and a few media appearances. Through this activity I met many musicians who played in a variety of genres including tamburitza.

In 1973 I was offered a fellowship to do graduate study at Indiana University and returned to the United States; by 1975 I was part of Dr. Dorson's "Gary Gang." It was inevitable that tamburitza would become a major focus of my research in the Calumet Region, but that likelihood was enhanced by a coincidence. My brother William March was a professor of Slavic languages at the University of Kansas. He told me

Uncle John Grbac posing with his tambura, Chicago, ca. 1930. (Richard March Collection)

Aunt Agnes Daniels in the studio of WJBK, Detroit, ca. 1945. She was the on-air host of *The Croatian Radio Hour* in that city for more than a decade. (Richard March Collection)

that the father of one of his students (Karen Opacich) was a tamburitza maker and musician in the Calumet Region. Milan Opacich (1928–2013) turned out to be an ideal informant. Generous with his deep knowledge and his time, Milan introduced me also to a dozen or more other *tamburaši* from the area.

During the two academic years from 1975 to 1977, I made more trips than I can count from Indiana University in Bloomington to the

Calumet Region, almost always stopping for a while at Milan's work-shop to get the latest news on the local tamburitza scene. In 1977 I completed my graduate studies in Indiana and, with Dr. Dorson's en-couragement as chairman of my dissertation committee, I applied for and received fellowships from International Research and Exchanges as well as Fulbright-Hays to conduct research for my PhD dissertation in Yugoslavia—on the tamburitza tradition.

In 1977–78, I was graciously hosted in Zagreb by the research center that currently is named the Ethnology and Folklore Institute (Institut za etnologiju i folkloristiku). In addition to office space and the free-dom to peruse their extensive library and archives, I had frequent stim-ulating discussions with helpful colleagues Krešo Galin, Stjepan Sremac, Olga Supek, and especially with Zorica Vitez, Jerko Bezić (1929–2010), and Dunja Rihtman-Auguštin (1926–2002). Moreover, they facilitated my fieldwork with many useful suggestions, contacts in the field, and even occasional joint field trips.

I had the opportunity to conduct research in several regions of Cro-atia, in Vojvodina, and in Bosnia. My field research was facilitated by my insider-outsider status: the combination of my family background (even my physical appearance is quickly recognized as Croatian), my earlier connections to the United States and Croatian tamburitza scenes, and my own musical abilities. (I even had opportunities to perform as a member of a tamburitza orchestra in the Croatian city of Sisak, like Gary, a steel-mill town.)

When I returned to the United States in 1978, my life took a differ-ent direction. I lived in Milwaukee, Wisconsin, from 1978 to 1983, and there I had the opportunity to observe and participate in the active tamburitza scene in and around that city. Between helping care for my son, Nikola, who was born in 1980, and full- and part-time jobs, with the help of my former wife, Mary Bruce, I managed to complete a draft of *The Tamburitza Tradition* in May 1981. I brought the manuscript to Dr. Dorson in Bloomington. I was shocked and saddened when a month later Dr. Dorson suffered a massive, fatal heart attack.

A few months later, Dr. Ilhan Basgoz agreed to become chairman of my dissertation committee. Dr. Basgoz acknowledged that I had written the work under Dr. Dorson's guidance, and it was obvious that the dissertation addressed Dr. Dorson's interests. Although his own scholarly approach was different, Dr. Basgoz requested relatively few changes. I defended the dissertation early in 1983 to earn my PhD.

In 1983, academic positions for a folklorist were limited. In July of that year, I was hired by the Wisconsin Arts Board to be that state agency's folk arts specialist. I enjoyed a twenty-five-year career in public folklore, working to enhance the appreciation and ensure the continued vitality of the folk arts of all the peoples of Wisconsin. My efforts included occasional work with *tamburaši* in the Midwest. Moreover, I became active in the Croatian Fraternal Union and a member of the Milwaukee-based Graničari adult tamburitza orchestra. In this way I kept abreast of developments on the tamburitza scene.

In 2003 Naila Ceribašić, my colleague from the Ethnology and Folklore Institute in Zagreb, suggested that I write an article on more recent developments in the tamburitza tradition. I did so, writing "My Little (Global) Village" for the journal *Narodna umjetnost*. Subsequently Naila suggested that I rewrite and bring up-to-date the entire dissertation. In

Richard March playing *brač* with the tamburitza orchestra of the Independent Crafts Guild, Sisak, Croatia, October 1977. (Richard March Collection)

2007 I was invited to present a paper on tamburitza, drawing from my previous and more recent research, at "Croatian Music of the 20th Century," a symposium in Zagreb, organized by Matica Hrvatska, an important Croatian cultural institute. Material from the "My Little (Global) Village" article and the Matica Hrvatska symposium paper are incorporated into this present book.

Writing in the early 1980s, I addressed issues concerning "authenticity," which were current in the field of folklore at that time, and discussed them in terms of the extant literature. My update of the work has been based largely on my ongoing personal experience as a participant in the tamburitza tradition, on more recent relevant scholarship, and on the wealth of new information created by tamburitza enthusiasts and made available on the Internet.

Over the past three decades, theoretical issues have been addressed in academic work in the humanities and social sciences, which have raised concerns regarding the roles of scholars and of scholarship itself as actors in the cultural matrix that is their object of study. The point is particularly applicable to my work as I have endeavored to be transparent with reference to my own role as an insider-outsider raised in the culture I studied. Moreover, especially in the fieldwork-based section of this book, I endeavored to reveal the experiential process and my interactions with participants in the tradition that have been the main sources from which I learned.

The lion's share of my fieldwork was conducted by a process of immersion in the tradition, frequent conversations with other participants, and by attending and observing events, taking a few field notes, snapping some photographs. By comparison, I did little recording of formal interviews or systematic media documentation of events. I include in the text many remembered statements from my informants with the approximate date of the conversation.

Of all the people and institutions mentioned earlier, Naila Ceribašić undoubtedly deserves the most credit for instigating this project and for toiling with me to improve my manuscript. Thanks also to Ivan Lozica, director of the Ethnology and Folklore Institute, for his support of the publication of the Croatian-language version of the book. Thanks also to Matica Hrvatska for reinvigorating my tamburitza enthusiasm by inviting me to speak at their 2007 "Croatian Music of the 20th Century" symposium. Thanks also to my longtime colleague and collaborator Jim Leary. Our discussions over the years concerning our shared passion—the traditional and ethnic musics in the Midwest—have been crucial to my capacity to undertake this effort. Equally crucial has been his canny perception that my transatlantic work nonetheless fits well into the series, of which he is an editor, sponsored by the Center for the Study of Upper Midwestern Cultures devoted to midwestern traditional music. Thanks to the Mills Music Library at the University of Wisconsin and to the University of Wisconsin Press, especially its staff Sheila Leary, Raphael Kadushin, and Matthew Cosby, for helping me to improve the manuscript. And I give many thanks also to my wife, Nikki Mandell, for her unwavering support and encouragement.

A Note on Language Usage

The terminology of the tamburitza tradition draws on words and linguistic rules from three languages. Throughout this book I use Serbian or Croatian words that are commonly used in English-language discourse about the tamburitza tradition. I have employed the terms as they are habitually used by American participants in the tradition. For some terms, like the word "tamburitza" itself, an anglicized spelling has become common, but the original spelling *tamburica* also is frequently encountered. Pronunciation varies too with some Americans using the English short "ă" sound in the terms and others employ the Slavic long "ā."

When forming the plural, in some cases, the Slavic plural is used—for example, *tamburaš*, a tamburitza player, becomes *tamburaši*, tamburitza players; tambura, singular, becomes *tambure*, plural. (The -i ending is the plural for masculine words, the -e ending is for feminine words.) In other cases, the -s plural ending from English is applied to Slavic words, for example, tamburitzas, instead of *tamburice*, or *bračes* instead of *bračevi* for the *brač* instrument. The plural of kolo, a line dance, is usually kolos in English rather than the Slavic plural *kola* (-a is the neuter gender plural).

Another issue is differences between the Serbian and Croatian place names; for example, a historical province divided between Serbia and Croatia is Srem in Serbian and Srijem in Croatian. For geographic names, if there is a common English version, like Belgrade (rather than Beograd), I use it. If not, I use the Croatian form. As is common in a discourse that blends elements from two or three different languages, usage varies from person to person, and even a single individual may be inconsistent. Readers may find the glossary at the end of the book to be helpful.

THE TAMBURITZA TRADITION

Homelands of the Tamburitza. (Map by author)

Introduction

Six young men, their faces stern with concentration, are picking out the fast and intricate melody of a folk dance on their tamburitzas, fretted stringed instruments that range in size from smaller than a mandolin to larger than a string bass. The musicians are wearing clean, pressed, pajama-like Slavonian folk costumes of coarse white linen with black vests and hats, but unlike their peasant forebears, they no longer use these costumes for daily wear. Today is a festive occasion, a regional folk fair. The young men are standing on an outdoor stage in a large park, in the most inconspicuous position possible—at the extreme rear corner of the stage. Although the musicians' skills are dazzling, they are not in the center of attention. The audience sitting outside in Slavonia's hot, early July wheat-ripening sun focuses its attention on the costumed folk dancers at center stage; their fast intricate steps seem to match the aesthetic of the intricate melody that the young musicians are playing.

Elsewhere, an octet of comfortably rotund Romani musicians strolls from table to table, some strumming a dynamic rhythmic accompaniment, others tickling intercascading countermelodies to the tune of a romantic song of sad love that they are singing. They receive generous tips from the patrons of this tavern, located in an old fort, only a stone's throw from where the Danube meanders across the broad Pannonian plains.

In yet another setting, nine men whose occupations range from truck driver to chemical engineer—amateur musicians all—are seated behind music stands, carefully sight-reading their parts to a recently penned "folk rhapsody." They are kept on tempo by the waving baton and out-loud counting of a high school music teacher hired to direct the group. Squeezed in beside the long table in the meeting room of the local artisans' guild, these men are devoting half of their weekday evenings to rehearsals for an upcoming community concert in their small industrial city in central Croatia.

In another small city thousands of miles away, in the steel city of America's great Midwest, school children are poring over sheet music, learning to pick out on their tamburitzas the right notes to a medley of well-known Croatian sentimental songs. They are instructed by a steel worker who is also a part-time professional musician and music teacher. He teaches a different group of youthful musicians four evenings per week.

A few more miles to the west, in an old-fashioned neighborhood bar and restaurant on the industrial southeast side of Chicago, four men, with modern, sponge-shielded microphones in front of them, nonchalantly sing and play "Hang on Sloopy," a recent rock 'n' roll hit accompanying themselves on beautiful old instruments, highly decorated with mother-of-pearl inlay, Farkaš-system tamburitzas created by the skilled hands of a master craftsman who took his apprenticeship in Graz, Austria, in the days of Franz Joseph.

The preceding musical events were characteristic of the tamburitza tradition in the 1970s and early 1980s when most of the research for this book was done. This folk tradition of the South Slavs has a recorded history extending back at least to the fifteenth century and is still the focal point of an active and expanding cultural movement. The tradition flourishes not only in the regions that contributed most heavily to the emergence and development of its present form—the Pannonian regions of former Yugoslavia: northern Croatia and Vojvodina—but also in other former Yugoslav lands where it has taken firm root wherever colonies of South Slavic, especially Croatian immigrants, have been established in many parts of Europe, North and South America, Australia, and New Zealand. In addition, the musical form has been adopted by non-Slavic enthusiasts for the tamburitza in cities as distant from southeastern Europe as Los Angeles, California, and Nagoya, Japan.

Today a type of tamburitza can still be found played by Balkan shepherds and wood-cutters; small tamburitza ensembles are an essential feature at village weddings in many regions. To an even greater extent, the tamburitza can be found in more urbane contexts. School orchestras and amateur "cultural and artistic societies" may play on the dusty square of a small town or on the stages of the finest concert halls. Professional Romani combos entertain in stylish restaurants and in dives. Radio orchestras and national folk dance troupes featuring the tamburitza perform on radio and TV and on international concert tours.

In North America, small ensembles entertain at weddings, christenings, and picnics. Children's orchestras perform in the halls of churches and ethnic lodges as well as at local folk fairs. Thus, the tamburitza tradition in its many manifestations, past and present, is the topic of this work.

Participant observation, library research, and interviews with informants were the principle research techniques. This study examines a folk tradition that continues to exist both in the original rural and the modern urban context. It is popular both in its original homeland and in immigrant enclaves in the United States and elsewhere. Among its practitioners are musicians who consciously perform tamburitza music as an expression of their past or ethnic heritage and those who perpetuate it simply through a love of music. This study describes culture change occurring in the course of urbanization and migration, relates social and economic change to change in a form of expressive culture, and examines the effect upon the expressive form of self-conscious awareness by the musicians and audience that the artistry represents their folklore heritage.

For many, including many participants in the tamburitza tradition, the question remains: Should this tradition be considered folklore? To answer we need a definition of folklore, but there has never been complete agreement among folklorists on a definition. Early definitions from nineteenth-century scholarship were based on mystical concepts: it was lore that spontaneously arose from a nation's soul or, according

to another school, survivals of savage thought-patterns from an earlier phase of human evolution (Dorson 1972, 18). These conceptions
have been rejected, for the most part, in later scholarship; as folklorist
Dan Ben-Amos has pointed out, the many definitions proposed by
twentieth-century folklorists tended to utilize three major characteristics of the lore as criteria: its social base (in common folk or peasantry),
its time depth (dating from antiquity), and its medium of transmission
(spreading orally or by imitation) (Ben-Amos 1971, 8).

Though there may be general agreement on these three criteria,
there is still considerable difference in emphasis by various folklore
scholars. For example, central European professors of folklore [*Volkskunde*] and the folklife specialists from the British Isles tend to emphasize a social base in the peasantry as the crucial criterion. It suits the
field data readily available to them; feudalism was finally abolished a
little more than two centuries ago, and central Europeans usually can
distinguish culture stemming from the feudal peasant class. Thus in
Europe, the concept of folklore is often identical to "peasant art," the
artistic aspects of traditional peasant life (Bošković-Stulli 1973).

While the Europeanists emphasize the arts of peasants, the African-
ists, or scholars who specialize in the folklore, anthropology, or ethnomusicology of the third world, emphasize time depth or traditionality
since they often investigate cultural phenomena in which partake both
the ruling elite and the common people of the societies they study
(e.g., d'Azebedo 1973). The class distinction is obscured.

Class distinctions are perhaps still vaguer to American folklorists
who work in a country that never knew actual feudalism. In addition,
the newer countries of the Americas have spawned more recent traditions so that Americanists emphasize neither a distinct peasant social
base nor great time depth but instead stress oral transmission as the
most crucial defining criterion of folklore (Dorson 1972).

These differences already are not inconsequential, yet the definition
question is further complicated by the emergence in the late 1960s of
a school of thought, spearheaded in articles by Dan Ben-Amos and
Robert Georges. They attempt to move away from defining folklore as
discrete objects and strive for a definition of folklore as a particular
process of small group communication (Ben-Amos 1971).

In terms of these varying but noncontradictory definitions, to what extent does the tamburitza tradition correspond to a strict definition of folklore? First, regarding the criterion stressed in Europe, the instrument, the music, and most of the repertoire performed stems from an origin in the peasant class; there can be no doubt that the tamburitza does not stem from an elite origin (Andrić 1968, 186). Second, the form of the instrument, much of the music, and many of the songs performed originated several decades or even more than a century ago, thus satisfying a second commonly cited criterion, time depth. Third, much of what the *tamburaš* learns is by ear, by listening to and imitating a mentor. In short, transmission through oral, aural, and imitative means is important to the tradition.

The preceding statements seem to place the tamburitza tradition in the realm of folklore, even according to stringent definitions. There are still some illiterate mountain shepherds who strum hoary melodies on simple handmade tamburitzas. These are, however, quite different aspects of the tamburitza tradition. To investigate only the nonliterate shepherd tambura player, one would have to ignore the most obvious manifestations of tamburitza, often in much more urbane contexts.

Today's tamburitza music is an expression of a more complicated way of life. For every shepherd musician whose rugged figure matches a romantic image of the primitive folk, there are dozens, perhaps hundreds, of educated and sophisticated *tamburaši*. For every player of the primitive *samica*, an instrument not suited for ensemble play and whose name means it is played solo, there are many more musicians who belong to large tamburitza orchestras who learn their repertoire from sheet music, which may include arranged folk songs in addition to elite compositions and transcriptions by classical composers like Franz Schubert or Aram Khachaturian (Kolar 1975, 76). Café entertainers use the tamburitza to perform an eclectic repertoire drawing on popular hits as well as traditional folk songs (Kuhač 1877). Even the primitive shepherd no longer seems so idyllic. Nowadays a shepherd is more likely to sing recently composed songs heard on the radio than old ballads of folk tradition. In the world of the present, the tamburitza has entered the mass media: radio and television broadcasts transmit the music across great distances so that sophisticated music can penetrate the most remote backwater. Recorded music travels still farther to reach distant audiences. Since the beginning of the twenty-first century, recordings and videos of tamburitza performances are being shared worldwide on the Internet. Once limited to oral transmission, the tradition has entered whatever medium of communication is available in its cultural environment.

The picture is further complicated because the tamburitza musicians of today have lost the innocence and purity attributed them by romantics. Nowadays the word "folklore" has entered the lexicon of most *tamburaši* along with a romantically based concept of what it means. Sometimes strident arguments rage between practitioners of the tradition as to whether a particular song, instrumental style, or form of presentation is "authentic folklore." Musicians make a conscious decision about whether to play new material or to stick to the old heritage. Many play both old and new, depending upon the context. Far from being a nonreflective, spontaneous creation as some scholars used to believe pure folklore should be, *tamburaši* make conscious, thoughtful choices to play this instrument, what to play on it, and how it should be played. A frequent criterion for the judgments of a significant segment of *tamburaši* is how it meets their concept of "authentic folklore" or "true national music" (Rihtman-Auguštin 1976, 11).

Finally, the forms of the instrument commonly in use today and how they are played (in ensembles of various-sized tamburitzas) trace their origins to the efforts of nineteenth-century nationalists, for the most part urbanites, who wanted, for political reasons, to "ennoble" Croatian culture with a folk-based but refined musical form, a proof of the autonomy of their national culture (Kuhač 1893). Suddenly the same tradition that once seemed folkloric—a spontaneous, orally transmitted traditional creation of the peasantry—now seems to be a forgery, the fabricated "folk soul" of a romantic nationalist movement, which is today spread by the entertainment industry.

Viewed holistically, either extreme view is untenable—that the tradition either is or is not folklore. The tamburitza tradition once existed as a "pure" folk tradition, but since the mid-nineteenth century the tradition has been saturated by the attempts of urban intellectuals to apply, modify, and convert folk music for use in cultural and political movements. Through their efforts, however, they promoted musical literacy, which, though never totally dominant, has become an important factor in the tamburitza tradition. In the days before sound recording devices, written notes made it possible to introduce new and varied musical ideas. Thousands of tamburitza students have learned to play using written music. Technical advances by instrument makers who became familiar with other fretted stringed instruments, such as the Spanish guitar or the Italian mandolin, transformed the tamburitza into a versatile instrument capable of playing a chromatic scale and executing new musical ideas.

Despite the efforts of the intellectuals or in some cases owing to their efforts, the folkloric tamburitza tradition continued to live on. Not only did some peasants remain uninfluenced and continue to make and play the original "primitive" forms of the instrument from which the nationalists had created the "ennobled" tamburitza, but the improved instrument, along with new songs and new musical ideas, have been selected, filtered, and adapted by the country folk to their own uses on the basis of their own aesthetics and placed in sociocultural niches of their own choosing. Small ensembles of peasant musicians used the "orchestral" tamburitza instruments to entertain at weddings, saint's days, and other village festivities, playing tunes and singing songs learned by ear, always a part of their local oral tradition. The peasant tamburitza ensembles and Romani bands spirited the music out the back door of the concert hall into which the intellectuals had endeavored to place it, and they brought it back, in a changed form, onto the village street or into the tavern and coffeehouse. Such ensembles moved into the traditional contexts occupied by the players of older traditional instruments (such as bagpipes in eastern Croatia or *guci* violin ensembles in central Croatia), sometimes completely replacing the older instruments in the local tradition.

There can be no simple yes or no answer to whether this music is or is not folklore, nor is it essential that there should be. The tamburitza tradition is an extant phenomenon, and it seems pointless to judge it in terms of preconceived criteria. What is important is that the theories and methodology of folklore study can fruitfully be utilized in research and analysis of the phenomenon.

~

The tamburitza tradition is a cultural form that emerged out of nearly a century and a half of continuous coexistence and mutual influence of a folk music tradition and a phenomenon that came to be known as folklorism. The term "folklorism" is the English translation of the German word *Folklorismus* (Greverus 1976, 183). In Europe the term carried negative connotations much like "fakelore," the term coined by American folklorist Richard M. Dorson to denote a genre of pseudo-folksy popular literature (Dorson 1972). To study folklorism's influence on tamburitza, there should be an objective understanding of folklorism, but unfortunately objectivity has been clouded by heated debate and condemnation of it coming from many folklore scholars and enthusiasts.

Warnings against the threatening ravages of folklorism appeared in the European press and even in scholarly journals. Maja Bošković-Stulli cited the titles of a few such diatribes: "Protiv lažnih narodnih pesama" (In opposition to false folk songs), "Stupidnost s okusom folklora" (Stupidity with the flavor of folklore), "Na raskršćima i razbojištima folklornog tržišta" (On the crossroads and crime scenes of the folklore marketplace), and, most impressive, "Borba protiv folklorizma jedan od uslova stvaralačkom razvitku savremenog folklora" (Struggle against folklorism is one of the prerequisites for the creative development of contemporary folklore) (Bošković-Stulli 1971, 171). In these Yugoslav-era examples, the titles revealed the overwhelmingly negative attitude toward folklorism articulated in Europe at that time.

Scholarly discussion of folklorism began in Germany in the early 1960s. In a pioneering article, Hans Moser suggested *Folklorismus* as an alternative to "applied folkloristics" (Bausinger 1961, 50–51). According to Moser, folklorism "involved a double phenomenon: general interest . . . in everything 'folk' and for all the pockets of 'folksiness' in which life still has particularity and authenticity, strength and color, or at least seems that it has" (Moser 1962, 180). Often relying on indirect transmission through the media, folklorism was usually presented in the form of selected attractive items that purported to originate in folk culture. Moser explained that where the "real substance" no longer exists, traditions may be invented (ibid.).

Though he proposed objective study of folklorism, Moser's negative feeling about it was strong and he lapsed into condemnations. He asserted that folklorism was "primarily commercial and firmly built into two very significant economic fields . . . the tourist and the entertainment industries" (ibid., 198–99). Books, sheet music, radio, and television broadcasts carry folklorism to its audience. Peasant handicrafts are marketed in urban department stores. Folklore ballet troupes perform stylized folk dances to an audience sitting beyond the footlights in concert halls.

According to Herman Bausinger, for something to be folklorism, "it is necessary that particular phenomena of folk culture be shown outside of their original base with new functions and purposes" (Bausinger 1969, 5). But Bausinger indicated that revived "folklore" may return to its original setting and resume its traditional function in a comparable cultural context. Such an occurrence Bausinger called "second existence" folklore, which he contended may be difficult to distinguish from folklorism or folklore. Bausinger held that there are no firm boundaries (Bausinger 1966, 70–71).

Bausinger was cautious regarding the much trumpeted "authenticity" of the folklore presented to the public. He noticed that in countries like the Yugoslavia of his era, where the agrarian economy had remained important, rural folk traditions remained a great part of cultural life in the form of revitalized folklore and folklorism. Scholarly ethnographic researchers were connected with the process of organizing events to exhibit peasant arts. Many of these researchers considered folklorism falsified kitsch, and they fully believed that there was an absolute standard to differentiate authentic folklore from folklorism. In this regard, Bausinger believed that the ethnographers and the less-schooled organizers of folkloric events were mistaken (Bausinger 1969, 2). The view of the event organizers was that folklore and folklorism were opposing phenomena. Folklore was pure, authentic, and "good"; folklorism was the degradation of authentic folklore and therefore "bad."

Ethnographers tended to "canonize" the form of a particular performance, often the earliest example to be documented in the ethnographic literature. They considered this example to be the *only* correct model for all subsequent performances of the folk arts of that locality. They ignored the fact that the original recorded performance might have been only one variant, created to fit a unique set of ephemeral contextual circumstances. For example, a village informant might have felt it appropriate to eliminate obscenities from a song's lyrics when being recorded by a university professor.

Insofar as staged performances were able to closely replicate an approved performance documented years ago, the ethnographic school viewed it as "authentic folklore," without regard to its context, not considering whether the performance took place on a village crossroads or on the stage of an opera house. The change of context did not render the performance as folklorism according to this view. And thus authentic folklore became folklorism, however, if the performers failed fully to emulate the original model.

Although contemporary scholars in the former Yugoslav republics have rejected these older notions regarding folklorism, proponents of these very notions had a significant influence on musicians and on members of folk dance groups and their audiences. As graduates of university ethnology programs, they held posts in museums, local administration bureaus, or cultural organizations. They were in direct contact with the performers; they organized folk festivals and set the criteria whereby a group might be eligible to participate. Some set up teacher-training systems, or were already teachers of folk dance and music groups. In this way, ethnographers directly intervened in the tradition. They were actors, not simply outside observers of cultural developments. They succeeded in gaining acceptance of their ideas among the public because they tended to be very dedicated and worked with fervor. Although discarded by contemporary scholars, the earlier ideas have had staying power among music and culture enthusiasts. The ideas that there is an absolute standard of right and wrong or that there exists a pure national heritage to be defended against pollution are easier to grasp than the more complex analysis of the process-oriented folklorists whose views now predominate in scholarship. Moreover, the earlier ethnographic concept ideally fit the underlying cultural and political aspirations that imbued the tamburitza tradition as well as other forms of folklorism: an assertion of the value and particularity of a national culture (Rihtman-Auguštin 1978).

In recent years, scholars whose view is attuned to the process-oriented theories of international folklore study have assumed leadership in staging major events like Zagreb's International Folklore Festival (Međunarodna Smotra folklora). They have relaxed the standards of "purity." Nowadays they include modern and hybrid artistic expressions in the festival program. The inclusion of modernisms and outside influences, which were anathema to the earlier ethnographers, they consider to be an inevitable consequence of cultural process, and indeed, evidence that the tradition is still vital, creative, and thriving.

Nonetheless, at the local level, the instructors of the "authentic folklore" groups who participate in the festivals usually still have the notion that there exist "canonized" versions of their local folk traditions, often preserved in written or media documents, which they carefully teach to insure the performances retain that fixed form. Moreover, the raison d'être of such groups is to present their locality's "authentic folklore" in a staged context. It is ironic that an influential segment of the "folk" has become the purists, and now the scholarly experts favor an eclectic viewpoint.

Existing literature on the tamburitza tradition is sparse. The earliest scholarly works on tamburitza are the treatises of Franjo Ks. Kuhač. His extensive descriptions of the *tamburaši* of the 1860s and 1870s are the earliest descriptive writings on the subject. Other early descriptions are contained in the ethnographic data assembled by Croatian ethnologists and their collaborants who used the ethnographic questionnaire assembled by Antun Radić, the founder of ethnology in Croatia, to describe as complete a picture as possible of village life. A few such writers mentioned the role of tamburitza in their descriptions of local village culture. The work of Ivan Lovretić in the Slavonian village of Otok is a good example (Lovretić 1897–1902).

The composer and musicologist Božidar Širola has a short section on tamburitza in his survey of Croatian folk music. Širola also documented the manufacture of *samice* in the Zagorje region (Širola 1935).

In the 1950s Josip Andrić, a tamburitza musician and composer, wrote several short, informative, historically oriented articles and a book on tamburitza music (e.g., Andrić 1955, 1955a, 1958, 1962, 1968). Julije Njikoš, an important composer of works for tamburitza, has written articles on the career of Josip Andrić, compiled numerous songbooks based on his field collections, and has written a biography of the most famous tamburitza pioneer, Pajo Kolarić (Njikoš 1995). Cvjetko Rihtman, from Sarajevo, has contributed important studies of soloistic tambura (Rihtman 1976).

In the 1990s Ruža Bonifačić wrote about the tamburitza as a Croatian patriotic symbol, not just historically but also importantly during the establishment of the independent Croatian state and the 1991–95 Homeland War (Bonifačić 1993, 1995). In his book *Tambura u Hrvata*, Siniša Leopold wrote a short history of tamburitza and compiled many Croatian folk songs (Leopold 1995). More recently, Nada Bezić produced a well-researched article with an emphasis on the development of musically literate tamburitza orchestras in Zagreb at the turn of the twentieth century (Bezić 2001).

In the United States, Walter W. Kolar, director of the Duquesne University Tamburitzans, has written a two-volume *History of the Tambura* (Kolar 1973, 1975). His work contains much specific data, the names and careers of individual American *tamburaši*, and for the European aspect, excerpts from the works of Kuhač and Andrić. Mark E. Forry discussed *tamburaši* and other South Slavic musicians in an article on *bećar* music in Los Angeles; in his doctoral dissertation on tamburitza in Vojvodina he analyzed notions of traditionality and self-conscious expressions of culture (Forry 1977, 1990). And I have written quite a few articles on tamburitza (March 1976, 1982, 1993, 2005, 2009).

This present book will attempt to be a broad, comprehensive study of the tamburitza tradition, emphasizing its historical and its current sociocultural aspects. The tamburitza has been known in the Balkans for five hundred years, but its recorded history has been spotty at best. Before the later nineteenth century, few literate people considered the tamburitza a matter of concern, hardly worth committing information about it to writing. Even in more recent times, little has been written about the instrument or the small groups and orchestras that use it. For many years, musicologists found tamburitza too crude, and ethnologists found it too modern.

Because of the paucity of synthetic studies, I have used a variety of other sources: concert programs and newspaper accounts, memoirs of distinguished musicians, instrument makers' catalogues, 78 rpm and LP phonograph records, CDs, DVDs, sheet music, photographs, and interviews with *tamburaši*. Good data from the past is relatively scarce compared to the abundant material available to document in the contemporary tamburitza scene. Therefore my geographic scope is somewhat wider in the historical segments than in the contemporary description. The geographic emphasis is on tamburitza in the vicinity of Zagreb and nearby areas of northern Croatia, and in North America, the American Midwest, especially the greater Chicago area, emphasizing the Calumet Region, two regions that are of major importance to the tamburitza tradition.

CHAPTER 1

The Soloistic Tambura
Comes to the Balkans

As the crow flies, it is scarcely 100 kilometers from the center of Zagreb, the Croatian capital, to Šturlić, a Bosnian village. The rough terrain, rivers, and mountains make the actual journey on land a good deal longer, but even so, given this degree of geographic proximity, the cultural distance between Zagreb (a "little Vienna") and Ottoman and Eastern Šturlić is nothing short of phenomenal. For nearly five centuries, until 1908, Šturlić and the Bosanska Krajina region of which it is a part represented the westernmost holdings of the Ottoman Empire, and today the region still is the home of a native Islamic culture. On the Turkish side of the border, Ottoman civilization made a lasting cultural imprint, yet just across the man-made line, in the lands that comprised the Austrian Empire's Military Frontier, only a few obviously Ottoman cultural elements can be found.

The Military Frontier was a region of fortresses and towers, populated by refugees from the southeast who were settled there by the Austrians to be the first line of defense against Turkish incursions (Clissold 1966, 27–31). For centuries, relations across this border were anything but cordial, a situation reflected in the belligerent and bloody epics sung on both sides of the line (Murko 1951). From 1918 to 1991, Bosanska Krajina and the neighboring Croatian regions of Kordun and Banija were part of Yugoslavia, but nevertheless strong cultural differences still remain.

I met villagers from Šturlić in Slunj, the largest town in Kordun, only about fifteen kilometers down a bumpy, unpaved road from Šturlić. The Šturlić villagers had crossed the old Turkish-Austrian border to represent their locality at a folklore festival with a lengthy title: The Fifth Exhibition of Authentic Folklore of Banija, Bosanska Krajina, Kordun, Lika, and Pokuplje (V. Smotra izvornog folklora Banije, Bosanske Krajine, Korduna, Like i Pokuplja). For the occasion, they had donned their old-fashioned costumes—no longer the norm for everyday use. The men wore loose-fitting tunics of hand-loomed white linen and baggy trousers of the same material. Under their sandals of woven strips of leather, they wore white woolen socks. The only color in the costume was the faded red of the black-tasseled felt fez and a colored sash about the waist. The costumes of the women were of the same linen and of a similar cut. The tunics were longer and had light brown stripes from a natural dye woven into the material, but the baggy trousers (*dimije*) and their footwear were practically identical to those of the men. Bright sashes, cloth flowers sewn around the edge of their white kerchiefs, and necklaces of beads and coins lent a little color and femininity to their garb.

I chatted with the Šturličani, and they sang a few songs for me to record. Following an ancient social custom, the women and men sang separately. The girls sang in a polyphonic style, which made use of a vocal drone and frequently the somewhat dissonant interval of the major second. The texts consisted of two-line verses of *deseterac*, the ten-syllable-line form of verse well known thanks to the numerous studies of South Slavic epic songs that are also typically sung in this form.

Misliš diko da me neće niko
A ja vraga svakome sam draga

Šaren ćilim u malenu sobu
Daj mi dragi usnice na probu

[You think, my dear, that no one wants me / But the devil with you, everyone likes me // A bright carpet in a little room / Let me try out your lips, my dear]

Members of
the folklore
ensemble from
Sturlić, Bosnia-
Herzegovina,
June 1978.
(Photos by
author)

The texts reflect sexual joking and teasing that goes on between the young women and men at the then still-vital folk custom of a communal work bee, called *prelo*, or *sijelo*, during which the tedium of repetitive handwork is relieved by song, jest, and socializing.

The men's singing was similar to the women's except that it showed a greater degree of influence of the more recent *na bas* singing style, a style that has become widespread in their region (Bezić 1976, 199).

A je lipa ona moja mala
A je lipa ona moja mala
Oj mati mati
Zar da moraš za sve znati?
Selom ideš, svašta čuješ
Dojde doma, mene psuješ.

[My little one is pretty / My little one is pretty / Oh Mother, Mother / Do you have to know it all? / You go around the village and hear all sorts of stuff / And you come home and curse me.]

Na bas singing, as in this variant of a song from Slavonia, emphasizes vocal harmonies within the interval of a fifth, and the harmonic progression moves from the tonic to a conclusion on a dominant chord, a more Western style of singing than the women's songs. Unlike the women's unaccompanied singing, the men sang to the rhythmic accompaniment of a stringed instrument, the *šargija*, a slender, long-necked Middle Eastern type of tambura (Gavazzi 1975, 42). The four steel strings of the pear-shaped wooden instrument are fastened by simple wooden tuning pegs, held only by friction in holes bored in the head; the thin copper wire frets are wound in double strands all the way around the neck. The long corpus of the resonator is carved out of a single piece of maple, a quarter section of a tree trunk. The spruce top is a thin board; there is no large sound hole, but instead there are four diamond-shaped clusters of small holes drilled, or perhaps burned, in the top. This instrument is locally made in Šturlić, but *tambure* of this exact type can be found in the countries of North Africa, the Middle East, and in Central Asia (Andrić 1958, 12). My interaction with the Šturličani, typical of the informal sharing of folk traditions that goes on at festivals, brought me into contact with the "nondeveloped" tambura, a type of instrument known from Morocco to Uzbekistan.

The instrument's very presence seems to evoke questions. How can this obviously Eastern instrument be a part of the folk tradition so close to central Europe? Where did the *šargija* originate? How and when did it come to this northwestern corner of Bosnia? Can this instrument, seemingly so different in appearance and musical sound and scale, really be the ancestor of the modern orchestral tamburitza?

The eminent Croatian ethnologist Milovan Gavazzi felt that the *šargija* may be considered the original form of tambura known on the Balkan peninsula (Gavazzi 1972). Its basic form has not been altered for centuries. Furthermore, Gavazzi maintained that the tambura was brought to the Balkans with the arrival of the Turks in the fifteenth century, a direct import. It did not appear in southeast Europe through a prior, gradual process of cultural diffusion from the Middle East as he felt was the case with the one-stringed *gusle*, which was probably known in the Balkans since the tenth century.

The ethnomusicologist Bozidar Širola agreed with Gavazzi. Writing in 1941, he emphasized just how recent was the adoption of the tambura by the South Slavs: "The tambura has spread a great deal in recent times. It penetrated from the East to the West around the beginning of the past [nineteenth] century. Bosnia and Herzegovina accepted it in the archaic form" (Širola 1941, 46). Širola's view was shared by Josip Andrić, a musician, composer for tamburitza orchestras, and historian of the tradition. Andrić believed that the instrument originated in Persia, spread throughout the Middle East, and from there was brought by the Turks into the Balkans (Andrić 1958, 12).

This seeming unanimity of scholars regarding the tambura's origin and diffusion belies the fact that that there was not always such agreement. During the later years of the nineteenth and the beginning of the twentieth centuries, there was a considerable polemic concerning the tambura's origin, in which more than purely scientific considerations often played a part. To justify the tambura's acceptance as a "national instrument," a few early scholars sought to prove that the tambura was known to the South Slavs since antiquity. The relative paucity of solid historical data on the instrument created favorable conditions for advancing highly speculative and romantic theories of origin, even by serious scholars like Franjo Ks. Kuhač, the founder of ethnomusicology in Croatia, and Vjekoslav Klaić, an important Croatian historian whose multivolume work *Povijest Hrvata* (History of the Croatians) is still standard reading for students of Croatian history (Klaić 1972).

In the first volume of *Povijest Hrvata* (1899), Klaić cited a well-known passage from the seventh-century writings of Theophylactus Simocattes, a Byzantine historian, which describes a legendary incident in Thrace in 591 CE during the military campaigns of the Byzantine emperor Mauricius. Simocattes noted that Mauricius's troops captured three prisoners who were carrying no weapons but had stringed instruments in their possession. They were brought before the curious emperor, who asked them who they were and what it was they carried. They replied, "We are Slavs and we live along the Western Sea (Adriatic). We play tambura because in our country there is no iron and we live in peace. We do not know the meaning of (war) bugles" (ibid., 26).

In the original Greek text of the passage, the name of the instrument is "kitharas." Klaić rendered the translation as "tambura," but Franjo Kuhač, who also mentioned the Simocattes passage more than twenty years earlier in his 1876 address to the Yugoslav Academy, translated the instrument's name as "gusle," the one-stringed, bowed instrument used to accompany South Slavic epic songs. Bulgarian scholars have rendered the translation as "gadulkite," the name of a Bulgarian folk instrument (Rihtman 1976, 218). Although each translator wished to use the passage to indicate the hoary antiquity of a favorite national instrument, it would be speculation to assert anything about the exact form of the instruments mentioned by Simocattes. It is evident, though, that they all had strings.

Although Klaić used the word "tambura" for the instruments mentioned in Simocattes's account, he may not have intended to make a definitive statement that an instrument anything like the modern tamburitza was in the possession of the sixth-century Slavs in Thrace. It seems that Klaić used the word casually, a convenient Croatian translation of kitharas. Perhaps his choice was spurred by his well-known affection for tambura. In addition to being a noted historian, Klaić was an accomplished musician and actively involved with amateur singing societies and orchestras in Zagreb (Andreis 1974, 208–9). The stature and accessibility of his *Povijest Hrvata* and the romantic image of musical, peace-loving Slavs contributed to the spread of the Byzantine passage in the form of a historical legend. The story still circulates today. In the central Croatian town of Sisak I heard an oral variant of the legend from a local tambura player in 1978.

The first study to deal with the origin of the tambura was prepared by Franjo Kuhač in 1876 and presented as an address to the Yugoslav Academy of Arts and Sciences. In his version of the Simocattes passage, Kuhač had the ancient Slavs carrying *gusle*, not *tambure*, but he used different arguments to prove that the Slavs had played *tambure* since antiquity. Kuhač stated, without supporting evidence, that the tambura is "the same as the ancient Greek pandura," and proceeded to dismiss a number of theories about the origin of the pandura. He denied that the instrument could have been invented by the ancient Greeks, the Hellenes, or the Arabs, but he stopped short of definitely attributing its invention to the Slavs. He maintained that "the Slavs were, in their way, the people who brought the tambura from their original homeland and spread it to other nations" (Kuhač 1898, 17).

Kuhač's theory is highly implausible. First of all, other nations who play the tambura—Arabs, Persians, Turkic peoples of Anatolia and Central Asia—do not live along a route between the Slavs' original homeland east of the Carpathians and the Balkan Peninsula. Second, the Slavs did not appear in the Balkans until the sixth or seventh century CE— more than a millennium later than the fifth century BCE—which Kuhač stated was the century when the Slavs supposedly arrived in that part of Europe (Clissold 1966, 11). Records exist that show that Middle Eastern peoples played the tambura centuries earlier than 500 CE, and since Kuhač himself cited these records as evidence, his argument is negated by archaeological evidence placing the Slavs' arrival in the Balkans a thousand years later (ibid.).

In 1898 and in the face of mounting contrary evidence, Kuhač modified his theory of the tambura's origin. In a study published by the National Museum of Bosnia and Herzegovina titled "Turkish Populace in the Folk Music of the Croats, Serbs and Bulgars" ("Turski živalj u

pučkoj glazbi Hrvata, Srba i Bugara"), Kuhač claimed that the Croats
and Serbs obtained the tambura from the ancient Greeks (Kuhač 1898,
17). He was still adamant that the South Slavs did not adopt the instrument from the Turks.

Kuhač argued that the Turks did not have any native folk music at
all but that all of their music was borrowed from the Arabs. Kuhač
stated that in the cases of other peoples who "progressed in the arts
to a greater or lesser degree, in perfecting their own [heritage] and
accepting foreign elements, they still retain some traces of their own
former musical practices. In the case of the Turks, this is not so!" (ibid.,
28). He continued, dealing specifically with the tambura:

> I do not deny that the Turks received the tambura from the Arabs, I
> only deny that the Slavs borrowed it from the Turks, because when the
> Turks came to Europe, the pandura had already been in use for five hun-
> dred years among the Slavs, who took it from the ancient Greeks. . . .
> It is probable that the Bulgarians obtained the tambura through the
> mediation of the Turks, but the Croats and the Serbs did not. This
> is proven on one hand by the skill of Croats and Serbs in playing the
> tambura and the perfection of the instruments themselves. Among
> the Turks and the Bulgarians the tambura is still primitive today and
> they cannot play it as skillfully, harmoniously or in ensembles as can the
> Croats and Serbs. (Ibid., 38)

It appears that Kuhač had preconceptions, based on political feelings. Clearly, he wanted to prove that the tambura could not have been
adopted by the Croats and Serbs from the culture of the recently ex-
pelled Ottoman invaders. Likewise, he wanted to show that the tambura
had been known to the South Slavs since antiquity. With due respect
to Kuhač's important contributions documenting traditional music,
his arguments here are erroneous. The Turkish people do indeed have
their native folk music traditions. They were extensively documented
by Béla Bartók in his 1936 field recordings in Turkey. The ancient Greek
pandura cannot be equated with the tambura. Today Macedonian
Slavs use the term "pandura" for an instrument more commonly called
"lauta" or "ut." This fretted stringed instrument has a large pear-shaped

resonator, a very short neck, and a peg head set at an angle to the fingerboard in the manner of the medieval European lute. It is a different instrument from the long-necked, small-bodied tambura (Gavazzi
1972). Moreover, there is no evidence that the South Slavs played the
tambura prior to the Turkish invasion in the fifteenth century, much
less five hundred years earlier.

Finally, the skill of the musicians and the "perfection" of the instruments, judged here according to Kuhač's own criteria and aesthetics,
cannot be indicators of the origin of the instrument. Perhaps Kuhač
referred to the development of Western-oriented tamburitza music in
Slavonia and Bačka, which featured ensemble play. As a son of Slavonia, no doubt this music appealed to Kuhač more than the soloistic
Eastern music practiced by the Turks and Bulgarians.

Modern scholars respect Kuhač for his important field collections
and organological studies as well as his analyses of the characteristics
of South Slavic folk music, but they reject this theory of tambura origins. Josip Andrić wrote in 1958:

> The tambura has not been ours since antiquity. Although in our period
> of romanticism it was held that our ancestors brought the tambura with
> them from their original homeland thirteen centuries ago when they
> migrated from east of the Carpathians to the Balkan peninsula, such an
> opinion was the result of a mistaken translation of a Byzantine histori-
> cal document [Simocattes]. It is however the case that for a full nine
> centuries from the time of the arrival of our ancestors [in the Balkans],
> there is not the slightest mention of the tambura among our people in
> any sort of document. (Andrić 1958, 13)

Andrić's statement is reinforced by the research of Koraljka Kos in
her extensive investigation of the depictions of musical instruments in
medieval frescoes in Croatian churches. Hundreds of instruments of all
sorts can be seen in the frescoes, typically shown in the hands of angels
or played by shepherds. Among the numerous stringed instruments
depicted, there are no plucked instruments with the long neck and narrow resonator of the tambura. Given the large number of instruments
shown in the frescoes, had the tambura been known in Croatia prior to

the fifteenth century, it is likely that it would have been depicted (Kos 1969, 167–270).

The view that the tambura was brought to the Balkans by the Turks in the fifteenth century is supported by early documentary evidence, although specific documents mentioning the tambura were rare until the later eighteenth century. Literacy was long confined to the clergy and aristocracy in this part of Europe, and written documents concerned matters those groups considered important, mostly affairs of state or theological issues. To them, the simple noise-makers played by lowly shepherds or peasants did not merit the attention of the literate. Therefore, where the tambura is mentioned in early documents, it is by chance or in passing.

Cvjetko Rihtman states that "Turkish tambura players and singers are mentioned in documents referring to Sarajevo in the fifteenth century" (Rihtman 1976, 219). Josip Andrić cites a travel account of the German writer N. Nicolai, who in 1551 crossed the Balkan countries in the company of the French emissary to Istanbul. Nicolai described young Janissaries, members of an elite Ottoman military corps, who were learning to play *tambure* (Andrić 1958, 13). In the same article Andrić also mentions a 1670 document, found in the archives of the Dalmatian city of Šibenik, which notes that two tambura players appeared in the town. Presumably they were traveling musicians from the interior.

These are only scraps of evidence but, by the mid-eighteenth century, documentary data becomes much more substantial. The spread of the Enlightenment into the Balkans resulted in an increase in literacy and a greater interest in writing about all secular topics, including the tambura. The instrument even became the subject of a controversy when the Slavonian writer Matija Reljković condemned its use. Reljković, born in a Slavonian village in 1732, was a career officer in the Habsburg army. He was imprisoned in Frankfurt beginning in 1757, during the Seven Years' War, and in the course of his incarceration he was able to acquaint himself with the way of life in a modern and developed part of Europe. While still a prisoner, he wrote *Satir iliti divlji čovik* (The satyr or the wild man), which he published in Dresden in 1762 (Reljković and Bogner 1974).

Imbued with the ideals of the Enlightenment, *Satir* was a didactic work and an early example of "applied folklore." In *deseterac* (the ten-syllable verse form used in folk poetry and beloved by the common folk), he attacked the "backward practices" of his countrymen in Slavonia hoping, perhaps, to change their ways. The Austrians had only recently driven the Ottomans from that region after more than a century of Turkish domination. Reljković viewed the illiteracy, the primitive agricultural techniques, and the folk customs of the peasantry as negative consequences of the Turkish occupation. He condemned village feasts, dancing the kolo and playing the tambura as "the devil's lesson taught to us by the Turks" (ibid., 82).

Reljković's writings show that the tambura was associated with the Turks and must have been well established in Slavonia at least by the mid-eighteenth century. Despite the popularity of *Satir*, Slavonians never heard Reljković's advice. They still play *tambure* in Slavonia, perhaps more actively than anywhere else. Slavonia and its neighboring provinces of Bačka and Srijem constituted an important center for the development and dissemination of the tamburitza tradition.

How and why did this area, the southeastern portion of the Pannonian plain, in the Sava and Danube River valleys, emerge as a major center of this musical tradition? Why and when did Croatian and Serbian peasants accept this Turkish instrument as their own?

The earliest documents mentioned by Cvjetko Rihtman and Josip Andrić associate the tambura with the Turks (Andrić 1958, 13; Rihtman 1976, 219). There is a degree of ambiguity in the use of the term "Turkish" in this part of the world. While there were a few ethnically Turkish soldiers, administrators, and artisans who came to the Balkans during the Ottoman era, the term *turski* (Turkish) was generally used to refer to a much larger group, the native Slavic Muslims who converted to Islam after the Ottoman conquest. They were particularly numerous in Bosnia-Herzegovina, where they constitute more than 40 percent of the population.

Various explanations have been advanced for the conversion to Islam of such a significant number of Bosnians. Historians cite the religious situation that prevailed in medieval Bosnia. Exposed to the competing religious influences of Rome and Constantinople, the situation was complicated by the development of an independent Bosnian Church. For more than a century historians contended the Bosnian Church was a manifestation of the Bogomil heresy. The Bogomils are said to have taken their name from a tenth-century Bulgarian priest named Bogomil ("Beloved of God"). He is said to have believed that the entire material world was an abomination created by Satan. To escape Satan's domination, man must avoid contact with the material and lead a strict ascetic life. The British historian Steven Clissold stated: "The Bogomils rejected the Old Testament, the Incarnation, the cross, the sacraments and the whole organization of the Christian Church. They formed a 'Bosnian Church' of their own, headed by a 'Bishop' and served by a semi-monastic body of devotees who spread their faith by acting as envoys or missionaries. Bogomilism became the faith of not only the common people, but of many land owners and nobles as well" (Clissold 1966, 58). At one point, the Bosnian ruler Kulin Ban was a Bogomil but was later forced to recant by the Roman Catholic Church.

Neither the Crusaders led into Bosnia by Peter the Hermit in the eleventh century nor the theological concessions offered by the Vatican could win the Bosnians' fealty to the Roman faith, and by the fourteenth century Bosnian Christians had grown into a powerful organization centered at Janjići in the Bosna River valley. Having endured the persecutions of both the Roman Catholics and the Orthodox, the adherents of the Bosnian Church apparently had little remaining sympathy for Christianity and had few qualms about converting to Islam following the Turkish conquest of Bosnia in 1463 (ibid., 58–60). Moreover, conversion conferred distinct practical advantages in Ottoman society. For example, Christians could not sue Muslims or testify against them in court (Malcolm 1996, 66).

More recent historical research has called into question that the Bosnian Church was actually an offshoot of Bogomilism; although the Vatican may have chastised Bosnian clerics for their dualistic tendencies, it did not declare the Bosnian Church heretical (ibid., 27–42). In Bosnia there was a high degree of religious independence from both Rome and Constantinople, and subsequent to the Ottoman conquest a large portion of the Bosnian population converted to Islam.

With the customary enthusiasm of new converts, the Bosnian Slavic adherents of Islam adopted a more zealous interpretation than that of the Caliph in Istanbul. And along with the religion, they eagerly embraced a host of other characteristics of Middle Eastern culture. The homes of the urban Moslems in Sarajevo, Mostar, and Banja Luka imitated the splendors of Istanbul. Fine Turkish-style architecture, furniture, and costumes graced the way of life of the well-to-do city dwellers. Intricate wood carvings, finely hammered copperware, and elaborately etched brass were among the marks of wealth and status in the Ottoman Empire. And the Moslem Slavs' acceptance of the Ottoman cultural complex included also the music and musical instruments, including the tambura.

Not all Moslem converts were wealthy or urban. There was mass conversion of peasant villagers, often at the behest of their feudal overlords. Moslem villagers imitated as best they could this favored complex of material culture. The patterns of fine silk urban costumes were imitated in coarse linen, and stubby wooden village minarets were a humble replication of the soaring minarets of Sarajevo's mosques. The classical Ottoman *saz*, a large finely wrought tambura with its deep, pear-shaped resonator pieced together from narrow strips of bent wood, was imitated in the village *šargija* whose back and neck were hewn from a section of tree trunk.

Despite the widespread acceptance of many Turkish traits, among the Slavic Moslems there has also been a great deal of retention of Slavic culture. Though many Turkish and Arabic loan words entered the lexicon of the Bosnians, the native Slavic language has been retained. There was no official Ottoman pressure to adopt the Turkish language. The concept of linguistic nationalism had not emerged during the Ottoman era. Religion was the primary distinguishing characteristic between peoples in the Empire.

Although some Christian and Jewish merchants became prosperous, the mass of the non-Moslem population were the so-called rajah, Catholic and Orthodox Christian peasant laborers subject to the authority of an Ottoman official. As Ottoman power began to decline, the rajah were subjected to ever-increasing burdens of taxation, not the least of which was the requirement to give up a certain number of their male children for reeducation as Moslems to fill future roles in the Ottoman bureaucracy or in the Janissary military corps (Clissold 1966, 64).

The receptiveness of the rajah to Ottoman cultural inventory varied considerably from place to place and time to time during the four centuries of Turkish rule. Although they shared Slavic origin and spoke the same language, the conflicts and animosities between the Christian and Moslem Bosnians reduced communication between the groups and diminished the desire to adopt elements of the other's culture (Murko 1951, 335). That the tambura was rejected by many Christians is evident from the writings of the Franciscan Grga Franičević. In the introduction to a collection of Bosnian and Herzegovinian folk songs, published in Osijek in 1858, Franičević stated, "To the Bosnian Moslem the tambura is the instrument of seduction, therefore the Christian folk believe it is a sin to make use of this device" (Kuhač 1877, 96).

The tambura was never widely accepted among the particular Catholic peasants in Bosnia-Herzegovina to whom Franičević referred. The rejection of the tambura should not be understood as a total disdain of everything Ottoman in their vernacular culture. For example, Ottoman influence is obvious in the traditional costumes of the Herzegovinian Catholics (Gavazzi 1972).

Christian receptiveness to Ottoman cultural influence varied and was also selective. Each community accepted or rejected Middle Eastern cultural items according to its own criteria. In general, Turkish costume seems to have been popular among the Christian subjects. According to some reports, the Ottoman authorities had to enact a law forbidding Christians from wearing certain garments and to limit green-colored clothes to Moslems (ibid.).

Concerning the tambura's acceptance in Bosnia-Herzegovina, the Moslems widely and readily accepted the instrument while the Roman Catholic and Orthodox Christians gradually and selectively adopted its use. The Eastern types of tambura—the *šargija*, *saz*, and *baglama*, to name the most common types—became a part of the local tradition first in the larger urban centers, then along the most-traveled trade routes, finally spreading to rural areas (Rihtman 1976, 220). In the northern and eastern portions of Bosnia, in the Sava and Drina River valleys, the *šargija* is still very much in use by Bosnians of all faiths.

North of the Sava River, in Slavonia, Srijem, and Bačka, events took a different course. These provinces fell to Ottoman rule following the rout of the Hungarian army at Mohács in 1526. For one hundred and fifty years the Ottomans controlled the Hungarian plains, but Turkish control of the area began to slip by 1683, after the lifting of the siege of Vienna. There followed a series of wars lasting until the early eighteenth century when the Austrians drove the Turks south of the Sava.

The extent to which the Christian populace of Slavonia, Srijem, and Bačka may have adopted the tambura during Ottoman rule is not known. The advances and counterthrusts of opposing armies and pillaging by Turkish irregulars caused many to flee the area. The population underwent dramatic changes in the decades-long period of wars that led to the expulsion of the Ottomans. From the south, Serbian and Croatian refugees who had aided the Austrians during their thrusts into Bosnia streamed north to escape the wrath of the returning Turks. In the lands where Habsburg rule was established, settlers of many nationalities from various parts of the Austrian Empire were encouraged to homestead in planned communities in areas depopulated by the decades of warfare. Germans, Hungarians, Czechs, Slovaks, Ukrainians, and others joined the South Slavs to make up an exceedingly multiethnic population.

The refugees from the south might have been those who brought the tambura with them from Bosnia, or perhaps some of the South Slavs already north of the Sava had begun to play tambura during their period of Turkish rule. Conclusive evidence is not available, but no matter how the tambura got there, Reljković's writings show the instrument certainly was popular in Slavonia by the eighteenth century.

Unlike the *šargija* of Bosnia that retained its original Eastern form and décor, the tambura in Slavonia began to lose many of its Middle Eastern attributes. Western musical traditions were influential in the Austrian-ruled zone. Villagers adjusted the frets on the tambura fingerboard to the tuning of a Western diatonic scale. The shape of the instrument and the style of ornamentation became more westernized as well. The adaptations of the instrument were far from uniform and no doubt came about gradually. Unfortunately, no *tambure* from the eighteenth century have been preserved. The oldest instruments in

museum collections were obtained by Kuhač in the 1860s and probably date from no earlier than the first decades of the nineteenth century.
These *tambure* exhibit a great deal of variety. Each village craftsman
who made *tambure* created his own combination of Eastern, Western,
and personal design elements using building techniques according to
his own experience, knowledge, and preferences (Kuhač 1877, 82).

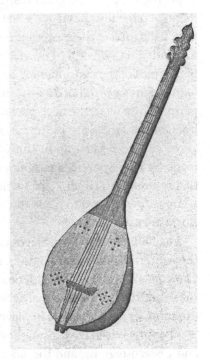

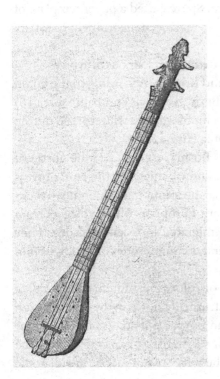

Sketches of *tambure* by
Franjo Ks. Kuhač from his 1877
presentation to the Yugoslav
Academy of Sciences and Arts.
(*Rad Jugoslavenske akademije
znanosti i umjetnosti* 39)

The modern-day, handmade soloistic *tambure* (commonly called *samice* or *dangubice*) are still quite similar to the Eastern versions of the *šargija*, with the exception of specific modifications. North of the Sava, the instruments are more rounded in shape and occasionally made in the shape of a miniature guitar. Often they feature only one sound hole placed under the strings near the middle of the top, like a guitar, instead of having a pattern of small dispersed holes as in the Eastern instruments. Generally they have a flat peg head, which is wider than the neck itself, unlike the Eastern type on which the pegs are inserted into a cylindrical extension of the neck and which is no wider than the rest of that part of the instrument. The most important difference has to do with the music produced by the instrument. The *samice* have wire frets permanently set in the neck positioned to produce a diatonic scale; the frets on the *šargija* are set to a Middle Eastern scale. External appearances can be deceiving. In the Croatian region of Lika I saw *šargije* made by Pajo Sporčić, a tambura maker from the village of Kuterevo, that resembled a larger-sized *samica*. Sporčić used a paper template of a *šargija* fingerboard to place the frets making an instrument to satisfy Bosnian customers.

The *samice* spread from Slavonia to the mountainous provinces along the western Bosnian border, Lika and Kordun. According to the noted Croatian ethnomusicologist Jerko Bezić, the *samica* probably spread to Lika and Kordun via seasonal agricultural workers who worked during the summer in the harvest in Slavonia (Bezić 1976).

The *šargija* is played throughout Bosnia, especially in the northern and eastern regions, and the *saz* is known chiefly in the larger towns and cities. Soloistic *tambure* also may be found today in industrial cities of former Yugoslavia and Western Europe to which villagers from the tambura's native regions have migrated in recent decades. They also turn up occasionally in the overseas communities of South Slavs in America and Australia.

There remains one other type of soloistic tambura, the so-called *tambura dvožica*, a two-stringed instrument known in the Banija region of central Croatia near the Bosnian border. *Samice* usually have four strings; *šargije* typically have five or six, but the *dvožica* resembles the *samica* in shape and decoration. The frets are not placed in a diatonic scale pattern but are all placed approximately equidistant from each other at intervals approximately equal to one inch. The scale produced on the instrument is similar to the scale used in the old-style local singing tradition in Banija and Kordun; it resembles the so-called Istrian scale used in the singing of Istria, a western, coastal Croatian region. The scale also turns up here and there in inland Croatia in the oldest songs and dirges.

It is difficult to determine whether the *dvožica* developed as an adaptation of the *samica*, which could have spread into the region from the east, from Slavonia, or an adaptation of an Eastern tambura coming from Bosnia, immediately to the south. In outward appearance, the *dvožica's* similarity to the *samice* seems to support a Slavonian origin. However, its two-string form is akin to the Eastern two-stringed tambura *ićitelj* or *ćitelija*.

The *dvožica* of Banija gives us an example of the development that occurs everywhere. Wherever the basic tambura was accepted in a region, its frets would be adjusted to suit the scale favored in the local village singing tradition (Rihtman 1978).

In summary, the tambura came to the Balkans as an item of Middle Eastern material culture brought by the Turks in the fifteenth century. Urban Moslem Slavs were probably the first Balkan Slavic people to adopt the instrument, followed by rural Moslems. Later, many Bosnian Christians adopted it. The villagers of Slavonia, Srijem, and Bačka who were subject to a much shorter period of Ottoman domination either adopted the tambura during or immediately following their period of Turkish rule. From this area the tambura subsequently spread to most of inland Croatia.

CHAPTER 2

A National Music
and the Illyrian Movement

On a March evening in 1978, I attended a concert in Samobor. Samobor is a small but growing town, thirty-some kilometers west of Zagreb, nestled along a rippling stream in the beautiful foothills of the Žumberak Mountains. In the old center of the town the flavor of Austrian days still seems alive. On the ornate facades of a neat row of shops and public buildings on the main street, décor dating from the Habsburg era prevails. One can easily imagine a carriage rumbling over the cobblestones, pulling up at a small elegant café, a well-dressed gentleman emerging to meet his peers for genteel company.

Across a small, manicured park from the main street stood the theater, a place to see popular films, American Westerns, and Italian crime stories as was evident from the coming attractions posters in the lobby. That particular evening, however, a well-dressed and mannerly crowd turned out not to see a film but to enjoy a performance by Samobor's best-known musical organization, the Ferdo Livadić Tamburitza Orchestra.

In the auditorium, seated upon a stage decorated with motifs of old Samobor, an orchestra of more than thirty tamburitzas was seated. The conductor, Željko Bradić, then in his forties, emerged on stage in black tie and tails. At the tap of his baton there was an expectant hush, and the downbeat brought forth the harmonious strains of romantic melodies. The concert seemed to reflect a glimmer of musical events of the

The Ferdo Livadić Tamburitza Orchestra, Samobor, Croatia, 1977.
(Courtesy of Croatia Records d.d.)

nineteenth century. The appreciative audience basked in the nostalgic
atmosphere created by the sounds of the Livadić Orchestra and the
old favorite, sentimental songs performed by operatically trained vocal
soloists.

It is hard to imagine a greater contrast to the *šargija* player from
Šturlić in terms of the music, the sort of event, and the people involved.
When one views the concert of an ensemble like Ferdo Livadić, it
seems incredible that this form of artistic expression might trace its
roots to the tradition of the Bosnian *šargijaš*. How could such a transformation have taken place?

The concert tamburitza orchestras today perform Stravinsky-influ-
enced compositions of composers like Tihomil Vidošić, Romantic-
era pieces of Franz Schubert, and even avant-garde creations by Ernö
Király and others. Some of the members of these orchestras also play
in informal combos in which they utilize the musical knowledge and
skills attained in orchestral performance to play a wide-ranging repertoire of newer and older popular and folk songs.

The world of the tamburitza is complex, and a better understanding of its many manifestations requires an examination of musical developments in Croatia and the Balkans during the past century and a half. It was during the course of the nineteenth-century national movement in Croatia (*Hrvatski narodni preporod*) that the musical aesthetics, national symbolism, and style of performance developed that remain dominant in modern tamburitza orchestras both in Croatia and in North America. Writers, politicians, and musicians developed a cultural ideology, which consciously tied all genres of artistic expression to the national movement. The newly developed fields of ethnology and ethnomusicology were enlisted in the service of the national revival. The far-reaching influences of the Croatian national revival affected all segments of society. Even today, such overtly nonpolitical expressions as landscape paintings and love songs may nonetheless be invested with and understood by a Croatian audience as having ethnic or national symbolism. The same is true of the tamburitza and its music.

The scope of the following historical survey includes a discussion of Croatian literary and musical developments, which, strictly speaking, are not part of the tamburitza tradition. The tamburitza, especially in its "developed" form, has never been isolated from other trends in the national culture. Though relatively little has been specifically written about activities associated with tamburitza, it is possible to extrapolate a good picture of them from writings concerned with other Croatian musical activities—notably "national" directions in classical music. Indeed, some of the same musicians who were involved with the tamburitza's development were also classical musicians or composers.

The national identity of the South Slavic peoples became articulated in intellectual movements of the nineteenth century. Aiming to spread their ideas to broad segments of the population, South Slavic patriots quickly grasped the usefulness of music and song to advance their causes. Folk music was especially useful since a vast majority of the South Slavs were peasants. In their writings, the patriots have enshrined certain forms of folk poetry and folk instruments, especially the *gusle* and the tamburitza, imbuing them with nearly sacred symbolic value.

The ideas of Johann von Herder influenced the movements, and in keeping with his Romantic nationalist concept, folklore was representative of the true national culture of the South Slavs (Despalatović 1976, 9). Those cultural expressions created by the peasantry, according to Herder, demonstrated a nation's unique heritage and cultural independence. They held that modern states should be nation-states; therefore cultural independence implied political independence as well. The performance and study of folklore was an integral part of the movements for the political liberation of the subject South Slav nations (ibid., 9–10).

Although for centuries there had been incidents that evidenced a degree of national consciousness, the nationalism movement among Croats began to take definite form in the second half of the eighteenth century. The work of three individuals is symptomatic of the state of the movement as well as indicative of the attitude of the educated people toward folklore: the works of the Dalmatian Franciscans Filip Grabovac and Andrija Kačić-Miošić, and that of the Slavonian officer Matija Reljković.

Grabovac and Kačić had a great deal in common. They were members of the same religious order, roughly contemporaries (Grabovac was born in 1697, Kačić in 1704), and both were natives of the impoverished hinterlands of the Dalmatian coast. In 1747 Grabovac published *Cvit razgovora naroda iliričkog iliti hrvatskoga* (The flowers of conversation of the Illyrian or Croatian people), an anthology of educational and entertaining writings in both verse and prose. The book has much to interest folklorists: Grabovac provides moral lessons on the goodness of Divine Providence by relating legends of miraculous rescues of the pious, and he composed historically oriented epic poems in a style close to that of the folk epics (Bezić 1965–66, 247–51).

Even though his work was successful artistically, Grabovac fell afoul of the Venetian authorities because in his epic songs he bemoans the fate of the Croatian people who (he proclaimed) must continually make war, yet the benefits of their fighting are usurped by their foreign rulers. This statement did nothing to endear him to the Venetian doge, and petty regional rivalries deprived Grabovac of a strong base of support even among his own countrymen. Some Dalmatians apparently felt that Grabovac praised the heroes of his own home town, Vrlika, at the expense of neighboring towns, so Grabovac was left without supporters. He was arrested by the Venetians and imprisoned in Venice, where he was tortured to death in 1749. His book was seized and destroyed, but several of the original four hundred copies remained at large, hidden in Franciscan monasteries (Barac 1963, 60–61).

The work of Kačić was obviously modeled after that of Grabovac, but Kačić took pains to avoid the fate of his fellow Franciscan. His book *Razgovor ugodni naroda slovinskoga* (Pleasant conversations of the Slavic people) resembles the second, poetic section of Grabovac's *Cvit*. Kačić composed epics in a folk style, many of which are similar in content and style to the oral epics of his region. In the poems Kačić was careful to refrain from criticizing the doge. He often praised him, in fact, more than was to the liking of later Croatian patriots (Despalatović 1976, 9).

Razgovor ugodni or *Pismarica* (Songbook), as it is still frequently called by Dalmatian villagers, was a tremendous popular success. Many of Kačić's poems entered the repertoire of folk epic singers, and versions of them are still available. His poems stressed the unity of the South Slavic peoples, and he exalted the exploits of Croatian, Serbian, and Bulgarian heroes (Ravlić 1967, 19).

Kačić succeeded in his goal, as did Grabovac, by retaining the ideas of the Enlightenment, using the folk poetic form to educate the common folk regarding their history, and creating a sense of national pride.

Matija Reljković, whose attack on the tambura as a manifestation of debauchery and ignorance was mentioned in chapter 1, had similar educational goals. In a sense it is ironic that in *Satir* he used folk poetry meters to censure the folkloric practices of village festivals, folk dances, and tambura music. The emerging Romantic school soon exalted these same practices, but to Reljković's Enlightenment mentality, they were primitive, backward, and prevented the cultural advancement of his home region (Barac 1963, 62).

While Enlightenment writers were still attempting to elevate the culture of the common people, Romantic nationalism burst upon the intellectual scene in central and southern Europe early in the nineteenth century. The Romantics were influential upon the South Slavs in two overlapping ways: they spread the philosophical precepts of Romantic nationalism to the Balkans, and they increased the appreciation of native culture by presenting an idealized picture of South Slavic peasants and their folklore to the larger European nations.

The influential ideas of Herder, Romantic nationalism's spokesman, may be summarized as follows: A *Volk* or nation is the natural unit of humanity; it shares a common history, culture, and language. Each *Volk* needs to fully develop its own culture thereby enriching all of humanity. Herder believed that the common people had preserved the true national culture while the elite had a culture largely based on foreign models. Thus the language, the oral narrative arts, and indeed any expression of the common folk should be the basis of the arts of a modern nation (Wilson 1975, 65).

It is easy to see why such ideas found fertile ground among the intellectuals of the subject nationalities of Europe. Their national identities were threatened by imperial assimilationist policies, and their native tongues were neglected in the arts and in public life. Folklore became part of the intellectual vogue. Herder himself collected German and other European folk songs, which he published in 1778 and 1779 in *Stimmen der Volker in Liedern* (Voices of the folk in song).

In 1774, the West's interest in Balkan folklore was suddenly stimulated by the success of *Viaggio in Dalmazia* (Travels in Dalmatia), a travelogue by the Italian writer Alberto Fortis. At the request of his English traveling companion John Symonds, Fortis wrote a long chapter on the life and customs of the Slavic peasants, whom he called *Morlacchi*, in the Dalmatian hinterlands. At the end of the chapter he included a text of an epic poem. This poem, *Hasanaginica* (The wife of Hasanaga), caught the imagination of the Romantics. Johann Goethe translated it to German, and Herder included *Hasanaginica* in addition to a second song from Fortis's book in his second edition of *Stimmen der Volker*. From there it was translated into French and English. The English rendering was done by Sir Walter Scott, and before long there was a European vogue for South Slavic poetry (ibid., 192–94).

The popularity of this poetry prompted Jernej Kopitar, a Slovenian who served the government in Vienna as a censor for Slavic language books, to encourage a young Serbian man-of-letters Vuk Karadžić to collect folk epic songs. Kopitar put Karadžić in touch with Jakob Grimm, whose influence helped make Karadžić an important nineteenth-century folklorist. The lexicographical work of Karadžić was in accordance with Herderian principles. His Serbian dictionary, the first ever compiled, was based on the language of the folk epics and the prose folk tales he had collected (ibid., 98–101).

In this intellectual climate, with the prevailing attitudes toward folklore, the Croatian national revival began. That revival deeply and permanently influenced the tamburitza tradition. Each of the present-day types of tamburitza performance bears the stamp of cultural ideas prevalent at one or another phase of this movement's development. The large tamburitza orchestras, for example, derive from an ideology that dominated early in the national movement, while the "folklore" ensembles owe their nature to another school of thought that was to emerge later.

At the beginning of the nineteenth century, the Croatian people were divided, politically weak, and their institutions of high culture were dominated by their foreign rulers. Among the contributing factors were the modernizing and social reform policies pursued by Emperor Joseph II in the late eighteenth century. These policies imposed a centralization of power and Germanization of the culture of the Empire. There was disagreement between Croatian and Hungarian nobles about the nature of Croatia's centuries-long connection to Hungary. There was much dispute about whether Croatia was a freely associated kingdom (*regna social*) as the Croats maintained or an annexed territory (*partes adnexae*) as the Hungarians argued. Such debates became newly pertinent. The Hungarians had also felt the Germanizing pressures of the emperor's rule, and they reacted with resurgent Hungarian nationalism. A later form of this nationalism was an effort to Magyarize their Slavic subjects (Črnja 1962, 299–303).

In 1809 Napoleon's French Empire occupied Slovenia, Istria, and Dalmatia, breaking the power of the Venetian doge who had ruled much of this area. It also destroyed the independence of the Dubrovnik city-state. For a brief period, 1809–13, the so-called Illyrian provinces existed as a separate entity in Napoleon's far-flung empire. This was the first political unit in which Slovenes, Croats, and Serbs were combined, and the idea of democracy was given some acknowledgment (Clissold 1966, 54). After Napoleon's fall, the provinces were taken over by the Habsburgs, who held them until their empire eventually disintegrated in 1918.

The various Habsburg provinces inhabited by Croatians were separate and were related to the central government in quite different ways. Inland Croatian territories for the most part were in the Hungarian portion of Austria-Hungary and sent representatives to the Imperial Council in Budapest. Most of the Adriatic coast and some nearby inland areas were under Austrian jurisdiction. A wide strip of territory, bending like a horseshoe adjacent to the border of Ottoman Bosnia, was known as the Military Frontier. This region was administered directly from Vienna under a special form of military rule. There was no single political unit to which all Croatians sent representatives (ibid., 37–38).

In terms of social and economic conditions, Croatia was still a feudal country. Despite a smattering of industry and trade, Croatia was primarily agricultural land. The farming and stock-breeding methods were backward, and the life of the peasantry was harsh. Constant Austro-Turkish wars in the area and government policies from Vienna and Budapest discouraged industrial development in Croatia (Vucinich 1975, 55–56).

The nobility was few in number. Taking into consideration the lay, ecclesiastical, and so-called peasant nobles of the Turopolje region, they constituted only 2.9 percent of the total population (Črnja 1962, 303). Many of the Croatian nobles did not consider themselves to be of Croatian nationality. Indeed, many did not even speak Croatian.

The lifestyle of the Croatian nobility underwent a change at the close of the eighteenth century. Previously they had lived in rather humble conditions compared to contemporaries of their class in Western Europe. Austria's wars with Prussia, in which the Croatian nobles participated, provided them an opportunity to become acquainted with conditions in Germany and other more developed parts of Europe. Their new awareness stimulated a desire to imitate the luxury and glitter of the way of life of the Western aristocrats. French-language tutors were included in many nobles' households, and music teachers became an influence on musical culture in Croatia. Noble families in Zagreb and Varaždin organized dances and concerts in which foreign guest artists sometimes appeared. The nobles followed developments in French and German art and literature. Zagreb and Varaždin grew pretentious, and both towns adopted the nickname Mali Beć (Little Vienna) (Andreis 1974, 139).

These developments had only a remote effect upon the peasantry who remained feudal serfs. In the towns, there developed a middle class of craftsmen and merchants, although they constituted a much smaller group than was the case in Western Europe at that time. With its colorful mixture of nationalities, Zagreb emerged as the largest town in central Croatia. Besides Croatians, there were Germans, Hungarians, Italians, Jews, Czechs, and Slovaks who made up a cosmopolitan multiethnic society. German became the common language in Zagreb, partly as a result of the policies of Joseph II. In 1789 German-language newspapers and magazines became Croatia's first periodicals. There was the *Agramer Zeitung, Luna,* and, by the early nineteenth century, even a theater magazine, *Agramer Teaterjournal* (ibid., 136).

The Hungarians were the first to react to those Germanizing pressures. They pressed for the exclusive use of the Hungarian language in all official capacities, not only in ethnically Hungarian territories but also in Slovakia and the parts of Croatia under Hungarian administration. Reacting to this aggressive Hungarian nationalism, the Croatian nobles vigorously defended the continued use of Latin as the official language in Hungary and Croatia. They threatened that they would use their own Illyrian language if Hungarian were adopted in Croatia. As long as they were able to forestall the Hungarians, however, they showed little interest in actually developing a Croatian literary language. In fact, the Habsburg censor Antun Nagy, who served from 1810 to 1818, complained that during his tenure he hardly ever received any sort of Croatian manuscript (Vucinich 1975, 58). From 1825 to 1830 the Hungarians gradually succeeded in forcing Vienna to accept their demands. Hungarian was made the obligatory language in schools and in government affairs throughout their kingdom. The prospect of rapid Magyarization finally lent urgency to the Croatian awakening known as the Illyrian movement (ibid., 68–69).

The movement involved linguistic, literary, and political struggles. The period has been the subject of many historical studies that treat Illyrianism in detail, but what follows here is only a general discussion of the main thrust of the movement, emphasizing the role of music, folklore, and folklorism.

In Zagreb, early stirrings of national feeling began in the closing years of the eighteenth century. The upper echelons of the clergy and the Croatian nobility played the leading roles. Bishop Maksimilian Vrhovac of Zagreb had been an active advocate of the Slavic cause as early as the 1790s, and later he became a staunch Illyrian adherent. Like Vuk Karadžić, he collected folksongs and proverbs. In the introduction to one of his published collections, Vrhovac asserted the Herderian principle that these narratives were the truest expression of the nation's soul (ibid., 70). Vrhovac was also one of the organizers of the first recorded revivalistic folkdance performance in Croatia. When Emperor Franz II and his wife, Karolina, visited Zagreb in 1818, they were greeted in front of the bishop's palace by a group of dancers and singers in peasant costumes performing a kolo dance, led by Count Janko Drašković, an important Croatian noble. In fact, Vrhovac had composed a "folksong" for the occasion (Bošković-Stulli 1972, 165).

The kolo, a type of village line dance, was added to the stylish forms of ballroom dance for the nationalist segment of Zagreb nobility. "Folk style" balls were arranged not just in Zagreb but also in the small provincial town of Slavonska Požega in the Military Frontier (ibid., 166).

LJUDEVIT GAJ AND THE ILLYRIAN MOVEMENT

These nationalist stirrings required a central focus around which to coalesce. This focus was provided by the establishment of a literary magazine in the Croatian language published in Zagreb by the man who came to be acknowledged as the most important figure of the Illyrian movement, Ljudevit Gaj. Gaj was the son of a pharmacist in the provincial town of Krapina, near the Slovenian border. Although he never achieved much as a literary author, nor was he a powerful politician, he was responsible for initiating, organizing, and promoting Illyrianism in Croatia between 1835 and 1843 (Despalatović 1975).

Like many of the other leaders of the Croatian national revival, Gaj was not ethnically Croatian. His father, Ivan Gaj, was a Slovak from the Tatra Mountains who moved to Krapina to open his pharmacy. Gaj's mother, Julia Schmidt, was a German-speaking Austrian, and German was the language spoken in their household. While still young, Gaj learned the Kajkavian dialect of Croatian spoken in his hometown (ibid., 27–29).

In his autobiography Gaj recalled that his mother imbued him with sympathy for the local peasants, and Gaj himself developed a great pride in his native Zagorje region. His perspectives broadened from the narrowly regional when he attended gymnasium in Karlovac, where he encountered the writings of Andrija Kačić-Miošić: "By then I had realized that my homeland laid also beyond the confines of Zagorje. . . . At Karlovac I saw men and women of the old stock, of the core of our Croat and Serbian nation. I listened to their vigorous language and when I read Kačić's *Razgovor ugodni*, the loveliness and dignity of the Illyrian tongue were revealed to me" (ibid., 34).

Despite his professed love for the Croatian language, German was the language of Gaj's first attempt at writing. In his work *Die Schlösser bei Krapina* (The fortress near Krapina), Gaj attempted to prove the veracity of folk legends about the old fortress on the hill above Krapina. He showed that the contents of the legend, as he collected it from local peasants, matched information recorded in old chronicles, which, he felt, proved the legend's historical veracity. It did not occur to him that the chronicler might have encountered variants of the same oral legends at an earlier time. Even though he did not prove what he hoped to, his work reveals an interest in folklore. He even cited a quotation from Scottish poet James MacPherson's *Ossian*, a fabricated "ancient epic" (ibid., 42–43).

Gaj pursued higher education in the city of Graz, where he befriended Mojsije Baltić, a Serb from the Military Frontier. Baltić introduced Gaj to Vuk Karadžić's collections of Serbian folk poetry, and Gaj was so impressed that he decided to collect folk poetry himself. He began to collect the narrative folklore of Zagorje, including material from other regions of Croatia as well, in the summer of 1827 and continued to work on the project for many years. Gaj's collection was never published, ignored for more than a century. It was rediscovered in the twentieth century when the folklorist Nikola Bonifačić-Rozin examined it and found the collection to be of high quality (Bonifačić-Rozin 1978). In these works Gaj concentrated on proverbs: more than 90 percent of his pages of manuscript deal with the five thousand or so proverbs he had collected. Gaj viewed proverbs as a sort of customary unwritten law of a nationality. In 1835 he wrote, "Who can note and discover the origin and causes of the actions and habits of a nation . . . if he does not know the most important and most commonly used words of the nation, if he does not understand the proverbs which once supplanted law and order?" (Despalatović 1975, 43). In his own writings Gaj frequently and skillfully made use of proverbs like "Besposlen pop i jariće krsti" (An idle priest will start baptizing goats) or "Kak pri jelu, tak pri delu" (The way one eats is the way one works) to advance his polemics.

In 1834 Gaj managed to make the necessary financial arrangements and obtain official permission to begin publishing the first newspaper and literary magazine in the Croatian language. At this early stage of Croatian letters, an initial problem was to reach agreement on a uniform literary language, since Croatian regional dialects differ substantially. At first, Gaj's publications used the Zagreb Kajkavian dialect and bore the titles *Novine horvatske* (Croatian news) and *Danica horvatska, slavonska i dalmatinska* (Morning star of Croatia, Slavonia, and Dalmatia). Less than a year later he abandoned Kajkavian, adopted Štokavian, the dialect spoken by a majority of Croats and Serbs, and changed the names of the publications to *Ilirske novine* (Illyrian news) and *Danica Ilirska* (Illyrian morning star) (Vucinich 1975, 95–96).

Gaj's keen interest in folklore was soon evidenced on the pages of *Danica*. In 1835 he contributed three articles concerning folk poetry. He explained Herder's idea of folk poetry as a valuable source for a literary tradition, especially for a people who possessed little written literature. According to Gaj, it was the patriotic duty of an Illyrian (meaning a South Slav) to be familiar with the folk poetry of his or her nation (Despalatović 1975, 88–89). He stressed that the folk poems could teach the Slavs about themselves, their history and customs, and he called for increased collecting efforts. Gaj also discussed various extant published collections, particularly Karadžić's, and adopted a policy of publishing poems from Vuk's collection in *Danica*. Gaj asserted that the folk poems reflected the heroism of the Illyrian people, their sufferings under foreign rule, the freedom of their spirit, their stormy history, and their love of music.

Gaj helped foster an intimate connection of folklore to the national revival. Like the German term *Volk*, the Slavic equivalent, *narod*, has a certain built-in ambiguity. It can mean either folk or national, and this very ambiguity helped the concept of *narod* to become central to the Illyrian movement. When the term "Illyrian" was outlawed by the Austrian authorities in 1843, Gaj changed the name of his newspaper to *Narodne novine* (Vucinich 1975, 98).

Illyrian writers sought to use the *narodni* language (Štokavian) and to write in the *narodni* spirit—a more elusive concept. Though writing and language were pivotal to the goals of the Illyrians, artists working in other genres were no less ardent to imbue their works with the *narodni* spirit.

The importance of the development of a national direction in music was clear to Gaj from early in his career. Musical life in Zagreb had developed rapidly at the beginning of the nineteenth century; dramatic and operatic performances in the German language grew more frequent. Between 1826 and 1833 the plays of Shakespeare, Goethe, and Schiller were performed by Zagreb-based troupes who traveled to Varaždin, Karlovac, and Rijeka; traveling companies from Western Europe presented operas. In 1827 the Zagreb Musikverein (music society) was established.

The Illyrians sought to influence the development of this fledgling musical life in Zagreb. They knew that music could awaken and strengthen patriotic feelings, and could play a part in affirming Croatian culture. Consistent with their ideas regarding language and literature, the Illyrians felt an authentic national music should be based upon folk music and folksong. Gaj expressed the Illyrian program in the field of music in an 1837 article: "Thus brothers and patriots, we have laid the foundation of Croatian music and indicated the direction to go. Let it swell out of the folk, or let that which is newly created be created in the spirit of our common people, but not so crudely and naively as with the commoners, but rather gentlemanly, refined and according to the principles of art and aesthetics. Then we will achieve that which other nations have not: a true national music" (Andreis 1974, 141). And here, Gaj stated the essence of what was to become the aesthetic strivings of the orchestral tamburitza tradition.

Even before his newspapers were published, Gaj recognized the need for a patriotic hymn to rally Illyrian sentiment. His efforts to create a "Croatian Marseillaise" finally bore fruit in 1833. Many years later in an interview with Franjo Kuhač, Gaj related how he had set out by carriage one winter day in 1833 to visit his friend Ferdo Livadić in Samobor. Livadić was a musically talented nobleman of German extraction. He had changed his name from Ferdinand Weisner under the spell of Illyrian enthusiasm. Gaj explained to Kuhač that as his carriage passed through a village, he could faintly hear the strains of a peasant band drifting across the fields. They were *guci*, a small ensemble consisting of two violins and a small, bowed string bass. All that Gaj was able to make out was the basic rhythm. At that moment Gaj claimed the words "Još Hrvatska ni propala" (Croatia hasn't fallen yet) came to his mind, and he immediately started to compose verses on that theme to the rhythm of the village *guci*.

Još Hrvatska ni propala dok mi živimo
Visoko se bude stala kad ju zbudimo
Ak je dugo tvrdo spala, jača hoće bit
Ak je sada u snu mala, će se prostranit.

[Croatia hasn't fallen yet as long as we are alive. / She will stand tall when we awaken her. / If she long has soundly slept, the stronger she shall be. / If now sleeping she is small, she will widen.]

It seems certain that the first line of Gaj's lyrics was derived from the Polish national anthem "Jeszcze Polska nie zginęła póki my żijemy" (Poland hasn't fallen yet because we are alive). Refugees from partitioned Poland's 1830 revolution had come to Zagreb, and this may have provided Gaj an opportunity to hear the song (Andreis 1974, 143).

As soon as Gaj arrived at Livadić's manor in Samobor, the two men sat down at the piano to make up melody for the lyrics. In a few minutes they had composed this well-known Croatian patriotic song.

Once created, Gaj sought to have the song performed in public. The problem was that no songs in the Croatian language had ever been performed for genteel company from a Zagreb concert stage. No one dared to sing it for fear of being mocked and ridiculed. But Gaj persuaded Sidonija Erdödy, the teenaged daughter of Count Erdödy, a Zagreb nobleman with Illyrian sympathies, to perform the song. On February 7, 1835, Sidonija sang the song during the intermission of a German play. The excited audience applauded and insisted that she repeat it again and again. Overnight the song became the rallying hymn of the Illyrians (ibid., 145).

It is ironic that the Illyrian hymn came into existence in this way. The lyrics were written by Gaj, a member of the Austro-Hungarian middle class of Slovak and German background. The melody was composed by Livadić, a German nobleman. Both of them had adopted Croatian identity through personal choice. The song was first performed and made famous by the daughter of a nobleman of Hungarian origin. The only connection to the Croatian peasant folk was the faint rhythm of a village band that Gaj heard as he traveled from Germanized Zagreb to the manor of a foreign noble in Samobor.

Many of the failures of Illyrian music to achieve the goals articulated by Gaj stemmed from the relative ignorance of the urban and intellectual classes concerning South Slavic folk music. Many of this class were neither Croatian nor Serbian; they were much more familiar with Western European classical music than with the folk music of peasants.

Vatroslav Lisinski and the First Croatian Opera

The most important and concentrated music effort by Illyrian adherents was aimed at establishing a Croatian opera company, which would perform operas originally composed in the Croatian language, a nineteenth-century national status symbol. The development of a national opera may be peripheral to the tamburitza tradition, but it merits attention here. Material from nineteenth- and twentieth-century Croatian operas became and still remains in the repertoire of many tamburitza orchestras. Selections from *Nikola Šubić Zrinjski* by Ivan Zajc and from *Ero s onoga svijeta* by Jakov Gotovac are frequent favorites. Furthermore, the opera influenced tamburitza musical aesthetics, including the music of small ensembles as well as orchestras. Many vocalists, especially females, who sing to tamburitza accompaniment seek to emulate an operatic vocal style.

The creation and staging of the first Croatian opera, *Ljubav i zloba* (Love and evil), was one of the halcyon achievements of the Illyrian movement. Moreover, the obstacles in the path of its staging, and the repression and ultimate destruction of its composer Vatroslav Lisinski by opponents of the Illyrians, is an instructive example of cultural politics in mid-nineteenth-century Croatia. Lisinski was, perhaps, the most important Illyrian musician. He was born in Zagreb in 1819; his father was of Slovenian ethnic background, his mother was Croatian. Lisinski's original name was Ignac Fuchs. Near the end of his short and tragic life, like many of his fellow Illyrians, he slavicized his name (ibid., 152).

Lisinski was a frail youth, a childhood injury having left him lame for life. He completed gymnasium and managed to obtain some higher education. Lisinski's gift for music was recognized early, and he took private lessons with some of the most distinguished musicians in Zagreb. Despite the best training local conditions could provide, there were few opportunities for a musical career in Zagreb at that time. As a result, at the end of his schooling Lisinski was obliged to take a job as a clerk in a government office.

In his free time he composed patriotic airs and with the encouragement and guidance of Alberto Štriga, an ardent Illyrian musician, Lisinski managed to put together his first opera, *Ljubav i zloba*. Symptomatic of the climate of the times, the first planned performance of the opera had to be cancelled because the male lead was shot and seriously injured when troops fired on a crowd of demonstrators, mostly Illyrian adherents, who were protesting irregularities in a disputed election.

After more than a year of delay the opera was performed in the spring of 1847, a benchmark in the course of the Illyrian movement. This and other achievements of the Illyrians came to fruition when repression of the movement was increasing and after the name "Illyrian" had already been officially outlawed by the Austrian authorities (Barac 1963, 116–22).

The opera revealed that Lisinski's potential talents had yet to mature. His work showed the desire to follow the new romantic musical trends, but his training tended to anchor him in the classicism of the previous century. Nonetheless, the opera was a popular success; Štriga was able to line up some wealthy patrons to send Lisinski to Prague for further musical education. Unfortunately his efforts were thwarted. He was refused admission to the conservatory in Prague because he, at twenty-eight, was considered too old. Lisinski did manage to take private lessons with the directors of both the conservatory and the organ school. Though he advanced musically, Lisinski was unable to obtain any sort of official diploma indicating his qualifications—a situation that proved disastrous to his late career. Lisinski's sojourn in Prague was difficult; the stipend sent by Štriga was never adequate to cover basic living expenses, and in 1848, with the outbreak of the revolution, the stipend payments ceased altogether (Andreis 1974, 153).

In 1849 Lisinski returned to Zagreb to find the political climate dramatically changed. Slavic nationalism was no longer tolerated; Germanization and centralistic power were enforced by absolute rule. Lisinski did not obtain the position of conductor of the orchestra at the music institute as he had been promised when he went to Prague. His lack of an official diploma rendered him vulnerable to the politically inspired exclusion. In fact, Lisinski never found any paid work at all. His only association with the music institute was to serve as an unpaid supervisor of the music school's classrooms. Because he was never robust, years of living with deprivation caused his health to fail. He died in obscurity in 1854 at the age of thirty-five. His second opera, *Porin*, though musically superior to his first opera, was not performed until decades after the young composer's death (ibid., 156).

Pajo Kolarić of Slavonia

It was in Zagreb, the center of Illyrian activity, that Ljudevit Gaj enunciated the goal of a folk-based national music and where Vatroslav Lisinski managed to produce the first Croatian opera. But it was in Osijek, the major city of the eastern Croatian province of Slavonia, that the tamburitza was first conceived as a symbolic national folk instrument.

By the 1840s echoes of Illyrianism had begun to spread from Zagreb to other Croatian cities. Some two hundred miles to the east of Zagreb, Osijek had few ties to the Croatian capital. Travel was difficult; there were no railroads, roads were primitive, and Slavonia was socially and culturally distinct from Zagreb. Previous to the development of the Illyrian movement, the prevalent sense of ethnic identity tended to be regional, Slavonian, as opposed to national, Croatian. Illyrian influence did not become significant in Osijek until 1842, and concrete achievements such as the establishment of a Croatian reading room and obtaining permission to found a Croat-Slavonian literary society did not come until 1847 (Rakijaš 1974, 8–9).

For many years in Slavonia, the development of musical life was connected to the emergence of a sense of national feeling. The Croatian Franciscans, who organized musical events both in and out of church, and compiled songbooks of well-known Croatian airs, were especially influential. The Gesellschaft der Musikfreunde (music lovers' society) in Osijek existed from 1830 to 1838, offering a program of music instruction on string and wind instruments. The driving force behind the organization was provided by Josip Krmpotić, a judge, who later distinguished himself as a strong supporter of the Illyrian movement (ibid., 9).

In Osijek, *tamburaši* were associated with the Illyrian movement from its inception. An early achievement was the publication in 1842 of *Tamburaš ilirski*, a collection of folk songs by Mato Topalović, a poet and Illyrian adherent from the town of Vinkovci who later became a professor of theology and Croatian language at the bishop's school in Đakovo (ibid.).

Perhaps the most effective agitators for the Illyrian cause in Slavonia were the *tamburaši* led by Pajo Kolarić. Kolarić was active in local politics, served as an alderman in Osijek, and was also a self-taught musician and song writer. In 1847 he established the first tamburitza society. It is probable that Kolarić was drawing on a Slavonian tradition of music making, which had developed and spread rapidly at the end of the eighteenth and beginning of the nineteenth centuries.

Slavonia, with its neighboring provinces of Srijem and Bačka, had emerged from Turkish rule in 1699 and had been severely depopulated by decades of military incursions, warfare, and pillaging. Once the Austrians established firm control in the region, they encouraged settlers from various parts of their far-flung empire to take up residence there. Slovaks, Hungarians, Ukrainians, Czechs, Germans, as well as Croatian and Serbian refugees from south of the Sava settled in planned, orderly villages. The Empress Maria Theresa is reported to have taken a personal interest in designing the rectangular town plans and the architectural style in the new settlements (Clissold 1966, 31).

The musical life of this multiethnic region was dominated by the famed Hungarian Romani ensembles known as *kapele*. These Romani bands consisted of varied combinations of violins, violas, cellos, a string bass, and the cimbalom, a large type of hammered dulcimer. The ensembles typically consisted of five, six, or more musicians who played the popular music of the day at town and village weddings and festivities. Usually referred to as "Hungarian Gypsy ensembles," these orchestras were by no means limited only to Hungary. They were frequent also in Slovakia, Rumania, and among the South Slavs living on the Pannonian plain (Andrić 1958, 13).

The tamburitza composer and historian Josip Andrić contended that the first tamburitza ensembles were created to be analogous to Romani violin and cimbalom groups. The Croatian ethnic groups known as Bunjevci and Šokci as well as the Serbs of Bačka already were familiar with the tambura *samica*. Taking a clue from the Romani ensembles, some thought that *tambure* might be organized in ensembles, and Andrić felt that that the first such experimental attempts likely took place near the end of the eighteenth century.

Tambure are fashioned in various sizes and each is assigned a role analogous to the members of the violin family. The *prima tamburica* is comparable to the first violin; the *brač* has the same name as the German word for viola, *bratsch*. The *čelo brač* is analogous to violoncello, and the *berde* functions like the string bass (see also chap. 3). Andrić, himself a Bunjevac, guessed that the Bunjevci, a Croatian minority group in Bačka, originated the first tamburitza ensembles (ibid.). These early ensembles must have aroused considerable enthusiasm. In the climate of anti-Hungarian feeling, then beginning to develop among the South Slavs of the region, the fact that tamburitza ensembles used a different instrument from Hungarian Gypsy orchestras must have been a factor in popularizing tamburitzas (ibid.).

Tamburitza orchestras were able to avoid the stigma of a social concept regarding musicians. Throughout most of the Austrian Empire professional popular musicians were thought of as a lower social status than their audience. Often members of the dominant ethnic or religious group refrained entirely from professional music making, leaving that task to lower-caste groups or ethnic minorities like Romani or Jews (Gojković 1972, 18–22). At that time the tambura was not an instrument associated with professional musicians. Typically they were played by amateur musicians belonging to the major ethnic groups. The amateur had a "respectable" occupation and played music for personal enjoyment; the Romani performer "degraded" him or herself, pandering to the wishes of the audience in order to receive money. These prevailing social attitudes and the association of the Romani with the violin created an incentive for the tamburitza to be the instrument of Slavonian amateur musical societies.

Most of what we know about Pajo Kolarić and his first documented tamburitza society comes from Franjo Kuhač. While he was still a boy in Osijek, Kuhač was inspired by Kolarić, both musically and politically. Kolarić, as a friend of Kuhač's father, visited the household on a number of occasions in the 1840s and took an interest in young Franjo's developing musical talents.

Kolarić was born in the city of Osijek in 1821, completed gymnasium there, and, lacking funds to study law, took a job in the office of the city government in 1840. Kuhač depicts him as a "fun-loving personality, a skillful but untrained baritone singer, an excellent tambura player and a fiery Illyrian patriot" (Kuhač 1893, 248). In 1847 Kolarić put together an amateur tamburitza ensemble of six young Osijek residents. These original instruments, completely Eastern in their basic form with the exception of thicker necks, are preserved in the Zagreb Ethnographic Museum.

According to Kuhač, "wherever there was a friendly get-together or some sort of patriotic special occasion, there was Pajo with his group, spreading the Illyrian idea and developing sympathy for the national movement." Kuhač felt that Kolarić's Croatian music and song won over many to Illyrianism. The songs Kolarić composed spread by word of mouth. The town's residents, typically German-speaking in that era, began to sing Kolarić's songs in Croatian, and these might have been the only Croatian words to pass their lips (ibid.).

The songs Kolarić composed were sentimental love songs typical of nineteenth-century popular music. The titles are characteristic: "Da znaš pravo srce moje" (If you knew my true heart), "Radi tebe ja na kočku stavio sam" (I risked everything for you), "Tko je srce u te dirno" (Who touched your heart). Several of Kolarić's songs became widely known and some are still performed (Njikoš 1957, 22). His compositions were typical examples of the *starogradske pjesme* (old town songs), the major form of urban popular music in the late nineteenth and early twentieth centuries. Recordings of *starogradske pjesme* are still commercially viable in Croatia and Serbia; the songs are commonly in the repertoire of amateur singing societies and may be sung in informal social gatherings, despite decades of exposure of Croatian and Serbian culture to jazz, rock, and other imported musical idioms.

Pajo Kolarić (1821–76). (Program for Đakovački Vezovi, Đakovo, Croatia, July 1978)

Although he was not musically literate, Kolarić had a great natural talent for melody; according to an analysis of his songs by the musicologist Božidar Širola, Kolarić's melodies showed many characteristics of Croatian folk melodies. As is typical of *starogradske pjesme*, these sentimental love songs, drinking songs, and patriotic hymns comprise Kolarić's opus.

Kolarić helped establish the connection of the tamburitza to Croatian national politics He was briefly imprisoned by the Hungarians in 1849, and Kuhač referred to him as a "brave agitator" during the revolutionary events of 1848 and 1849. In 1861 Kolarić became a city councilman in Osijek and was involved in local electoral politics until his death in 1876.

Kuhač commented upon the role of *tamburaši* during the revolutions: "*Tamburaši* have no small effect upon the folk; thus in the crucial years of 1848–1849 they helped a great deal to fire up the Slavonians to support Ban Jelačić and our national politics; knowing well what they were doing, they called upon students, clerks and other educated people to start tamburitza societies. During those fateful years there were many such folk/national musicians, and many of the most outstanding patriots of Slavonia were leading members of these societies" (Kuhač 1877, 81). It was politics as much as music that drew members to the tamburitza societies. Kolarić's orchestra promoted South Slavic patriotism and resistance to foreign rule.

The Croatian national revival that culminated in the Illyrian movement of the 1830s and 1840s had a decisive influence on folklore study in Croatia. Moreover, Illyrian ideas gave rise to the goal of producing a folk-based, but refined, musical tradition featuring the tamburitza as a symbolic Croatian national instrument. More than a century and a half later, Croatian and Croatian American musicians continue to pursue this goal.

CHAPTER 3

The Tamburitza Matures and Migrates to America

T he accomplishments of the Illyrian movement proved to be crucial in determining the nature of the tamburitza tradition, especially in its soon-to-develop orchestral form. In Zagreb, the Illyrians developed a musical ideology still influential today, and in Osijek, South Slav patriots established the first urban tamburitza orchestra with self-conscious nationalistic pretensions.

Because of the then-prevailing isolation of Osijek from Zagreb, there was not adequate time for Kolarić's orchestra to become known or imitated in Zagreb before the sudden, imposed end of the Illyrian movement. Following a short period of stagnation, the tamburitza movement gained momentum. Organized orchestras and informal combos proliferated during the later decades of the nineteenth century and during the early years of the twentieth until 1914.

In geographic terms, the ensembles ceased to be only a regional phenomenon of Slavonia, Srijem, and Bačka. As they spread to western Croatia, Bosnia, and Serbia the increased demand for the instrument stimulated the manufacture of *tambure*, creating full-time tamburitza makers who sought to improve and perfect their product.

Since the period of the increasing popularity of tamburitza orchestras coincided with the period of mass migration of South Slavs from Habsburg lands to North and South America, Australia, and New Zealand, it is not surprising that tamburitza ensembles cropped up in these immigrant colonies. Musical activity in tamburitza orchestras and vocal choirs became the most important focus of immigrant cultural activity.

It took until 1914 for the seeds planted by the Illyrians in the 1830s and 1840s to grow to full maturity. The growth and development of tamburitza groups started slowly, picked up momentum, and finally snowballed by the beginning of the twentieth century. In the 1850s, though, the first decade after the crushing of the Illyrians, tamburitza activity faced a hostile political climate. Hungarian revolutionary zeal carried with it a certain chauvinism that favored Magyarization and cultural assimilation of the Slavic subjects in the Hungarian kingdom. It is characteristic that the noted Magyar leader Lajos Kossuth declared himself unable to find Croatia on the map and stated emphatically, "I know no Croatian nationality" (Clissold 1966, 34). The so-called April laws, passed by the Hungarian Diet in 1848, greatly limited Croatian autonomy and aimed to incorporate Croatia within the administrative system of Hungary. Therefore, while turbulent unrest began to shake the Empire, it was in the immediate interests of the Slavs in the Hungarian kingdom to support the Habsburg Crown against the Hungarians.

Public opinion in Croatia became intensely anti-Hungarian. The newly appointed *Ban* (viceroy) of Croatia, Baron Josip Jelačić, was an Illyrian adherent but also a conservative noble and loyal to the emperor. He favored Croatian independence from Hungary but wanted Croatian lands to remain in the Habsburg Empire on an equal footing with Hungary. These views brought him into conflict with the Hungarians, especially the radical nationalists. In September 1848, Jelačić crossed the Drava River into Hungary with an army of forty thousand Croatians, including a contingent of Serbian volunteers, thus precipitating the war that ultimately crushed the Hungarian revolution.

As a faithful servant of the emperor, Jelačić expected that Croatia would be rewarded with increased unity and autonomy. The Habsburgs, however, realized that Illyrianism represented as much of a potential threat to their rule as did Hungarian nationalism, and all non-German nationalities were therefore equally suppressed. A young Franz Joseph installed a repressive absolutist regime in the 1850s, which became known as the Bach period, so named after Alexander Bach, the minister of the interior who enforced harsh policies (Macartney 1969, 426).

One contemporary observer commented that "the Hungarians received as punishment what the other races received as reward" (Clissold 1966, 35). Franz Joseph and Bach endeavored to destroy local autonomy and the privileges of the national nobility, which led to widespread Germanization. German became the official language in schools and government offices; German-speaking Austrians were sent to the Slavic provinces to dominate the local bureaucracies (Macartney 1969, 494). Slavic cultural activities were curtailed. The newspapers were government controlled and only one Croatian magazine, *Neven*, was allowed to continue publishing (Andreis 1974, 184).

The suppression of Vatroslav Lisinski typifies the way in which Illyrian cultural activities were stamped out. He never received the promised position as conductor of the Zagreb Music Society's orchestra and eventually was forced out of even his unpaid association with the music school. The final blow came in November 1852, in connection with a concert prepared for Franz Joseph's visit to Zagreb. At the last minute, Lisinski was replaced as conductor by Anton Schwarz, a person openly hostile to Lisinski and Illyrian ideas. The scheduled performance of Lisinski's opera *Ljubav i zloba* was cancelled, and an Italian opera company was specially invited to perform Donizetti's *Lucretia Borgia* (ibid., 155).

ORGANIZING TAMBURITZA SOCIETIES

During the absolutist period, conditions for organizing urban tamburitza societies, with their Illyrian association, were not good. It seems that informal tamburitza groups were beyond the power of the government to control. Small tamburitza ensembles increased in popularity, spreading among rural peasants and artisans in towns (Kuhač 1877, 76).

Political conditions changed abruptly in the 1860s when military defeats in Italy and Prussia forced the weakened Habsburgs to abandon absolutism, making concessions to the resentful repressed nationalities. In 1867 they came to terms with the Hungarians, establishing the Austro-Hungarian dual monarchy, and Croatia was once again divided between the Austrian and Hungarian spheres. The inland Croats again felt the pressures of Magyarization, especially during the tenure (1883–1903) of the notoriously anti-Croatian Ban Károly Khuen-Héderváry.

There was some political room to maneuver between the competing interests of the Austrians and Hungarians to secure more cultural autonomy for the South Slavs. Through this political process, Zagreb managed to emerge during this period as the true cultural center of Croatia. In 1861 the Zagreb Theater was declared a national institution; the Yugoslav Academy of Arts and Sciences was established in Zagreb in 1866, fully fifty years before the establishment of a Yugoslav state, indicative of the ideals of South Slavic unity stemming from the Illyrians. In 1874 Zagreb University was founded, a magnet for future generations of the Croatian intelligentsia (Clissold 1966, 38).

The musical scene was reinvigorated, especially vocal music. To sing in Croatian remained a powerful symbolic act of defiance to Magyar or German rulers. Croatian national feelings stimulated the formation of choirs, and renewed calls were made for the establishment of a Croatian opera company. Josip Andreis characterized singing societies as the vanguard of the national movement during that period: "In 1862, the amateur singing society Kolo was founded and it remained a very important performing body for a long time (until the end of the Second World War) giving frequent concerts, taking part in performances of larger vocal and instrumental compositions and stimulating composers to write more and more complex compositions. The programs of its early concerts included rousing songs, marches and other patriotic choral songs designed to awaken and strengthen national consciousness. Later programs included . . . pieces for tamburitza orchestra" (Andreis 1974, 187). Even before the end of absolutism and the founding of Kolo, in the provincial city of Karlovac, the choir Društvo karlovačkih pjevača (Karlovac singers' society) was established in 1858, and in 1868 its name was changed to Prvo hrvatsko pjevačko društvo "Zora" (First Croatian singing society "Zora"), thus reflecting an open Croatian orientation. Such choirs spread quickly to other provincial towns and even to larger villages, becoming a central institution of cultural life. The choruses branched out in their artistic activities, nurturing not only music but also theatrical arts. They staged comedies, dramas, and operettas. In the context of these cultural organizations, tamburitza orchestras were founded that organized formal concert programs. According to ethnomusicologist Grozdana Marošević: "In Karlovac the first [local] tamburitza society Hrvatska was founded in 1886, which was . . . until the beginning of the 20th century a significant presence in the cultural and recreational life of the city. After 1890, within the society a [female] ensemble called gospođica-tamburašica (Miss Tamburitzan) also was active. The [tamburitza] society collaborated with 'Zora' . . . and with the [local] Ramberg string ensemble. In the 1890s additional tamburitza societies became active [in Karlovac]" (Marošević 1986, 346).

To link these societies, in 1874 the Croatian Singing League (Hrvatski pjevački savez) established its headquarters in Zagreb (Holjevac 1967, 88–89). Aside from Kolo, there was another Zagreb group, the revitalized Illyrian music society that became active again, known as Vienac after 1868. Other choirs in Zagreb were Sloboda (founded in 1873) and a university choir Mladost (founded in 1900). In Dalmatia, the Zvonimir choir was founded in Split (1884), and in Dubrovnik, Gundulić (1893). In Osijek there were two choirs, Lipa (1876) and Zrinski (1899). One of the most important choirs, Zora, was founded in Karlovac in 1876. These musical organizations continued to proliferate.

Enthusiasm for musical activity increased and new repertoire was created. There was a lot of excitement about the new Croatian vocal and instrumental music of Ivan Zajc and his successful establishment of a Croatian opera company. Franjo Kuhač had begun systematic ethnomusicological study among the South Slavs, conducting extensive field research. His published song collections became a source of material. In 1890 Vienac organized a concert of folk songs from various parts of Croatia, Serbia, and Vojvodina, arranged for choir with all of the songs taken from Kuhač's *Južno-slovjenske narodne popievke* (Andreis 1974, 187).

This type of musically oriented cultural organization became a model for amateur cultural activity in the South Slavic immigrant communities of North America. In 1902 the Zora singing society was established in Chicago, named after the choir in Karlovac, no doubt by immigrants from the Karlovac region. In 1910 Chicago's Zora joined the Croatian Singing League. In 1911, taking the example of Czech

American singing societies who founded Ednota českih pjevačkih društava (Union of Czech singing societies) based in Chicago, they formed
the Savez hrvatskih pjevačkih društava u Americi (League of Croatian singing societies in America) (Holjevac 1967, 89). The league
strengthened connections in the Croatian American community. Croatian American choirs from different cities frequently traveled to perform as guests on the concert program of a similar choir. Typically, the
singers were house guests in the homes of members of the host choir
and a postconcert social party was organized by the hosts at the hall of
a fraternal lodge or a church.

The achievements of Ivan Zajc were influential on the tamburitza
tradition. It is reported that Zajc looked favorably upon tamburitza
orchestras. Such orchestras played tamburitza arrangements of his
operatic works, notably the song "U boj u boj" (To battle, to battle)
from the opera *Nikola Šubić Zrinski*. According to Josip Andrić, Zajc
composed four pieces specifically for tamburitza (Andrić 1955, 3–4).
It is even more significant that Zajc made the aesthetic criteria of
Romantic nineteenth-century classical music the dominant aesthetic
in Croatian music. In the city, in towns and villages, classical orchestras, village choirs, and amateur tamburitza societies all came to accept
the operas of Zajc as the ultimate musical model to emulate.

Zajc was born in the port city of Rijeka in 1832. His father was a
military band leader of Czech origin. He grew up surrounded by music
and excelled in music lessons as a child, but his father wanted the boy
to study law. Finally his music teachers persuaded the elder Zajc to
allow his son to get a higher education in music.

From 1850 to 1855 he studied at the Milan Conservatory, where
he was one of the most distinguished students. His opera *La Tirolese*,
composed as a part of his final examinations, won the student competition and was staged at the conservatory in 1855. The deaths of his
parents following his graduation brought Zajc back to Rijeka, where
he stayed until 1862. He became the conductor of Rijeka's municipal
orchestra and taught stringed instruments at the Philharmonic Institute (Andreis 1974, 193).

At this time Zajc began to develop Croatian national consciousness. He was a member of Hrvatska čitaonica, a Croatian reading and

discussion club that advocated Croatian national interests. He composed dance tunes for the club's social events including a quadrille
titled *Zivjela Hrvatska* (Long live Croatia) (ibid., 196). Zajc began to
feel that Rijeka was too provincial for him to fully develop his skills,
and he moved to Vienna with his family in 1862.

Vienna at that time had five opera houses. The operettas of Offen-
bach and von Suppe were in style, and soon Zajc was able to establish
a reputation for himself as a composer. At the end of 1863, his opera
Mannschaft am Bord (All aboard, boys) was successfully staged. During his eight years in Vienna, he became one of the more popular composers of operettas. His comic opera *Die Hexe von Boissy* (The witch of
Boissy) was a major hit.

Zajc's decision to leave Vienna and move to Zagreb was neither
sudden nor unexpected. Zajc frequently associated with Croatian university students studying in Vienna. Among them were writers like
August Šenoa and Ivan Dežman, who later became important literary
figures. They constantly reminded him of his duty, his patriotic mission to use his musical talents to improve the culture of his Croatian
homeland. He moved to Zagreb in 1870 and was offered the positions
of director of the newly established Croatian Opera and the director of
the Glazbeni zavod music school. He directed the opera until 1889 and
the music school until 1909, when he retired (ibid., 198).

Zajc and other Croatian composers of his era continued in the direction set out by Illyrian musicians. Though their ideology called for a
national music based on the music of the peasantry, these composers
simply knew too little about the music of the peasantry. Like Livadić
and Lisinski, Zajc was imbued with and a master of classical European
music. Compositions were made "national" or "folk" (*narodni*) by the
use of Croatian in song texts, patriotic titles of songs, or instrumental
pieces, the patriotic sentiments that might be expressed in the lyrics,
heroic themes from Croatian history in opera librettos, or by the performance of virtually any kind of music on the national instrument, the
tamburitza. A true fruition of Gaj's musical ideology, based on Herder's
ideas that art music should be based on peasant folk music, was not
possible to achieve until much later, after the ethnomusicological works

of Franjo Kuhač appeared and had time to enter the intellectual mainstream of Croatia (Rakijaš 1974, 28).

Franjo Kuhač

Franjo Kuhač has been mentioned so far in every chapter of this study.
Indeed, it would be difficult adequately to treat any subject in the field
of Balkan music and to ignore his work. Throughout his long, produc-
tive, and controversial career, he produced 191 published books and
articles plus 19 unpublished manuscripts. He established in Croatia
the necessity of field research to gain knowledge of traditional music.
In some of his works, he included information on the cultural context
of performances. He used the technique of grassroots oral history by
interviewing the surviving members of the Illyrian movement and
Illyrian musicians in preparation for his historical study of Croatian
music in the 1830s and 1840s (Kuhač 1893).

Franjo Ksaver Kuhač
(1834–1911). (Courtesy of
the Institute for Ethnology
and Folklore, Zagreb)

Kuhač was a fervently patriotic Croatian, although he was of German ethnic background. His parents, Joszef and Terezia (Piller) Koch, were born in Nemet-Bolje in Hungary, where their families had migrated to sometime between 1720 and 1740. After their marriage they moved to Osijek. Kuhač used the name Franz Koch until he was thirty-seven; Koch and Kuhač both mean "cook" in German and Croatian, respectively (Rakijaš 1974, 15).

His gift for music became apparent early, as did his Croatian sentiments, despite his German background. In 1847, when he would have been twelve or thirteen years old, he foreshadowed his rich career of notating folk music. At the urging of his father's friend Pajo Kolarić, he wrote down the folk song "Miruj miruj srce moje" (Be at peace, my heart) (ibid., 10). Kuhač's strong Croatian nationalist sentiments became apparent in 1848. He participated in demonstrations in Osijek, an event which may have prompted his parents to send him out of town to a teachers' school in Donji Miholjac. In 1850 he went to Pécs, a larger town with more musical life where his uncle Filip Koch was a clergyman. In 1852 he went to Buda, where he entered the music society's school (Hangaszegyesuleti Zenede); he studied under the composer Károly Thern for only two years, although six years were required to receive a diploma. From 1855 to 1858 he traveled extensively, visiting important cultural centers, Leipzig, Weimar, and Vienna, where he increased his musical knowledge through contact with noted composers like Franz Liszt, Carl Czerny, and Eduard Hanslik. His restless nature was to cost him; having failed to obtain a diploma from the Buda school hindered him in later years and contributed to his material insecurity (ibid., 13–14).

In 1859 Kuhač was living in Osijek once again when his uncle died, leaving Kuhač the sizable sum of 12,000 forinths with the stipulation that the money was to be used for cultural purposes. Kuhač decided to spend the next twelve years traveling during the warmer months to collect the folk music of the South Slavs and neighboring peoples. He carried out fieldwork in Croatia, Slavonia, Srijem, Istria, Dalmatia, Slovenia, Vojvodina, Bosnia, Herzegovina, Serbia, Montenegro, Macedonia, Bulgaria, Austria, Italy, and Hungary. As Kuhač put it: "I traveled for twelve years, every year for five, six or more months and so spent my entire fortune, which was by no means a small amount of money. On January 1, 1870, I started to work on my collected songs, harmonizing them and adding piano accompaniment, as well as indicating the variants of particular texts which were to be found in previously published songbooks" (ibid., 19).

In 1871 Kuhač moved to Zagreb. He obtained a position of piano instructor and music theory teacher at the Music Academy and supplemented the meager stipend for his work by writing music and theater reviews for Zagreb's two leading newspapers, Narodne Novine and Agrammer Zeitung. He made enemies, however, for his critiques were often very harsh, so in 1874 he was fired from the newspapers (ibid.). In 1876 he resigned from the Music Academy in a dispute with the director Karl Klobučarić. Kuhač was insulted, possibly by a reference to his incomplete education. Kuhač also complained about the pro-German cultural sympathies still dominant in the academy (Andreis 1974, 215). It is an irony typical of Austro-Hungarian Croatia. The native German Croatian patriot Koch/Kuhač was pitted against the alleged German culture supporter Klobučarić, whose surname is surely of Slavic origin.

Kuhač never again held a steady job. Although he obtained the support of institutions and patrons for many of his projects, he was forced to spend his wife's dowry to publish his most important work—his four-volume collection Južnoslovjenske popievke, issued between 1878 and 1881; a fifth volume was published posthumously in 1941. At one point Kuhač was forced to be a traveling life insurance salesman, something he complained about bitterly in a letter (Rakijaš 1974, 20).

His difficulties may have stemmed in part from the fact that he was, justifiably or not, identified as a follower of nationalist leader Ante Starčević's Stranka prava (Party of rights), considered by the authorities to be a radical Croatian nationalist organization. Kuhač denied that he was involved in politics, but in spite of that he was unable to obtain a position in any of Zagreb's cultural institutions. He remained an active independent scholar to the end of his life, publishing his last major book, Osobine narodne glazbe naročito hrvatske (Characteristics of folk music, especially Croatian), in 1909 at the age of seventy-five. He died in Zagreb in 1911.

Kuhač was a pioneer in ethnomusicology. His *Zbirke*, compiled from his original fieldwork, from fieldwork submitted to Kuhač by collaborating music enthusiasts, and from material published in earlier songbooks, remains a valuable source of data on South Slavic folksong (Marošević 1989, 107). There are aspects of his work that are fully acceptable, conceptually and methodologically, to modern ethnomusicological practice.

It was his goal to assemble data for an accurate picture of the state of South Slavic folksong at the time of his collecting efforts, sometimes including examples of songs that did not suit his cultural-political goals. For example he included a Slovenian song from the Austrian province of Styria that was "sasvim po njemačkom kroju" (completely German in style) because he wanted to show "kakav je u istini narodni piev sada, a kakav je bio prije, a ne kakav bi imao biti" (how folk song truly is now, and how it was before, but not how it ought to be [cf. Marošević 1989, 123]). On the other hand, his distaste for "foreign" influences on Slavic folksong might have been a factor in the paucity of material collected from Međimurje, a northeastern Croatian region, where Kuhač felt the singing tradition had become greatly influenced by Hungarian music. Kuhač was explicit about his Illyrian-inspired goal that the collections were intended to serve classically trained composers and musicians to create a true South Slavic national (*narodna*) art music. He had no qualms about "improving" the harmonization of simple folk songs, and his piano arrangements of the songs are sometimes overly complex, seeming to overpower the simple folk melodies. Believing in the cultural unity of the South Slavs, he had no compunction about sometimes combining melodies that he had collected in one area with texts from another, distant region—from what would be different countries today.

Kuhač organized the collection according to the theme of the text (i.e., love songs, wedding songs, drinking songs, etc.), including in these categories songs from various countries and regions. He thereby obscured the fact that many regions were underrepresented and failed to illuminate the stylistic particularities of regional music traditions. Since in those days Kuhač did not have a phonograph or tape recorder, his notations sometimes were understandably incorrect. Moreover, while Kuhač recognized the existence of the nontempered scales of certain regions' folk music, he did not understand them nor did he have a system for notating them. It is to his credit, though, that he did not consider music in these scales "accidental" or "wrong." Finally, some of his analytical works are overly opinionated and marred by exaggerated nationalism. Still, Kuhač's work represented a giant step, a major achievement, and a resource to both performers and scholars of South Slavic folk music (Rakijaš 1974, 24).

Early Tamburitza Combos

It is a happy coincidence that the sudden growth of the tamburitza tradition took place during the years of Kuhač's extensive fieldwork from which we get our earliest detailed glimpse of the tradition. In his 1877 address to the Yugoslav Academy of Arts and Sciences, he discussed informal tamburitza combos of the 1850s and 1860s:

> Some twenty years ago the tambura was accepted in Croatia once again, and now the folk already have quite a lot of them. Tambura is played mostly by the common folk (peasants) and by the lower classes of townspeople, especially barbers' boys and police, but you can also see it in the hands of soldiers, high school students, clerks and even nobles. Slavic women and girls very seldom play it, but those in Turkish harems often play tambura and mostly very well. All of the aforementioned play tambura solely for their own entertainment, but professional playing is done only by "real *tamburaši*," that is those folk musicians who play in taverns in groups of four, five, up to twelve men. These groups mostly stay in one place but a few travel as well, so that some fifteen years ago [1861] *tamburaši* from Novi Sad dared to travel all the way to France and Belgium. (Kuhač 1877, 76)

Kuhač wrote an indication of the social position of tambura players:

> Besides two or three tambura groups in our country who do nothing but play, there are many more that practice some other trade, and thus do not live exclusively from playing music. This segment of tambura

players descend directly from the folk; they are bricklayers, carpenters, roofers, basket-makers, fishermen, peddlers and the like. (Ibid.)

He described the process through which *tamburaši* learned their music, as well as the sources of their repertoire:

> When the end of autumn nears, the group gets together, or better said, it is called together by the *prima* player who is also its director. After some practice, the group puts on its performances which take place each and every evening and don't stop until about Easter. For the duration of the whole season they practice together to learn new pieces and new songs. Whatever one of them may have heard during the summer from the folk, from a gypsy orchestra, from a singing society, or made up by himself, he presents to the judgment of the group. If the proposed piece is considered proper and good, the whole group practices it—of course without knowledge of written notes. In this way the *tamburaši* give evidence of their good ear and I might say musical instinct. They are quite proud of their own ability and skill, thus claiming to be true representatives of folk or national music. (Ibid., 77)

Next Kuhač listed a number of frequent performance settings:

> Aside from in taverns, tambura groups play also at weddings, work bees, house parties and public dances of the humbler sort, public holidays and below the windows of people who would somehow offer them a treat. (Ibid.)

In a further discussion of tamburitza repertoire, Kuhač revealed his fervent nationalism and railed against the performance of non-Slavic material:

> At public performances, the program alternates folk dances, marches, fantasias and masterworks. For the most part, they play Slavic music, but at times non-Slavic pieces are heard. Often these are poorly done; their waltz, a slow German idea, is very funny and it could not be otherwise owing to the nature of tamburitza accompaniment. They know

well themselves that Slavic *tamburaši* were not born for foreign music, especially for foreign dances. But since they may encounter during their performances all sorts of audiences [meaning nationalities] and since they often play at dance parties, they can manage to play a waltz, a polka, a mazurka and so forth. If they are allowed to put together the program according to their own desires, you won't find anything other than Slavic music. (Ibid., 78)

Continuing on the subject of repertoire, Kuhač discussed the spontaneous, humorous, and satirical songs that are still today an important part of tamburitza performances:

Tamburaši sing mostly patriotic songs, but they are also prone to humor. They nurture funny songs with a special love. Usually the texts of these songs are made up by the *tamburaši* themselves so that their form may be poor, but they contain beautiful witticisms and various political or other sorts of jabs. Sometimes it is amazing how well *tamburaši* are acquainted with our public events and issues and how well they cut them up satirically. It is very difficult to collect such songs from them, because it is their principle that the sung word may be denied to the police, but the written or dictated word could be adequate evidence against them. As soon as the novelty of these songs wears off, they are forgotten, even by the *tamburaši*, and thus they disappear. Had anyone been able to collect all of the songs of this sort in our country, let's say from 1845 to today, there would be enough material for some sort of Croatian "Demokritos." (Ibid.)

From Kuhač's data, we know that the tambura was firmly established by the late 1860s not only in Slavonia, Srijem, and Bačka but also in western Croatia, including the city of Zagreb. Kuhač compiled a list of musicians he considered to be the ten greatest *primaši* (players of the high-pitched lead tamburitza). Although eight of them were from the eastern provinces of Srijem, Bačka, and Banat, and just two from Banija in the west, this proportion probably reflected Kuhač's Osijek residence during his period of intense fieldwork. That there were many *tamburaši* in western Croatia is plain from another list that Kuhač presented.

Kuhač obtained the list from Mijat Novak whom he describes as a seventy-six-year-old man from Petrinja (in Banija, southeast of Zagreb). The list, compiled in 1869, comprised the names of "all excellent *tamburaši*" from that area, including Zagreb. The sixty-four names include twenty-three from Zagreb, fourteen from Sisak, fifteen from Kostajnica, and a smattering from other nearby towns. It is puzzling, however, that Novak, from Petrinja himself, listed only two *tamburaši* from that town, excluding even Vasil Eror, whom Kuhač had included on his list of the ten greatest *primaši*. Novak also listed the occupations of the musicians, a wide range from farmers to craftsmen to office clerks. Most frequent are eleven shoe or sandal makers, ten barbers, eight farmers, five tailors, and only three of the sixty-four were full-time *tamburaši*. The first and family names of the musicians can be a useful, if somewhat imprecise, indicator of their nationality. A majority of the names seem to be Croatian with a few likely to be Serbian. This is despite the fact that there was a substantial Serbian minority in the Banija region (ibid., 79–80).

Kuhač described the typical instrumental combinations in small tamburitza ensembles, ranging in size from three to ten players. He indicated four musical roles named for the instruments in the tamburitza family: *primaš*, *čanguraš* (*kontraš*), *bugarijaš*, and *berdetaš*. The instrument names differ somewhat from the nomenclature for the Farkaš and Srijemski system tamburitzas that came later.

Kuhač gave us a vivid and detailed picture of the early tamburitza ensembles. It is likely that the rapid spread of this type of ensemble play was facilitated by the already wide distribution and popularity of the *samica*. Crudely hewn *samice* sold by woodworkers at town and village markets are still a popular inexpensive toy for young children. Several skilled tamburitza players informed me that their first musical experience was playing a simple *samica*. It is easy to imagine that once the concept of ensemble play was known, it was not difficult for a few musicians, already skilled on the *samica*, to learn to play together as a group. A good example of the process of ensemble creation has been preserved in the recollections of Pero Z. Ilić, a Serbian composer and music teacher born in 1868. Ilić's home town, Sremski Karlovci, was an important educational center that attracted gymnasium students from other provinces. In letters to Josip Andrić, Ilić described not only the formation of the first tamburitza ensemble in Karlovci but provided an example of how the ideas for technical improvements to the instruments came to town:

> In my home town, Sremski Karlovci, young men used to play *tambure* which had a pear-shaped form and a long neck (*samica*). On such a tambura there were four strings, arranged in two courses tuned to the same note. The fingerboard had thin wire frets placed in such a way as to produce the seven notes of the major scale. There were, at that time, larger and smaller *tambure* but they were all called by the one name tambura.
>
> In my father's home there usually boarded some poor schoolboy, normally from Croatia, Dalmatia or Bosnia. Thus a certain Mojsije from Dalmatia boarded with us who knew how to play bagpipes, violin and tambura. He had some sort of a guitar with four strings tuned in an open A chord. That instrument served exclusively as accompaniment for a melody using two chords ... Mojsije called that instrument "kontra" ... and its players "kontraši."
>
> In the fall of 1875, a lot of refugees escaped from Bosnia where a rebellion had broken out, going to Croatia and Srem and a large number of them came seeking refuge in Sremski Karlovci. Among these refugees was a young man, Marko Capkun, who brought two *tambure* with him. The smaller he called *ićitel* and the larger he called *šarkija*. ... The frets on the fingerboard were not of wire but rather of stretched gut, pulled through little holes on the neck and tied behind. On the upper part of the neck, the frets were arranged in half steps. Marko played some melodies which required half steps. It seemed to me, those were the first half steps in the tambura's development. At that time in Sremski Karlovci there was a woodworker Josif who made *tambure samice*, and seeing Marko's *tambura ićitel*, he began to make ones like it. But instead of the pear shape, he made them in the shape of a tiny guitar. Already in 1876 the Karlovci violin player Laza began to play such a tambura.
>
> A certain bird catcher, Joza, who played together with Laza besides catching and selling birds, engaged in tambura making. In 1877 or 1878 he built a big tambura—much bigger than a guitar, stretched two

thicker and two thinner strings on it and called it *tambur bas* or *berdon*. Now Laza, the musician, put together his first tamburitza ensemble like so: he played the little tambura, which they called *prima*, and his play was accompanied by three to five *kontraši* with one *tambur bas*. (Ilić 1955, 5–6)

Ilić described how Mojsije brought back from Dalmatia an improved *kontra*, which he called *brač*, after his school vacation in 1879. Later the Ilić family moved to Belgrade and later to Smederevo, where he recollects the names of *tamburaši* in those Serbian towns, indicating the spread of tamburitza ensembles to the south and east from Bačka, much as the data from Kuhač indicate a spread to the west (ibid.).

European ethnologists prefer to distinguish village traditions from town fashions, yet in the early development of tamburitza ensembles such a clear-cut demarcation does not seem to be possible. From Kuhač and Novak's data, it is evident that both peasant villagers and town artisans were among the first *tamburaši*. In towns and villages, the setting for tambura ensembles was often the tavern or inn. Even in the present day, the similarities outweigh the differences between taverns, whether they are at a village crossroads, in a small provincial town, or in the humbler quarter of the city. In a sense, taverns are a bridge between village and town society. The town taverns are frequented by villagers on their trips to market. While in town, villagers often patronize an establishment run by one of their landsmen. Peasant boys and girls often find their first urban employment working in taverns. Village taverns, meanwhile, may be the most "urban" institution in the rural setting. It is here that tradesmen or other travelers passing through would stay, bringing news from other parts. Even when there are no outsiders present, this is an important setting for socializing and communication among the villagers. While a noisy bagpipe might have been appropriate at a village wedding or an outdoor dance, by the late nineteenth century the softer, tinkling music of the *tamburaši* had captured the taverns. Their musical sound as well as their humor and their political and social satire was at home in the permissive environment of the tavern. It may be that from the start, *tamburaši* were among the most sophisticated and witty members of their communities.

URBAN TAMBURITZA SOCIETIES

Following in the footsteps of the widespread acceptance of the tavern groups, which seemed beyond the power of the government to stamp out, urban tamburitza societies began to proliferate. Ivan Sladaček (1820–99), an Osijek-born contemporary of Pajo Kolarić, may have been the first to bring musical literacy to the tamburitza tradition (Andrić 1958, 26). He organized a tamburitza orchestra, which played from music scores, in the Slavonian town of Vukovar. Their music, the first known musical scores for tamburitza orchestra, were written by Sladaček himself. Sladaček's orchestra performed in a Zagreb tavern in 1880 in what Josip Andrić called "the first tamburitza concert" in the Croatian capital.

There had been, no doubt, tamburitza playing in Zagreb prior to 1880. Mijat Novak's list compiled in 1869 had the names of twenty-three "excellent *tamburaši*" from Zagreb. These *tamburaši*, however, did not gain the attention of the crème of Zagreb society. They probably played for working-class people in taverns and parties. The 1880 performance by Sladaček may have been the first in Zagreb to attach pretensions and conventions of classical concerts to tamburitza, although such concert style of performance had existed years earlier in Slavonia. In 1865 the Prvo osječko tamburaško društvo (first Osijek tamburitza society) was established. Conducted by Franjo Kuhač in 1866, the ensemble performed on the occasion of the opening of the Osijek Upper City Theater (Rakijaš 1974, 15).

Two years after Sladaček's Zagreb performance, another Osijek native, Mijo Majer (1863–1915), had a major influence on tamburitza activity in the Croatian capital. Majer, who came to Zagreb to study at the university and had learned to play tamburitza in Osijek as a member of Pajo Kolarić's six-piece band, established Hrvatska lira (Croatian lyre), a twelve-member student tamburitza society in 1882 (Andrić 1958, 26).

In 1955 Josip Andrić interviewed a ninety-year-old surviving member of Hrvatska lira, Dr. Vlado Košćica. Košćica's account revealed the enthusiasm for tamburitza among young Croats during the 1880s as well as the difficulties they faced from the repressive measures of Khuen-Héderváry's government:

I was just a high school kid when the *tamburaši* from Vukovar [Slada-
ček's group] played on St. Mark's square in the Remer Tavern, on the
spot where now the Assembly Building stands. There were four of them:
bisernica, brač, bugarija and *berda*. The *primaš* was skillful. He had big
hands and firmly gripped the instrument. We boys on the square outside watched the playing through the window. It was then that I got the
urge to learn to play the tambura. . . . When the university tamburitza
orchestra was founded in 1882, I was in the sixth year of gymnasium.
The members of Hrvatska lira were an inspiration to all of us school
kids. After graduation in 1885, when I entered the university, I immediately joined Lira whose director was Milutin Farkaš. In 1887 there was
the attack with a boot on Ban Khuen, so the government broke up the
university group Hrvatska lira. Then, along with Farkaš, we started a
tamburitza group for the singing society Kolo. (Andrić 1955a, 12–13)

The Kolo group's appearance at the 1889 World's Fair in Paris was an
early high-profile performance in an international setting. This was an
important landmark in tamburitza history, which enhanced the status
and contributed to wider acceptance of tamburitza orchestras in Croatia. Košćica described how the decision was reached to go to Paris and
the difficulties with authorities that they had to overcome:

I still have the *brač* which Kovačić [Mato Kovačić, an early Zagreb tamburitza maker who died in 1888 of tuberculosis. His widow Terezija
continued to operate the company until her death in 1914, and her
second husband Mirko Koenig continued operations until 1925.]
made for me in 1886. It cost twenty forinths with the case included.
With that *brač*, I was in Paris when the tamburitza orchestra Kolo
played at the World's Fair in 1889. We arranged that tour in accord with
Nikola Faller [a Croatian composer and later, the director of the Zagreb
Opera] who was studying music in Paris at that time. That year in
Zagreb a concert was scheduled by some Hungarian cimbalom players
and on their posters it was printed that all proceeds from the concert
would go to defray expenses for their trip to Paris. Svinglin [another
Lira member] and I immediately said, "If the Hungarian gypsies are
going to Paris, why shouldn't we go too?!" And so we went. In Paris our

conductor was Slavšia Katkić, who they [the Austro-Hungarian author-
ities] wouldn't allow to go with us. But nevertheless, he managed to get
to Paris after us, supposedly on a private matter—so thus, we did have
a conductor. (Ibid.)

The spread of organized musically literate tamburitza societies seems
to have been amazingly rapid. In the 1860s and 1870s several societies existed in Slavonia, Srijem, and Bačka. In the 1880s they were in
Zagreb, and by the 1890s and the first decade of the twentieth century,
they seemed to be everywhere. According to Andrić, by the end of the
nineteenth century there wasn't a single larger town in Croatia, Dalmatia, Bosnia, Herzegovina, or Slavonia without a tamburitza orchestra
(Andrić 1958, 26). Tamburitza orchestras were present not only in the
areas Andrić mentioned but also in Serbia and Slovenia.

In Slovenia, according to Adolf Grobming, a Slovenian composer
and arranger of choral music, in the period from 1890 to 1920 there
were tamburitza orchestras in Ljubljana, Maribor, Trieste, Gorica, Celje,

Jadran, the amateur tamburitza orchestra, Dubrovnik, Croatia, 1923.
(Richard March Collection)

Kranj, Trbovlje, and in the Karnten province of Austria. "From the large towns, the tamburitza wave burst upon the surrounding villages so that in the first decade of our century, every larger settlement had its own tamburitza orchestra" (Grobming 1955, 10–11).

The underlying impetus for the formation of tamburitza societies playing patriotic repertoire on the national instrument was as much a Slavic opposition to Austrian, Hungarian, and Italian political and cultural hegemony as it was an appreciation for music. The common interests of the South Slavs opposing foreign domination prompted leading Croats, Serbs, and Slovenes of the Habsburg Empire to feel an increasing sense of unity, which was to culminate in the formation of Yugoslavia after World War I. The tamburitza was a part of this movement. It was a symbol of cultural equality and of independence from the then-dominant non-Slavic hegemonistic groups.

The tamburitza carried connotations of a Slavic national movement in that non-Slavs in close proximity to tamburitza-playing Slavs showed very little inclination to accept the instrument. The Hungarians and Donauschwaben (German-speaking settlers in the Danube region) had scarce interest in tamburitza. In contrast, another Habsburg-ruled Slavic nationality, the Czechs, even though the tambura had not been part of their folk tradition, established a few tamburitza orchestras despite their geographic separation from the South Slavs (Andrić 1958, 26).

Tamburitza was indeed part of a specifically anti-Habsburg Slavic movement because, among Serbians, it was primarily in Banat and Bačka, Habsburg territory, where the orchestras developed. Tamburitza groups were quite rare across the Sava and Danube in the nearby Serbian Kingdom (Ilić 1955, 6).

Although most tamburitza societies promoted nationalism, there were also tamburitza groups that promulgated socialism. Marko Nešić (1870–1938), an important figure in the musical life of Vojvodina, a tamburitza orchestra leader and the composer of several still-popular pieces ("Neven kolo," "Djuvedjije gde ste," "Idem kući a već zora"), organized Sloboda (Freedom), a socialist tamburitza society in 1910. In 1929 the group's name was changed to Radnik (The worker). Their repertoire featured the socialist anthem "Internationale," "Udružimo snage naše" (We join our forces), a Nešić original titled "Radnički pozdrav" (Worker's salute), and other overtly socialist numbers (Vuko-savljev 1960, 34).

Another socialist tamburitza society that was active from 1910 to 1925 was the tamburitza orchestra of the Samostalna sindikalna rad-nička dvorana (Independent union workers' hall) in Mostar, the main city of Herzegovina. According to a short report on their activities by Franjo Korlović, a group member, they played socialist hymns like "Budi se istok i zapad" (The East and West are awakening) and com-positions by Croatian composers like Ivan Zajc (Korlović 1959, 3). Like the nationalist groups, the socialist tamburitza societies also were subjected to government repression.

Tamburitza Instruments

The rapid proliferation of tamburitza orchestras created a demand for instruments, stimulating artisans to increase production. And these instruments needed to be more sophisticated than the simple *samica* with its diatonic major scale. The orchestral compositions favored by the leaders of tamburitza orchestras were more complex than diatonic folk songs. Following the principle of Gaj's musical ideology, these orchestras sought to play music based upon, but more refined than, the original peasant music. Tamburitzas that could play chromatic scales were required to execute accidentals and key changes that were included in the newly composed pieces. The tamburitza orchestras were not attempting to play "authentic folklore," and at that time no one had yet espoused the elimination of elite musical concepts from tambu-ritza performance. Quite the contrary, to ennoble the tradition, as it were, orchestral *tamburaši* eagerly made use of genre classifications from classical music. There were tamburitza concertos, overtures, and arias.

This music demanded a more versatile and more standardized fam-ily of tamburitza instruments. The process of improving the instruments had begun spontaneously, before the explosive spread of tamburitza orchestras. Ilić mentioned the arrival of half-step fretted *tambure* in Sremski Karlovci in 1875 (Ilić 1955, 6). An even earlier account comes from Milan Stahuljak, a member of a family originally from Slavonia. Stahuljak cited a letter from his father, Ivan Stahuljak, which in 1855 he sent home from Vienna where he was studying law. His landlord (only his surname Weisz is recorded) was a piano maker by profession. Weisz built a pear-shaped tambura for Stahuljak, fretted in a tempered scale, a great improvement for it allowed a player to change keys without retuning, which was not possible on a diatonic tambura (Stahuljak 1960, 36).

Although tamburitza instruments never have become rigidly standardized, by the late nineteenth century the instrumentation of tamburitza orchestras became increasingly less idiosyncratic with the development of larger-scale manufacture of the instruments by full-time tamburitza makers. Kuhač reported on the situation in the 1860s and 1870s: "It used to be every *tamburaš* made his own instrument and that is still partly true today [1877], but the majority buy *tambure* from people who make them as a trade. Tambura makers may be divided into two categories: trained instrument makers who make violins and guitars too, and the others who were *tamburaši* first and later turned exclusively to making *tambure*" (Kuhač 1877, 82). Knowledge of violin and especially guitar making must have had a profound influence on the modifications made to improve the tambura's versatility. Kuhač indicated there were five such trained tambura makers: two in Pest, and one each in Sombor, Novi Sad, and Zagreb. Kuhač contended that the informally trained tambura makers could be found in "every larger South Slavic town." He named nineteen towns as examples, mostly in Croatia or Vojvodina, but a few were in Bosnia and one was in Bulgaria (ibid., 83).

Kuhač also reported on an unusual situation that developed in Zagreb where prison inmates became important tamburitza makers: "The notorious outlaw Joso Udmanić was a skilled tambura maker, thus from the Zagreb prison he made hundreds of *tambure* which were then sold by the guards. Before Udmanić, the making of *tambure* was not only allowed but was the general practice, so that one prisoner would learn this skill from another. After Udmanić used his tambura-making tools to bore through a wall, prisoners were forbidden to make *tambure*" (ibid.). That tambura making was generally associated with prison is supported by Kuhač in this anecdote: "I once heard one Gypsy ask another, where was their comrade Palko, to which the second one answered, 'Making *tambure*.' 'Is he happy,' asked the first Gypsy. The second one answered, 'No way!' Thus he meant to say Palko was in jail" (ibid.).

Kuhač maintained that the *tambure* made by the highly skilled instrument makers were indeed better, more beautiful, and accurate in pitch, nevertheless many members of the tamburitza groups preferred to order instruments from the "second class" makers because their products were stronger and longer lasting. Though Kuhač does not mention it, they also might have been less expensive.

Beginning in the late eighteenth century, the form of tamburitza instrumentation underwent a gradual process of change to facilitate ensemble performance of Western music. The type of instruments Mijo Majer brought to Zagreb for the Hrvatska lira orchestra became known as the Farkaš system of tamburitza, after Milutin Farkaš, who succeeded Majer as director of the orchestra around 1900. Farkaš published an early influential tamburitza instruction book (Farkaš 1906). As the first somewhat standardized system of orchestral tamburitzas, their details merit scrutiny.

The instruments of the Farkaš system retain similarities to the diatonic *samice* in their basic form. The major distinction is the addition of the needed frets to enable playing a chromatic scale. It is easy to see how the Farkaš instruments are, in a sense, *samice* retrofitted for chromatic playing in an idiosyncratic and complex manner. It is not surprising that the Farkaš system has largely fallen into disuse, replaced by less complex, more versatile systems.

The melodic lead instrument, called the *bisernica* (little pearl), is high pitched and small, about 55 centimeters (22 in.) long. Like a *samica*, it has two double courses of strings all tuned to the same note. Unlike the *samica*, the body of the instrument is not pear-shaped but typically fashioned in the shape of a tiny guitar. The *bisernica*'s first five frets, placed in half-step intervals, pass all the way across the fingerboard, beneath both courses of strings. Beyond the fifth fret, which produces the interval of a perfect fourth to the open string, the remaining twenty-one frets are shorter, only lying beneath one or the other of the two courses of strings. These half-frets are placed, as *bisernica* players are apt to say, like the black and white keys on a piano. The notes on the lower course of strings are equivalent to the white keys, the naturals, while the upper course's frets produce the sharps or flats. As with the *samica,* a player's fingers must move up and down the neck to play a melody. The difference is that the upper course of strings, which is used in diatonic *samica* playing to produce a drone accompaniment, has been converted into the source of sharps or flats on the *bisernica.* In ensemble play, that drone is not needed since other instruments produce the accompaniment.

The next instrument of the Farkaš system is called the *kontrašica.* It is physically identical to the *bisernica,* but it is assigned harmony and countermelody parts in the manner of an orchestral second-violin section. The Farkaš *brač,* the next instrument, plays lower melodic and harmony parts. It is a somewhat larger instrument, 85–100 centimeters in length (33–40 in.), with four strings in two courses and very similar in its shape to a large *samica.* The first seven frets, set at half-step intervals, are long, fully crossing the fingerboard, followed by a short fret under only the upper course for each flat or sharp, and a long fret for each natural. There are twenty-two frets in all. Larger *brač tambure* (termed third and fourth *brač*) handle still lower musical parts. They are tuned a fourth lower and feature only long frets.

Rhythm parts are handled by a guitar-shaped instrument, the *bugarija,* also known as the *kontra.* The *bugarija* player always strikes chords across all four strings, which are usually placed with one double course and two single strings tuned in a major triad, an open chord. All frets are long and set in half steps. There may be first, second, and third *bugarije,* ranging in size from 75 to 105 centimeters (30–41 in.). Bass parts are played by the *berde čelo* and the *berde.* A Farkaš *berde* typically is shaped like an immense guitar with four steel strings. It is played standing upright using a large leather pick. The *berde* and *bugarija* work together as a rhythm section. The *berde* generally plays the accented beats while the *bugarija* chords are struck on the weak beats. The *berde čelo* is a rarely used instrument since the significant *brač* parts render it redundant. At 175 centimeters (69 in.), it is smaller than the towering 190–200 centimeter (75–79 in.) *berde.* Both instruments feature two courses of double strings tuned in the interval of a fourth or fifth. The tone of the bass parts has a metallic, piano-like ring, produced by the metal wire double strings pressing on wire frets.

In the mid-1920s, most tamburitza orchestras adopted Srijemski system instruments, which rapidly supplanted the Farkaš system. The exact origin of these modernized *tambure* is not known. The name of the system (Srijemski) implies that they originated in the historical Pannonian province now divided between the nations of Croatia and Serbia: Srem is the Serbian pronunciation while Srijem is Croatian. Josip Andrić believed that they evolved out of the three-toned *tambure* used earlier in Bačka. The Srijemski instruments feature five or six strings in four courses. (There is only one double course, the highest pitched strings if there are five strings, and two double courses if there are six strings.) The smallest instrument, equivalent to the *bisernica*, is called *prim* or *prima*. The other instruments have the same or similar names to the remaining Farkaš instruments, *brač*, sometimes called *basprim*, *čelo brač*, *bugarija*, and *berde*. On all of the Srijemski instruments the four courses of strings are tuned in the interval of perfect fourths with the exception of the *bugarija*, which like its Farkaš counterpart is tuned in an open chord. With few exceptions, the Srijemski *prim* is pear-shaped, though individual makers have produced variations of that shape. For example, tamburitza makers in the Prigorje town of Gračani on the northern edge of Zagreb square off the upper part of the sound box where it connects to the neck. In the United States, the tamburitza maker Milan Opacich makes a *prim* according to the templates that the immigrant instrument maker Ivan Hlad developed in the 1920s. Hlad's design features a scroll on the upper side of the sound box, near its connection to the neck, and a cut-away on the lower side, to make it easier to play on the highest frets.

There is more variety in the shape of the Srijemski *brač*. They may be in a narrow or wide pear-shape, but most common is the shape of a small guitar. The larger Srijemski instruments, the *čelo brač* and *bugarija*, are almost always guitar shaped, some having two violin-like f-holes, others with a single central sound hole. The Srijemski *berde* is generally made to resemble a string bass with a violin-type shape and f-holes, unlike the guitar shape of the Farkaš *berde*.

The greater range, versatility, and ease of playing have made the Srijemski instruments more attractive to most musicians. The four courses of strings each tuned a fourth apart enable a musician to play many full melodies in one left-hand position, without the need to slide the hand up and down the neck. A few tamburitza societies have retained their Farkaš instruments, and some individuals who originally learned on Farkaš instruments remained loyal to them, but on the whole, the Srijemski system has replaced Farkaš.

A third system of orchestral tamburitzas was originated by Slavko Janković, a noted musician, athlete, judge, and musicologist born in 1897 in Novi Mikanovci near Vinkovci in Srijem. His system's *tambure* resemble Srijemski instruments but are tuned in perfect fifths, like violins, in order to take full advantage of all four fingers on the player's left hand. In the post–World War II period, the system was adopted by many schools in Croatia, where it remains in use. Virtually no informal band musicians use Janković instruments and even in some school orchestras there has been a resurgence of use of the Srijemski system (Željko Bradić 1978).

In the 1890s tambura manufacturing increased rapidly to meet the growing popular demand for the instruments. As Kuhač indicated, individual craftsmen operated in most towns in Croatia, Slavonia, and Vojvodina. Sisak, a small industrial city southeast of Zagreb, became a particularly important tamburitza-making center. Jadran Jeić, a librarian and musician from Zagreb, mentioned the important role of nineteenth-century Sava River boatmen from the Sisak area who encountered and brought back *tambure* with them from their river voyages to Srijem, Bačka, and Banat (Jeić 2010). In Sisak, a steel-mill town, the tamburitza industry took on a more industrial model of production, nonetheless retaining elements of handcrafting. By the mid-1890s there were three major tamburitza makers in Sisak: Maksim Gilg, Janko Stjepušin, and the Dobranić and Vardian Company. These firms employed a number of skilled master craftsmen as well as workers who took care of various less sensitive steps in the process.

Janko Stjepušin understood the sound business practice that was necessary to increase general interest in tamburitza in order to create more demand for his products. Therefore he began to publish a small monthly magazine in 1904. Each issue featured advertisements for Stjepušin instruments and a chatty article on a topic of interest to *tamburaši*. The Gilg factory, founded in 1894, was still in operation in

1978 when its owner, Katerina Gilg, showed me two instrument catalogs published by the firm. The earlier catalog is dated 1914; the other is undated, but Mrs. Gilg indicated that it had been published in 1934 or 1935. The 1914 catalog shows that Maksim Gilg produced four lines of Farkaš-system instruments: Gradjanska, Velegradska, Svietska, and Biserne (urban, metropolitan, world, and pearl). The higher-end lines utilized better wood and had more decorative inlay. For a cost comparison in the Austro-Hungarian currency of that era, the Gradjanska *bisernica* cost only nine krune ($1.80) while the *berde* cost 80 krune ($16.00), but in the top line, Biserne, the smallest instrument cost twenty krune ($4.00) while the *berde* cost 200 krune ($40.00) (U.S. dollar equivalents are shown at the 1913 exchange rate). On a background of dark stained wood or black celluloid, mother-of-pearl was placed in the shape of ornate scrolls, flowers, or leafy vines. Gilg advertised that he would place "names, last names, or other writing" on the instruments for the low price of 20 filirs ($0.04) per pearl letter. In 1914, the only stringed instruments Gilg sold were Farkaš tamburitzas, although he did carry triangles, tambourines, ocarinas, and castanets. In the 1930s catalog, in addition to Farkaš and Srijemski tamburitzas, Gilg sold violins, guitars, Hawaiian guitars, and mandolins.

Both editions of the catalog featured letters from satisfied customers. In 1914 these came from Croatia, Serbia, Bosnia, Bohemia, and the cities of Auckland, New Zealand, Dunlo, Pennsylvania, and Kenosha, Wisconsin, in the United States. The letters from overseas tamburitza societies were symptomatic of the times, a period of massive emigration. Gilg's catalog specified how to order instruments from "America, Australia, and other overseas countries." In the 1930s edition, Gilg mentioned that one-third of his business was with overseas Croatian and Serbian immigrant groups.

The Tamburitza Migrates to America

In the early 1890s Croats and Serbs had begun to immigrate to North America in large numbers. Earlier, migration had been sporadic and on a small scale. Individuals and small groups, mostly from the seafaring culture of the Adriatic coast, settled in California, the northern Pacific

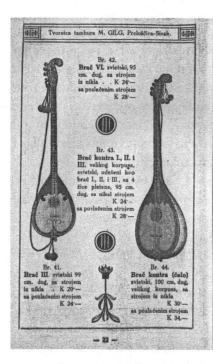

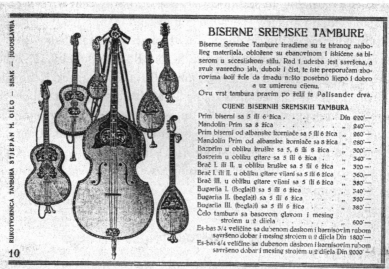

Pages from the sales catalogs of the Gilg Tamburitza Factory showing Farkaš and Sremske tamburitzas. (Richard March Collection)

coast, the delta of the Mississippi River, and New York City. There they worked as fishermen, farmers, seamen, and dockworkers. Many of the early immigrants, most of whom were males, supported family left behind in their home villages, visiting as often as possible.

In the 1890s a combination of bad economic conditions in the homeland and the requirement of American industry for large numbers of unskilled laborers prompted massive migration, not only from coastal Croatia but from its inland regions as well. Exact numbers are difficult to determine: no statistics were kept on the number of emigrants leaving Croatia until 1898, and even then only a minority of those leaving actually was counted. American figures on immigration also are imprecise. The Croatians and Serbs arriving from the Habsburg Empire were often counted as Austrians, Hungarians, Italians, or even Turks. On the basis of an analysis of existing statistics, Josip Lakatoš estimated that some five hundred thousand people emigrated from Croatia before World War I. This figure is generally accepted as realistic (Čizmić 1974, 10).

A majority of the immigrants from Croatia were Croats, but there were also many Serbians, especially from Lika, Kordun, Dalmatinska zagora, and Banija, regions of today's Croatia where there was a substantial Serbian population. Serbs also came in significant numbers from Habsburg-ruled Vojvodina, Bosnia-Herzegovina, and Montenegro. Before 1945, however, very few Serbs from the Serbian kingdom emigrated. Thus, before 1918, Croatian and Serbian immigrants alike came from the European regions where *tambure* were popular.

As in Austria-Hungary, in the United States the South Slavs found that they faced discrimination and disdain from the established, native-born Americans. The immigrants settled mostly in the smoky industrial cities and stark mining towns of western Pennsylvania and the Great Lakes states. The immigrant colonies had a disproportionate number of men, often living in crowded, barracks-like conditions in boardinghouses. In some boardinghouses, the worker's bed never got cold—the night shift worker plopped into it shortly after the daytime worker, who used the same bed, arose.

There is a good deal of scholarly and popular literature on South Slavic immigration to North America (ibid.), but surprisingly little on tamburitza activity. Perhaps the most important social institution among the early immigrants was the saloon. Some contemporary observers attacked the immigrant saloons as exploitative and encouraging waste and debauchery (Sirovatka 1907, 42), but trusted saloon keepers performed many of the services of a banker and travel agent as well as a translator and counselor. The saloon provided a space for socializing and festive events, space that was especially important for the many immigrants who lived in very tight quarters. As in the old country taverns, the American saloons became an ideal venue for tamburitza combos.

At the beginning of the twentieth century, living and working conditions in America were difficult for the new immigrants. They not only faced discrimination but also risked death and dismemberment in hazardous jobs in factories and mines. To provide some security, immigrants formed mutual protective societies for burial and life insurance. They also formed singing societies for spiritual and cultural uplift. Analogous pressures to those that prompted the formation of singing societies in Croatia were present also in the New World. In Europe and in North America, Croats and Serbs needed to validate the value of their culture and to resist denationalizing pressures from the government and the country's elite (Holjevac 1967, 82).

The singing societies were formed by humble people, former peasants, many barely literate. They turned to the beauty of folksong and music not just out of nostalgia for their homelands but also in the belief that love for music could most effectively unite their communities, promote education, and represent their culture favorably to other nationalities in America.

Some of the immigrants must have been familiar with the choirs and music societies in Croatia, and avidly endeavored to establish them in America. The Chicago area, one of the largest South Slavic ethnic communities in the United States, is a good example. The first Croatian American choir, Zora, was established there in 1902, and they were instrumental in organizing an American Croatian singing league in 1911. In 1907 a socialist choir, Sloboda, was formed, and in 1915 another choir, Zvonimir, was set up. In the nearby steel-mill town Gary, Indiana, the Preradović choir was formed in 1914; they were one of very few such choirs still active in the 1980s. Another socialist choir, Dalmacija, was established in 1922 and in 1924 Jadran was organized. In South Chicago two more singing societies came into existence, Velebit in 1925 and Gundulić in 1926. From the names of some of the choirs, it is possible to surmise the region of origin of most members— in Dalmacija and Jadran (Adriatic) they would be Dalmatians; in Velebit, named for the largest mountain in Lika, they would be Ličani. Gundulić, a famed poet from Dubrovnik, was probably honored by choir members from southern Dalmatia. Many immigrants felt strong ties to their regions of origin, and regional clubs were common (ibid.).

The repertoires of the choirs were similar to those of their European counterparts. As members of the Hrvatski pjevacki savez, they were able to receive from Croatia the same published song arrangements. As in Europe, many of the new American choirs formed drama groups and tamburitza ensembles.

By the early years of the twentieth century, tavern combos and orchestral tamburitza groups were active in the States. A good deal of material on the establishment, activities, and noted members of early tamburitza groups in the United States was compiled by Walter W. Kolar in volume 2 of his *History of the Tambura* (Kolar 1975). Kolar asserts that the earliest documented tamburitza performances in the United States took place in 1900. In that year, Franjo Zotti, a well-known immigrant "banker" and saloon keeper, organized a tour by Sokol, a seven-piece tamburitza combo from Sisak, led by Ivan Očvarek. Zotti sought to book Sokol into elite venues. In an advertising brochure for the tour, Zotti stressed that Sokol had performed for the crowned heads of Europe, and in 1900 they played in the roof garden of the elite Waldorf Astoria hotel in New York. It is not known if any of the members of Sokol stayed in the United States or if they performed for immigrant communities. Kolar also presented a photograph, dated 1900, of an immigrant family tamburitza combo, a four-piece group showing Frank Hofer with his two daughters and an unrelated *berde* player.

In the first decade of the twentieth century, an organized tamburitza society, Gorska vila (the mountain fairy), was established in Johnstown, Pennsylvania. The handwritten membership rules of this group have been preserved. They indicate that the members each were required to pay a small fee to their teacher/director, and members needed to learn how to read music.

The singing of improvisational, satiric, or humorous songs commenting on everything from politics to male-female relations were brought to America with the immigrants. Such songs usually are ephemeral, as Kuhač pointed out. But it is fortunate that columns by a writer who used the pen name of Pero Tamburica have been preserved. Pero wrote for *Hrvatski glasnik* (Croatian herald), published in Pittsburgh. His columns were in verse form, and they seem very improvisational, just the sort of lyrics that would have been sung to the tambura in Pero's native region of Srijem. From this little song, it seems clear that he actually played tambura and sang:

Ja sam Pero Tamburica
Ravnog Sriema sin
Zato pjevam male pjesme
Da ugodim svim.

Mila moja tamburica
Zasviraj mi malo
Ne bi li se po svem svjetu
I za mene znalo . . .

Onda pjevam da sve ori
Od malih pjesmica
A ti meni sekundiraš
Moja tamburica

[I am Pero Tamburitza / A son of broad Srijem / That's why I sing little songs / To please everybody. / My dear tamburitza / Play for me a little / In order that throughout the world / They would know about me. . . . / Then I sing so that all resounds / From my little songs / And you accompany me / My tamburitza.]

Many of Pero's songs deal with European and American politics of the period from 1912 to 1916, which included the first years of World War I. He expressed Croatian nationalist sentiments, seeing Franz Joseph and the Austro-Hungarian government as enemies of the

Croatian people, and he espoused sympathy for the Serbs. When it came to politics in his ethnic community, Pero urged the formation of a Croatian League. Pero seems to be from the very mold of the political *tamburaš* in Europe that Kuhač described in 1877.

But politics was not everything. Some songs deal with affairs of the heart—"Perina ljubav" (Pero's love) and "Našim frajlama" (To our young ladies). Other songs depict various aspects of life in the Croatian community of western Pennsylvania. "Pero i kum Vlado" (Pero and his godfather Vlado) depicts a chance meeting of Pero with his godfather on a streetcar in Pittsburgh. Pero winds up infuriating Vlado when he suggests that Vlado is talking too loud "as our people tend to do." Another song compares the business prospects of Croatian and Serbian grocers, butchers, and saloon keepers. Everyone wants to get groceries on credit and argues with the butcher, but the saloon keeper is paid in cash, he makes a lot of money, and everybody likes him. Some songs deal with very mundane subjects: winter is coming and Pero needs a warmer coat, or Pero became ill and had to be treated at a hospital.

In one of his songs, Pero paints a vivid picture of a festive event in Johnstown, Pennsylvania's Croatian community: the presentation of an amateur drama followed by a social dance. He describes a pattern for social events that still persists in the Croatian American community and mocks some stereotypical characters:

Ja sam Pero Tamburica
Koj sam prije bio
Makar da sam ovih dana
Dosta vino pio.

Danas hoću da vam pjevam
O Johnstownu gradu
Kak je tamo naš "Rodoljub"
Izveo paradu.

Cijeli Johnstown uzruja se
I veliki i mali
A svi žurno guraju se
K hrvatskoj nam hali.

I uz pjesmi i uz svirku
Rodoljubci marni
Igrali su i predstavu
"Ormar začarani."

Svi su glumci bili dobri
Baš im za to hvala
Ali sve je nadkrilila
Naša Luce mala.

Aoj Luce, mala Luce
Što si tako mala
"Da sam veća igrat tako
Možda ne bi znala.

Vide Mate dugih nogu
Pod divan se stišo
Da se boji od ljubavi
Da ne bi pokišo.

A što da ja jošte rečem
O onim drugima
Nego kad se ponajljepše
Zahvalim i njima

Oj Johnstownu, mali gradu
Ti si naša dika
Radi tvog hrvatskog rada
Hvala ti velika

Za predstavom slijedilo je
Plesanje lagano
Tako krasno plesat znade
U Johnstownu samo.

Pazi onog "Meta" malog
Što se vrte znade
Da i oni drugi hoće
Tako da urade.

Jos Smokvina taj konstabler
Primorske je "dite"
Al' mu ipak vrsak nosa
Crvenog vidite.

On ne voli naša pića
Vina i rakije
Iz praznoga taj vam čovjek
Nikada ne pije.

A naš pekar stari Stanko
Misli da je mlad
Pa bi i on zaplesati
Zelio si rad.

Momci plešu vesele je
I gospe i puče
A iz ruke pa u ruku
Leti mala Luce.

Sve do jutra trajala je
Lijepa ti parada
Osvijetlala jeste lice
Johnstowna grada.

[I am Pero Tamburica / who I was before / Even though these
days / I've had a lot of wine. / Today I want to sing to you / About
Johnstown city / How our club there "Patriot" / Put on a parade. / All
of Johnstown is excited / Both the large and small / Everyone
hurriedly pushes / To the Croatian hall. / Along with song and dance
/ The worthy "Patriots" / Put on the play / "The Enchanted
Wardrobe." / All the actors were good / Thanks to them for that / But
our little Lucy / Outshone everyone. / "Oh Lucy, little Lucy / Why
are you so small?" / "Were I larger maybe I wouldn't / Know how to
act so well." / See long-legged Matt / Squeezed under the divan / He's
afraid that from love / He might get soaked. / And what can I say
about the others? / But to thank them all. / Oh Johnstown, little city,
/ You are our glory / Because of your Croatian activities / Many

thanks to you. / After the play there followed / Slow dancing / Only in Johnstown / Do they know how to dance so beautifully. / Watch out for little "Matt" / who knows how to spin around / Others would like / To do as he does. / Then there's Smokvina the constable / A child of the seacoast / But the end of his nose / Is always red. / He doesn't like our drinks / Wine and plum brandy / That man will never drink / On an empty stomach. / And our baker, old Stanko / Thinks he is young / That's why he wants to dance so much. / Young men dance, it is merry for both the fine and common / And from arm to arm flies little Lucy. / It lasted clear 'til dawn / That beautiful parade / It lit up the shining faces / Of Johnstown city.]

CHAPTER 4

Ethnologists and the
Politics of Folklore Festivals

In the later part of July each summer, the streets of Zagreb fill with hundreds of colorfully clad celebrants. Everywhere you turn on the public squares, in parks, sometimes even on streetcars, bright embroidery on stiff linen meets the eye and the rich tones of peasant song are heard. The residents of Zagreb tend to think of themselves as an urbane and cosmopolitan lot, but during the Međunarodna Smotra Folklora (International Folklore Festival) Zagreb belongs to the villagers. The quiet of the baroque-era streets of Zagreb's old upper city is routinely shattered by a folk bagpiper or by the voices of apple-cheeked peasant women singing in an ancient mode.

Groups of peasants from all over Croatia, from the other former Yugoslav republics, and from various European and overseas countries perform the folksongs and dances of their native villages. For many years, the *smotra's* guidelines allowed only certain groups to participate, all of whom were pre-screened by experts to assure that only "authentic" lore be performed by "authentic" villagers. No urban revivalists were supposed to participate. Only villagers who performed the traditions of their own immediate region were to be included.

In addition to the songs and dances, most groups still also perform instrumental music. There are various wooden flutes, one-stringed *gusle*, and bagpipes, but perhaps the most frequent instruments are the *tambure*. Tamburitza ensembles have come from Slavonia, Posavina,

93

Brochure from the 1978 International Folklore Festival. (Richard March
Collection)

Medjimurje, indeed from most of inland Croatia from Bela Krajina in Slovenia and Bačka and Banat in Vojvodina. There have been *samica* players from Banija, Lika, Kordun, and Slavonia, *šargijaši* from Bosnia, and players of the *ćitelija* and *šarkija* from Kosova. The Zagreb *smotra* and smaller regional festivals continue to be very important events in the tamburitza tradition. In fact, folklore groups are one of the most common contexts in which *tambure* are played.

Nearly every larger town in Croatia features a *smotra* at some time, usually during the warmer months of the year. These authentic folklore festivals and the performances of the participating groups differ markedly from the concerts of tamburitza orchestras and from the jam sessions and shows staged by small tamburitza music groups. The folklore groups comprise yet another distinct facet of the tamburitza tradition, a facet based on different aesthetics, different creative roles, and different musical and political ideas.

Croatian ethnology scholars had a key role in the development of this component of the tamburitza tradition, in a conceptual, political, and practical hands-on manner. Authentic folklore groups, *smotre*, and the field of ethnology developed hand in hand in Croatia. Antun Radić, the founder of ethnology in Croatia, began his efforts just before the turn of the twentieth century. He developed an ideology that placed a high value on the traditional peasant way of life, including the artistic creations of their societies. His goal was to instigate the documentation of the totality of the village-specific peasant life in all villages. By the 1930s, ethnologists who followed Radić were advocating not only the documentation but also the continuation in active practice of that traditional peasant way of life (Sremac 1978, 102–4).

Unlike the Gaj ideology, which sought to "ennoble" folklore through adopting elite conventions and aesthetics, the ethnological ideology sought to preserve what was understood as the original peasant ways, in every detail. The ethnologists' concept often falls back on the term "izvorni folklor." Though I translate it as "authentic folklore," the word "izvor" means wellsprings in Croatian. By analogy then, "wellsprings folklore" implies a pure, unadulterated product, swelling from peasant culture like natural spring water. If it is as worthy and valuable as pure spring water, it must be guarded constantly against pollution, even from so-called ennobling efforts, which might spoil the folklore and render it impure. This idea could not have gained acceptance without the development of the field of ethnology. Not only was it ethnologists who espoused the idea, but the data from their work; the documented inventory of peasant culture was needed to establish the canon of that authentic folklore to which the ethnologists would exhort villagers to adhere (Radić 1897, 1–88).

Before World War I, ethnologists had exerted little influence upon the tamburitza tradition. A tradition of playing *tambure* had been established throughout most of inland Croatia, in sections of Serbia and Slovenia, as well as in South Slavic immigrant communities in North America. There were soloistic *tambure* and two developed forms, tamburitza orchestras and informal tamburitza ensembles. The orchestras were led by cultural workers and musicians who tried to fulfill the Gaj musical ideology to the best of their abilities. The tavern combos generally were comprised of nonideological, spontaneous musicians who played whatever was of interest to their varied audiences and music that was pleasing to the musicians themselves. Both types of groups shared the agenda of advancing South Slavic, especially Croatian, national interests—either in the more genteel settings of the orchestras or in the rough-and-tumble political commentary and satire of the tavern combos.

In 1914 World War I swiftly engulfed Europe, causing death, suffering, and great dislocations in European life. That year, the Sisak tamburitza maker Janko Stjepušin bitterly complained in his monthly newsletter that the war caused a virtual halt in tamburitza activity in Europe (Stjepušin 1914, 1).

In the United States, though, people were not subjected to a war on their home soil, so immigrant tamburitza activity flourished. From 1916 to 1918 dozens of commercial recordings were made by tamburitza groups for the Columbia and Victor record companies at their studios in New York and Chicago. Because Serbia was a Western ally against the Central Powers, some of the songs and tune titles expressed support for Serbia and for the Yugoslav movement that was developing in American immigrant communities. For example, the Serbian American *tamburaš* Vaso Bukvić recorded "Srbobran Marš" (Serb-defender march) and "Jugoslavenska Himna" (Yugoslav hymn) in June 1916. Ten months later, in April 1917, a group named Tamburaško pjevač [sic] recorded songs that referred to the Serbian army's retreat across Albania, "Tamo daleko" and "U Albeniju," and pro-Yugoslav sentiments may have been one reason the Serbian singer Obrad Djurin recorded "Slovenec sem" (I am a Slovenian) and six other songs in the Slovenian language in October 1917. Stevan Zerbes recorded the old Serbian patriotic song "Čuj Dušane" (Listen, Dušan) and "Na Balkanskom Bojnom Polju" (On the Balkan battlefield) in May 1918 (Kolar 1975, 26; Spottswood 1990, 931–78).

After the end of the Great War in November 1918, the century-old seeds of romantic nationalism at last bore significant fruit. The venerable multinational empires in Europe, the Prussian, Russian, Austrian, and Ottoman, crumbled, and diplomats met in Versailles to try to carve out equitable boundaries of nation-states. According to Herder, nation-states were the natural units of humanity, but when they had to be delimited by specific borders, their "natural" shape was not so apparent (Palmer 1970, 150–72). To justify their claims to territories, the diplomats presented evidence of the national identity of the peasant population of the area. Now the dialect, customs, and folklore of the peasants of a disputed region became matters of relevance in the diplomatic struggle that followed the war. Ethnology entered the realm of European diplomacy.

The important ethnological work *Balkansko poluostrvo* by Jovan Cvijić was first published in French in 1917—ethnological ammunition for the diplomatic battle at Versailles that culminated in the formation of the kingdom of Yugoslavia under the Serbian Karadjordjević dynasty (Cvijić 1918). Ethnology emerged suddenly as a factor in European politics, but this scholarly field did not spring up miraculously out of the war's ashes; it had been developing quietly for decades.

Antun Radić (1868–1919) laid the foundations of ethnology in Croatia when he established *Zbornik za narodni život i običaja* (Journal of folk life and customs). The journal began to come out as a regular publication of the Yugoslav Academy of Arts and Sciences in 1896. In the second issue, Radić published the extensive questionnaire and fieldwork guide "Osnova za sabiranje i proučavanje građe o narodnom životu" (A basis for the collection and study of data on folk life), which comprised eighty-eight printed pages (Radić 1897).

A fully completed questionnaire contained a total picture of village life in a particular location. Beginning with topography, climate, and the physical characteristics of the population, Radić then devoted the majority of pages to questions on cultural aspects of life: language, a total inventory of material culture, means and methods of work, lifestyle, family and social relations, customary law, annual and life cycle customs, amusements, folk poesy, narrative, and belief.

Radić explained that the best collectors would be literate peasants who could record data already known to them, using the organizational scheme of the questionnaire. He urged village school teachers or priests, who might have been born elsewhere, to enlist the aid of knowledgeable local peasants in filling out the questionnaire. Manuscripts were to be sent to Radić for publication in the journal. Radić even included directions on such matters as the format, margins, and on which side of the page to write.

Subsequent issues of the journal published the collected material of Radić's collaborators. Only a few of them managed to complete the entire questionnaire, but some of the most successfully developed field studies were "Otok" by Ivan Lovretić, "Poljica" by Franje Ivanišević, "Prigorje" by Ivan Rožić, and "Samobor" by Milan Lang. The journal published data drawn from the entire South Slavic area. Some very important collections were from Montenegro and from Moslem villages in Bosnia (Marošević 1997).

Social-scientific work seldom develops in a political vacuum, and from the beginning Antun Radić's ethnological efforts coupled with efforts to create a potent political force of the Croatian peasantry. In 1904 Radić and his younger brother Stjepan founded the Croatian peasant party (Hrvatska seljačka stranka, HSS), which was organized to advocate the interests of the peasantry. The Radić brothers legitimized their leadership roles by invoking their own peasant origins: both were born in Trebarjevo Desno, a village in the Sava River Valley southeast of Zagreb.

In 1899 Radić began to publish a chatty biweekly magazine, Dom (the home), subtitled "the Croatian peasant's magazine for conversation and learning." Here Radić commented on political and cultural events in Austria-Hungary, Europe, and the world with regard to their possible consequences for Croatian peasants.

According to the historian Jaroslav Šidak, Radić's aims in both his scientific and his political work were to bring about a "reconciliation of the upper classes and the folk" on the basis of a mutual acceptance of folk culture. Radić claimed to be striving to create a "renaissance" in the development of Croatian culture, "in which there will be felt everywhere not the spirit of foreign traditions but the spirit of the great masses and the fertile spirit of the folk" (Šidak 1968, 391–92).

Radić supported the idea of brotherhood among the South Slavic nationalities on the premise of the absolute integrity of the various peoples' cultures. To Radić, unity did not mean homogenization, and he condemned every form of chauvinism.

He was inspired by the pan-Slavic ideal and the struggle for a more equitable position for Slavs within the Habsburg Empire. He condemned such disparate phenomena as clericalism, class struggle, and capitalism, all essentially divisive to the unified "folk." Still he was no revolutionary. He believed in working within the boundaries of the existing social order (ibid.).

After Antun's death in 1919 at the age of fifty, his brother Stjepan became the dominant figure in the HSS and was responsible for bringing the party great popularity in the 1920s and 1930s. Stjepan Radić allied the HSS at one point with Vladimir Lenin's Third International—not a very close ideological match—but Stjepan later played a part in the formation of an alliance of similar peasant parties from several European countries, known then as the "Green International."

FESTIVALS OF MUSIC AND FOLKLORE

Consistent with the Peasant Party's goals and its ethnological orientation, the stimulation of village cultural activities was an important part of their political strategy. Cultural activities were not only important as a means to attain a specific political agenda but were an integral part of the party's goal to achieve a modern Croatian society based upon the tenets of traditional peasant culture. To that end, Seljačka sloga (United Peasants), a cultural wing of the HSS, was organized. Seljačka sloga sought to encourage and stimulate traditional village arts and to raise the consciousness of all Croatians, villagers and urbanites alike, as to the importance and value of these pursuits. As early as the 1920s, the efforts of village choirs were assisted by Seljačka sloga (cf. Ceribašić 2003 and Čapo Žmegač 1995).

Active since the late nineteenth century, village singing societies sang composed material, used written notes, and were led by a choir director. The efforts of such village-based choirs were connected to the efforts of similar urban singing societies. Together they were organized in the Hrvatski pjevački savez (Croatian singing league) (Sremac 1978, 101). In 1926 the village choirs organized themselves into a separate "parish" within the Croatian Singing League, which they named Matija Gubec, honoring the leader of a sixteenth-century peasant rebellion. The primary goal of the group was to promote Croatian folk songs in artistic choral arrangements. "Matija Gubec" put out a monthly magazine, *Hrvatska narodna pjesma* (Croatian folk song), which published the music to folk and patriotic songs, from which the village choirs could learn new repertoire. Also, in Zagreb, they organized a special instructional course for choir directors.

Matija Gubec also organized a number of choir festivals in Zagreb. At the 1927 festival two choirs from Bačka, among the easternmost Croatian settlements, appeared and performed their local songs without relying on written arrangements or a choir director. Rudolf Herceg, the secretary of Seljačka sloga at the time, was delighted by the performances because they seemed to meet so closely with Antun Radić's goals of preserving authentic village culture. He requested that at subsequent festivals, each choir should sing at least a few such unarranged songs. This goal was achieved by the 1929 festival. The performances of 1927 by the groups from Bačka are the first specifically noted instances of on-stage performance of unarranged, original folk songs performed by the villagers who were themselves the tradition carriers (Sremac 1978, 102).

There was a pause in activity from 1929 to 1935. During that period, a dictatorial form of government was imposed in Yugoslavia by the Karadjordjević dynasty. In 1928 Stjepan Radić was murdered in the halls of the Yugoslav parliament in Belgrade by a Montenegrin representative. The political turmoil that followed ended in the 1929 crackdown, and the HSS was outlawed.

Changing circumstances obliged the government to restore some political liberties, and the choir festivals resumed in 1935 after the lifting of the ban on HSS and its cultural activities. In 1935 Seljačka sloga assumed full responsibility for organizing the festival under the new name Smotra seljačkih zborova (Festival of peasant choirs). This began a tradition of using the word "smotra" to designate all such events, favored because it is a Slavic root word, unlike the word "festival," from Latin. From 1936 to 1940 the event was called Smotra hrvatske seljačke kulture (Festival of Croatian peasant culture). Eight *smotre* were organized in Zagreb during this period while in provincial towns about 150 local *smotre* were held before Yugoslavia was engulfed in World War II causing another hiatus (ibid., 107).

Prior to World War I, in Austria-Hungary, overcoming the political and cultural domination of Croats and other South Slavs by the non-Slavic Hungarians and Germans became the goal of the Croatian cultural activists. The Slavic nations in Austria-Hungary were united in this effort. After Croatia became a part of Yugoslavia, under the rule of Serbian kings and politicians, the nationality of the hegemonistic power was also Slavic. Emphasizing Slavic unity and Slavic language may have been adequate as a symbol of resistance to the rulers in Vienna or Budapest. After the formation of Yugoslavia, the Serbian royal regime became the political adversary of Croatian interests. Therefore, a more detailed Croatian cultural specificity was required to symbolize resistance to the Belgrade regime.

Once again, in the 1920s and 1930s, much as in the nineteenth century, artistic and cultural activities became a major focus of political opposition. In the Illyrian period, urbanites and aristocrats were the key figures, but by the 1920s peasants and politicians of peasant origin became the backbone of the Croatian movement, and the HSS became the most popular political party.

Because the HSS model of cultural development was based on ethnology, activist ethnologists entered the fray, striving to develop a pure Croatian folk culture, which they believed by now had become contaminated by numerous, often hard to recognize but nonetheless pervasive and threatening foreign influences. The ethnologists advanced the cause by assuming control of the folk festivals. The *smotre* already had become a popular focus of cultural activity for Croatian peasants. Many villagers were eager to form music groups in order to participate in the festivals. During the later 1930s the ethnologists proved themselves able to have a strong influence.

In 1935 at the first *smotra* of the 1930s, eight choirs (which had previously performed at in the 1920s festivals) were joined by five choirs from newly established branches of Seljačka sloga. A majority of the choirs were from villages in the immediate vicinity of Zagreb, but a few were from Posavina, the Sava River valley. Two of these Posavina groups, from Jasenovac and Sunje, also danced their traditional kolo dances. Along with folk song, dance now had ascended to the stage, performed by the villagers themselves.

After the 1935 *smotra*, a special committee met, chaired by the HSS president Vlatko Maček. Other participants included the leader of Seljačka sloga, Rudolf Herceg, the ethnology professor Milovan Gavazzi, his graduate assistant Branimir Bratanić, and such prominent musicians as Zlatko Grgošević, Rudolf Matz, and Zlatko Špoljar. At the committee meeting, specific proposals passed that had a major influence on the form and nature of following *smotre*. It was agreed that only unarranged songs were to be performed, and the use of a choir director was forbidden. Along with folk songs, each group should present traditional dances, instrumental music, and customs. The performances were to take place in "original" folk costume, and the entire program would be subject to prior approval by a panel of experts consisting of ethnologists and musicians. Furthermore, it was decided that smaller, regional *smotre* should be organized from groups that best fit these criteria (Bratanić 1941).

Ethnologists and politicians had the strongest influence in establishing the guidelines for the subsequent *smotre*. For musicians and composers, performing only unarranged folk songs represented a step backwards, from greater to lesser musical sophistication and complexity. The musicians continued to sponsor separate choir festivals, which featured composed and arranged material, but after the 1935 meeting, the choir festivals split in their development from the folk-lore *smotre*.

The 1936 *smotra* turned out to be immensely popular. It included fifty-two groups, mostly from northern Croatia, one group from Bosnia, and a choir of Burgenland Croatians, a Croatian minority and inhabi-tants of southern Austria since the fifteenth century. The following year the number of participating groups was limited to twenty-five, and the panel attempted to have geographically balanced representation with at least one group from every Croatian region. By limiting the number of participating groups, the panel was able to enforce its guidelines more strictly and to exclude groups that did not meet the criteria. If they wished to participate in the *smotra*, the groups were required to make sure their presentations met the standards of the panel of experts. The panel members felt their action would have far-reaching effects. According to Rudolf Herceg, "if we work in this way, in ten years we will be able to precisely formulate Croatian cultural individuality with an eternal source in the peasant folk and their ancient customs" (Bratanić 1941, 8).

Branimir Bratanić, who later became head of the Ethnology Depart-ment at Zagreb University, was a young and enthusiastic graduate stu-dent in 1936. He took an active role in the organization of the *smotre*. He published numerous articles in the Seljačka sloga magazine that gave advice to peasants regarding the best way to organize a regional festival. The articles offered insight into the idealistic but sometimes unrealistic views of the 1930s HSS cultural activists. Bratanić presented a more tempered view later in his career.

Noting that a *smotra* is a special kind of event, distinct from tradi-tional festivals, Bratanić set down guidelines as to what may and may not take place. For example, "At a *smotra*, drinking should never be allowed. A *smotra* is serious work, a relevant exam on the success of our work, even though it happens to show the merriest side of human life" (ibid., 14). He insisted that a *smotra* should always be an independent event, not part of any other festivity, with no outside sponsorship, not dedicated to anyone's honor, and it ought not fall on the same day as any other festivity. If it should happen that the *smotra* must take place on the same day as another celebration, it should be at a different place and at a different time—"the *smotra*, by all means, in the morning" (ibid.). The songs must be exclusively those from that particular village or region. According to Bratanić, if songs from another region are known in a village, they were "mostly brought in by soldiers," they are "foreign feathers and many of them are bad" (ibid., 19). He encouraged especially the singing of old ceremonial and work songs, and urged peasants to ask the old men and women of their villages for the words and melodies, as well as seeking the advice of Seljačka sloga in Zagreb.

Groups that wished to participate in the Zagreb *smotra* had to send the texts of the songs they intended to perform to Seljačka sloga for approval and archiving. Bratanić emphasized the importance of utilizing only the oldest forms of handmade musical instruments and costumes. He condemned newer styles of embroidery. Footwear was very important: "If only one man in the village wears *opanci* (peasant sandals) then the entire choir should wear them at the *smotra*, both men and women." Bratanić also attacked the style of curling women's hair as "ugly and foreign" (ibid.).

The purpose of these guidelines, of course, was to produce an event at which only "pure" Croatian folk culture would be presented, cleansed of foreign influence. Even the tamburitza ensembles of Farkaš or Srijemski instruments fell afoul of Bratanić's guidelines. Those instruments were made by specialized craftsmen, often town residents; Bratanić urged that only *samice* or other soloistic, handmade *tambure* be included in a *smotra* program.

The contemporary political situation in Europe of the 1930s does much to explain the desire for a strong affirmation of Croatian cultural autonomy. Croatian cultural independence was demonstrated not only to the Belgrade regime but also to other external enemies who had designs on Croatian territory. Moreover, rhetoric about "pure" national culture was beginning to show up in the discourse of the fascist regimes entrenched in several European countries, including Italy and Hungary, neighboring countries to Croatia. The murderous dark side of what such rhetoric might lead to had yet to be fully realized.

At the beginning of one of his articles in the Seljačka sloga magazine, Bratanić mentions that a group of Croatian students on tour in Italy were told by their Italian guides that Croats were actually Slavicized

Italians and that Il Duce would soon liberate them. The Croats could not convince their guides otherwise. And Bratanić maintained, if judging only by city ways, the Italians' thesis cannot be disproved. "Style comes from Paris and London, politics from Rome, Moscow, or Berlin" (ibid., 16). To prove cultural autonomy, he stated, Croatians needed to rely upon peasant culture because "our culture, insofar as it is truly ours, is only the peasant culture" (ibid.). Bratanić considered Croatian city ways, long influenced by Austro-Hungarian cosmopolitanism, an undesirable foreign intrusion.

Another reason to present *smotre* was not only to present culture on stage but to return it to its original village context. Bratanić urged peasants to return to their old ways. For example, he urged peasants to make homemade folk costumes their everyday wear, and he advocated the rejection of all industrially produced products. In an April 1936 article in the party magazine, Bratanić maintained that to preserve and maintain folk costumes "means the development of your own folk culture. . . . Folk costume is sturdy and lasting, practical and beautiful and it shows what we are capable of accomplishing by ourselves" (ibid., 33). He admitted that it might seem like a lot of work to produce so much handmade fabric, noting that in the old days it was easier when peasants lived in big extended-family collectives, called *zadruge*. He went so far as to propose that the Seljačka sloga organization become the modern-day version of the *zadruga*, and he reaffirmed the belief that all of a peasant's material and spiritual needs can be fulfilled in the village itself, using its own resources.

An example of an attempt to revitalize disappearing peasant customs was reported in the June 1936 issue of Seljačka sloga's magazine: "Under the guidance of the folklife expert Professor Milovan Gavazzi, the newly established mixed choir of the lodge [in a village near Dugo Selo] rehearsed that ancient folksinging custom [St. John's night] which remained in the memory of only the oldest people in the village" (ibid.).

And yet another reason to produce *smotre* was to "peasantize" or "Croatianize" the culture of the city. In the words of the Croatian literary scholar A. H. Žarković, "The question how shall we carry out the rebirth of culture in the city on a true folk foundation is a great historical task of our generation" (ibid., 18). This effort represented Radić's original goal of uniting urban and rural Croatians under the banner of peasant culture.

To demonstrate cultural autonomy to external enemies, to revitalize fading aspects of peasant culture, and to create an urban intellectual culture on a "folk foundation" were the lofty goals of the ethnologist-led movement with *smotre* of Croatian peasant culture as its signature event. To free the country and its culture from foreign domination, the folklore had to be cleansed of foreign contamination. Yet Croatia was not an isolated island. Croatia and its neighboring countries are located in a part of Europe that has been subject to repeated migrations, centuries of intense and constant interaction of different nationalities and fluid boundaries, and have generally included numerous peoples and cultures in a single political state. Some regions, notably on the Pannonian plains, are so culturally mixed—a result of resettlement policies of the Austrian or Ottoman Empires—that no single ethnic group constitutes a majority. In short, in southeastern Europe there have existed conditions conducive to cultural contact and interchange but not conducive to cultural "purity." Even the Croatian ethnologists engaged in this effort to revitalize "pure" Croatian culture used geographic rather than national zones to divide southeastern Europe—the Adriatic, the Dinaric, and the Pannonian zones.

Because many of the cultures of the area share many traits, it is hard to eliminate "foreign" influences that have been ingrained in local cultures for a very long time. Indeed, it is easier to identify modern traits from urban industrial culture. In actual practice, then, the ethnologists concentrated their attack on modernisms. They could identify newer popular songs, mass-produced instruments like accordions and tamburitzas, and factory-made clothes, fabrics, and dyes. Changes from newer creations arising in village culture, such as contemporary songs and dances, and new embroidery designs and patterns were also attacked even though they may have been originated by creative villagers well-grounded in peasant culture. The *smotra* organizers seemed to have decided that there should be no change in village culture so that the culture of a golden age must be preserved and protected.

Bratanić eloquently expressed his negativity toward modernity. Maintaining that the specialization of skills brought on by industry has made us dependent on other specialists for most of our various needs, he concluded that modern civilization actually destroys culture because "creative capability is the most important thing in culture." Bratanić felt that modern culture makes humans into specialized machines and is responsible for creating "in the big modern cities something which cannot be found anywhere among the peoples of Africa, Asia, or Australia . . . people without culture, wild men" (ibid., 34).

Real culture should be a harmonious whole, but civilization develops only one small part of that whole. Bratanić advocated for universality of folk culture. In answer to the question "Is 'little' culture possible?," Bratanić stated, "It is difficult to re-create folk culture if civilization has already destroyed it. In that sense we Croatians, like some other more 'backward' peoples are in an unusually fortunate position. We do not have to create such a folk culture; we have it already. It is our peasant culture" (ibid., 36). His romantic view of peasant culture also reflected the ideology of the planners of *smotre* up to World War II.

After the liberation of Yugoslavia from Axis occupation, the work of Seljačka sloga was revived and encouraged by the new socialist government. Regional festivals were organized, and in 1946 a large *smotra* was held in Zagreb with Marshall Tito in attendance. The vigorous activities of village folklore groups echoed in the city as well. Numerous urban amateur folklore ensembles started up, and in 1949 Lado, a professional folk dance troupe, formed in Zagreb.

In connection with the third conference of the International Folk Music Council held in 1951 in Opatija on the Adriatic coast, a large folklore exhibition took place. The following year, in Pula, another large festival was held in connection with the establishment of the Society of Musical Folklorists of Yugoslavia.

The rest of the 1950s showed a period of diminished folklore activity. Government ideology shifted as peasant culture was viewed as a backward relic to be soon replaced by the industrial culture of socialism. This imposed view proved to be short-lived. By the early 1960s the policy changed again, and folkloric cultural activities enjoyed official sanction and encouragement. By 1966 there was enough activity on a regional level to begin the Međunarodna smotra folklora in Zagreb, the newest incarnation of the interwar *smotre*.

A panel of experts, including Bratanić and Milovan Gavazzi, organizers of the 1930s *smotre*, was organized to select the participants.
Since the prewar *smotre* were based on Croatian nationalist ideas and
in opposition to modern industrial development, it is interesting to
note what might have been the changes in the *smotra* that were adopted
to bring the event into line with the new government's socialist ideology. Surprisingly, there was very little change. The revived event
avoided the taint of officially disapproved Croatian nationalism by
billing itself as an international festival. Groups from all the Yugoslav
republics were invited as well as groups from other European countries. The new *smotra*'s implied slogan proclaimed "Brotherhood and
unity of the peoples of Yugoslavia and the world," replacing "Pure
Croatian peasant culture." Partisan songs, composed in the course
of the national liberation struggle, were now deemed acceptable as
an expression of the folk. Otherwise the concepts of who and what
should be included in a *smotra* changed little. The panel of experts still
screened prospective groups in advance and endeavored to exclude
modern or urban elements, requiring that the villagers themselves
present only that folklore which the panel judged to be indigenous to
their region (Jakelić 1978).

The concepts of the panel did not take into account the significant
migrations that took place at the end of World War II. Many villagers from poor mountainous regions were resettled in fertile lowland
river valleys, many occupying the former homes of the German minority that had been forced out at the war's end. Families who might
have lived in mountainous Lika and were resettled in Slavonia would
be expected to participate in groups performing the Croatian Slavonian repertoire that was documented early in the twentieth century.
Any Lika repertoire or hybrid Lika-Slavonia expressions did not fit the
panel's criteria. In addition, villagers from all regions now streamed
into the rapidly expanding cities. New folkloric expressions arising from
the culture of the recently urbanized villagers, such as the so-called *narodnjak* songs—a form of popular music containing elements of traditional folk music—were not allowed. Thus, any folklore that had
arisen from recently created cultural contexts was excluded (Rihtman-
Auguštin 1978, 8).

Villagers from Slavonia at the folklore festival in Đakovo, Croatia, July 1978. (Photos by author)

Now no one claimed that the *smotra* might spark a Croatian cultural renaissance based on the old peasant ways, but nonetheless, folklore groups were encouraged by local governments and often assisted financially. To this day they continue to be viewed as a positive activity for youth and a valuable asset in the cultural life of the village. Many village groups seek to emulate the choreographed stage performances of Lado, the professional folk dance ensemble. Often the village groups had two repertoires, one of which they called "authentic" and the other "choreographed." They utilized their authentic repertoire when they were to be screened by ethnologists for participation at a *smotra*, but at local festivities in their home regions, ironically, they would be more likely to perform their diverse and somewhat more polished choreographed repertoire (Rajković 1978).

In many instances the authentic repertoire still persists and remains quite similar to the material performed by the current group members' grandparents decades ago. Thus the panel system succeeded in creating a concept of their own authentic folklore, known to the villagers and perpetuated for the purpose of having a chance to participate in *smotre* (ibid.).

Still, newer elements relentlessly penetrated the groups' repertoires so the panel was obliged to bend its guidelines. By the 1970s any cultural element that could be shown to have been accepted in the life of that village fifty years earlier could be presented at the *smotra*. The most important concrete effect of that rule was to allow Farkaš and Srijemski tamburitzas and accordions into the performances by many groups (Jakelić 1978).

The current directors of the *smotra* have discarded the exclusionary notions of the earlier ethnologists, and since the 1990s they include modern and hybrid forms of folk expression in the *smotra* program. And now, after nearly a half century of annual stagings, the *smotra* has acquired a well-known identity based on its earlier guidelines, which the majority of the current participants accept. Nowadays most of the village groups continue to rehearse their authentic folklore repertoire and bring it to the festival in Zagreb (Vitez 2011).

CHAPTER 5

The Tamburitza Tradition
Takes on American Ways

I n Gary, Indiana, Broadway has always been the main drag. Plotted
in 1905, it is a geometrically perfect straight line, aligned straight
south from the steel mills; the sooty sulfurous coke plants and
basic oxygen furnaces are perched on the south shore of Lake Michigan. Broadway runs under the railroad tracks, through the struggling,
half-abandoned downtown, through the neighborhood stores and store-
front churches of midtown, the heart of the black community, then
over the freeway into the ethnically mixed Glen Park neighborhood,
where European immigrants, who arrived since the 1970s, and old immigrants from the early 1900s rub shoulders with middle-class blacks
and American-born steelworkers. Broadway runs on past the new, hast-
ily constructed shopping centers; here and there stands an old frame
farmhouse, its rural-delivery mailbox beside the road testifying that
this was still farm country not so long ago. Farther south on Broadway,
the ex-farm suburbs finally give way to the true countryside, and Broadway gets lost in the furrow of a Hoosier state soybean field.

This was Gary in the 1970s when I carried out the bulk of the fieldwork for this book. The town and its surroundings, the Calumet Region,
are industrial America in the extreme, plagued with grime, crime, and
racial tensions. About halfway along Broadway's run from the steel
mills to the soybeans, Jenny's Restaurant operated in Glen Park. Amid
Slavic foods and drinks, Gary's "Hunkies," mostly Croatian and Serbian

Americans, enjoyed their ethnic cuisine, often accompanied by tamburitza music (March 1976).

Inside, the restaurant was long and narrow. In the evenings, a few customers enjoyed late suppers, and others sipped brandy or beer. On a wider patch of open floor, the four musicians of the Drina Orchestra created for themselves a stage-like area. There Milovan "Mel" Dokich played violin, Milan Opacich played *čelo brač*, Matt Jurich strummed a *bugarija*, and Jack Tomlin plucked a bass violin. Mel and Matt began musical apprenticeships at an early age as the sons of *tamburaši* famous in the 1920s and 1930s, Djoko Dokić and Matt Jurišić. Jack, whose family owned a flooring business that operated out of the same building decades earlier, learned *berde* and *čelo brač* in a youth tamburitza ensemble led by Ivan Stefanac, a noted local musician. Milan had to develop most of his considerable musicianship on his own, all eyes and ears at the performances of his boyhood idols: the Skertich Brothers and the Popovich Brothers. Both boys had been steeped in tamburitza music their whole lives.

These men, now all passed on, typified the active combo *tamburaši* of the 1970s. These part-time musicians were bearers of a tradition of American tamburitza music, which since the 1920s had developed its own style and aesthetic preferences; distinct societies and cultures flourished in the ethnic communities of American industrial cities (Jones and Holli 1981). The South Slavic communities in a steel-mill town like Gary differed markedly from rural life in a Croatian or Serbian village. The transplanted villagers and their progeny intuitively changed the music to suit and be expressive of their American environment.

In the period between the two world wars, *tamburaši* in Yugoslavia were aware of the concept of "authentic folklore." *Tamburaši* accompanied the dancers and singers of village folklore ensembles, which participated in the popular *smotre* of that era. Not all *tamburaši* played in this type of ensemble. Large orchestras continued to perform classical-style compositions, and tavern combos entertained with an eclectic repertoire. It would not have been uncommon for many adaptable *tamburaši* to play in more than one group—"authentic" material at a *smotra*, orchestral material with a tamburitza society, and diverse repertoire in a tavern band.

During that same interwar period, *tamburaši* in America were exposed to very different influences. There were no ethnologists among the former peasant millworkers and miners who made up the bulk of the immigrant population. The cultural polemics linked to Old Country politics raised by the ethnologists and politicians of the Croatian Peasant Party were less understood and seldom discussed in America.

The earliest *tamburaši* in America differed little from their European counterparts. Most had recently arrived in the United States. Time and extended exposure to American influences gradually developed into a distinctly American tamburitza tradition. Diminished contact with the homeland speeded the divergence of the American tradition from the European. Restrictions on immigration after 1924 all but halted the flow of new Croatian and Serbian immigrants to the United States (Higham 1988, 300–330). Without a continuing influx of immigrants, up-to-date knowledge of conditions and issues in the old country villages began to diminish. And certainly, since the pre–World War I departure of the bulk of the immigrants, there had been substantial changes in the homeland. The issues associated with the old Austro-Hungarian politics had evaporated, and the immigrants did not have firsthand experience or deep knowledge of the newly emerging issues in the Yugoslav state.

American *tamburaši*, insofar as they attached political conceptions to their music, generally continued to embrace the Gaj ideology to ennoble and uplift Slavic culture (see chap. 2). In Yugoslavia, Croats had become part of a new state where Slavs made up an overwhelming majority. In that country, Slavic language and generalized Slavic culture alone were insufficient to invoke Croatian cultural particularity, the new political symbolism of tamburitza in Croatia.

In America, most of the South Slavic immigrants were marginalized, exploited workers, toiling in mining and heavy industry, and living in a dominant English-speaking society. The immigrants and their culture were subjected to both ill-spirited and well-meaning threats. Spokesmen for pervasive nativist movements castigated Slavic immigrants as uncultured, inassimilable, and "un-American," not to mention "bad-smelling" and "Europe's inhuman rubbish" (ibid., 54–55). Educators and reformers sought to "uplift" the newcomers by obliterating the "strange," "radical," and "undesirable" traits of the immigrants' culture (Bodnar 1985, 190–92). Thus, as it had been in Austria-Hungary, efforts to affirm the value of their Slavic culture to a Germanic language-speaking overclass were still needed and appropriate in the English-speaking United States of the 1920s.

In America, something as far from the concept of "pure" Croatian peasant culture as the latest popular song in Serbian or Croatian none-theless might have been understood as an affirmation of Slavic culture. *Tamburaši* playing the same popular song that might have represented cultural affirmation in America likely would have been castigated by a cultural specialist in Europe as a foreign or modern degradation of pure Croatian culture. The American *tamburaši* heard no voices restraining them from modernity and eclecticism. On the contrary, the inclusion of Slavic performers in the emerging American entertainment industry provided them an incentive to diversify their musical expressions.

TAMBURAŠI AS TOURING ARTISTS

In the later decades of the nineteenth century, American entrepreneurs strove to develop an increasing "commercialization of leisure." Their interests in monetary gain blended, in many instances, with a reformist impulse to replace the rowdy and disreputable heavy drinking in saloons that had heretofore been the working man's primary leisure-time activity (Rosenzweig 1983, 171–83). Reformers suggested attending the-ater performances as an alternative to the saloon, yet lacking other venues, many of the mid-nineteenth-century performances still had to be staged in saloons themselves (Widen and Anderson 2007, 1–5). During the late nineteenth century there developed a wave of theater construction. The theaters of the 1850s and 1860s were often danger-ous wooden firetraps, illuminated as they were by candlelight and then the newly developed gaslight. By the later 1870s and 1880s, though, masonry theater buildings were built with safer illumination.

Entertainment entrepreneurs promoted an expanding popular cul-ture, viewing the American public as ticket-buying consumers of their productions. The advent of motion pictures in the twentieth century accelerated and spread theater construction, which increased attendance while creating simultaneously a competing entertainment product to the live shows (ibid., 28–51).

A widespread American interest in "exotic" cultures had been developed and nurtured through the proliferation of international expositions such as the Chicago World's Columbian Exposition of 1893, the St. Louis World's Fair of 1904, and the San Francisco Pan-Pacific Exhibition of 1915. These events featured constructed "native villages" populated by authentic residents of the countries represented (Rydell, 87–91). This was not exclusively an American phenomenon. Though they did not yet feature "exotic villages," the London World's Fair of 1851 has been considered the first such event, and as we read earlier, *tamburaši* from Zagreb performed at the 1889 Exposition Universelle in Paris.

To Anglo-Americans, tamburitza musicians qualified as "exotic," and understandably, *tamburaši* sought any musical employment opportunities available to them in the United States, even as "exotics." At the beginning of the twentieth century, tamburitza groups like Ivan Očvarek's touring group from Sisak were able to perform for mainstream and elite American audiences. Other ensembles such as the Zvonimir Orchestra, the Elias Serenaders, and the Sloga Orchestra, whose members were permanent residents of the United States, found work as touring acts in the vaudeville variety shows staged in American theaters and the educationally oriented Chautauqua tent-show entertainment circuits in the era from 1910 to 1945 (Kolar 1975). Owing to the strains of life on tour, each group experienced continual changeover in personnel. For example, Zvonimir, one of the earliest groups, had twenty-three different musicians as members between 1906 and 1928, even though at any one time they included only five to seven members. Zvonimir's name had a patriotic as well as musical ring; it is the name of a famed early Croatian king, but it is also the equivalent of the Latin name Aurelius, derived from the root word meaning bell, *zvono*.

Zvonimir began touring in 1910, featuring exclusively instrumental music at that time. Under the leadership of their musician/manager Petar Savich, they were able to market the sound of their Farkaš tamburitzas as a form of elegant European dinner music at some of America's swank hotels, the Willard in Washington, DC, the Baltimore Hotel in Kansas City, and Hotel Utah in Salt Lake City (Crnković 1933). The group performed as a pit orchestra at silent movies and accompanied opera singers and ballet dancers. Once they were even co-billed in a Chautauqua lecture program with the famous American populist politician and presidential candidate William Jennings Bryan (ibid.). For the most part they performed in the tent shows, local auditoriums, and movie houses of small towns across America. In 1923 they took their most extensive tour, playing in Australia and New Zealand.

In the earliest pictures of the group, their garb was a stylized version of folk costume. In later photographs, they appear in tuxedos and black bow ties. By the mid-1920s, the costumes became more flamboyant. One publicity photograph shows a five-member Zvonimir ensemble (down from seven members in 1915) in satin shirts with huge rounded collars, cummerbunds, and satin strips down the seams of their dark pants. Each musician sported a broad-brimmed Spanish hat with a shiny hatband. A pair of "Spanish dancers" (actually Anglo-Americans), an act they accompanied, are posed before them, the man staring with romantic intensity over the shoulder and into the eyes of his female partner whose silk-stockinged left leg is seductively exposed to mid-thigh between the strands of her fringed skirt (ibid., 28).

On the entertainment circuits, Zvonimir and the other tamburitza ensembles nurtured their image as an exotic European act, similar to entertainment curiosities like the troupes of Hawaiian steel guitarists and Swiss yodelers often featured in vaudeville shows of their era. Zvonimir's ornate pearl-inlaid instruments and their sometimes gaudy costumes contributed to their appeal to the general American public.

The Elias Serenaders, another group with a long career on the Chautauqua circuit, developed a different image, a family-based group with an educational and ethnic-cultural appeal. They always performed in stylized versions of Croatian folk costumes, played many of their programs in school and college assemblies, and consciously sought to increase Americans' knowledge of South Slavic culture, delivering short explanations in English about the performance. The nucleus of the group was the family of Charles Elias Sr., the group's founder (Elias Jr. 1981). Elias, whose original name was Dragutin Ilijaš, was born in

Suhopolje in Slavonia in 1886 and immigrated to Milwaukee in 1903 (Kolar 1975, 33). Working as a barber by day, he spent his evenings studying music at the Meyer Music School. He formed a number of tamburitza ensembles between 1910 and 1924 in the Milwaukee area, and also in Virginia and in northeastern Minnesota in the Iron Range, where he resided from 1915 to 1922.

In 1924 Elias accomplished a significant achievement in his musical career when he published *Škola za tamburaše* (School for tamburitza players), the first tamburitza instruction book to come out in the United States. The value that Elias placed on education is evident in the motto on the title page of the book, "U nauci je spas!" (In learning is salvation!) (Elias 1924). That same year he formed a five-piece ensemble, which included his son and daughter. They obtained a contract from the Redpath Lyceum Bureau to tour on the Chautauqua tent-show circuit. The Chautauqua adult education movement founded in western New York in 1874, initially as a program for educating Sunday school teachers, began in 1904 to lend its name to otherwise largely independent touring educational shows, featuring lecturers and musical performances. The method of presenting multiday programs in rural communities that may have lacked any substantial performance facilities is attributed to Keith Vawter, a Redpath Lyceum bureau manager. The shows were presented in tents pitched "on a well-drained field near town." Speakers and performers would make a circuit performing in each of the Chautauqua tents located in several nearby towns in a particular region. After several days of programs, the tents would come down and move to a different area. By the mid-1920s when Circuit Chautauquas were at their peak, they appeared in more than 10,000 communities to audiences of more than 45 million; by about 1940 they had run their course (http://sdrc.lib.uiowa.edu/traveling -culture/inventory/MSC150.html, accessed 2011).

From 1924 until 1941, the Elias Serenaders performed throughout the United States and Canada, continuing under the leadership of Charles Elias Jr. after his father's early death in 1937. The final tours of the Elias Serenaders, which lasted until 1945, were arranged under the auspices of the USO (United Service Organizations) to entertain American forces in the Pacific during World War II (Elias Jr. 1981).

Charles Elias Jr. (1911–83).
(Photo by Timothy Sharko)

Charles Elias Jr. did not cease musical activities after disbanding the Elias Serenaders. From his home base in Kenosha, Wisconsin, he became the music instructor and conductor of junior tamburitza orchestras including the Silver Strings of Milwaukee and the Waukegan (Illinois) Junior Tamburitzans, remaining active in that role until his death in 1984.

Both Charles Elias Sr. and Jr. were important composers of light classical pieces for tamburitza orchestra, usually arranged in seven parts. Among the hundreds of Elias compositions are suites of folk song melodies, polkas, waltzes, marches, and overtures. Elias compositions are still performed by tamburitza orchestras, especially in the Wisconsin-Illinois region where they were most active (Kolar 1975, 34).

The era of vaudeville shows and Chautauqua circuits passed, ending the involvement in them of tamburitza ensembles. Nonetheless, the opportunity these venues provided to *tamburaši* to become professional touring artists had a lasting effect on the nature of the tamburitza tradition in America. A good number of musicians found it possible to concentrate fully on musical endeavors and to develop their skills to a high level. Subsequent to their careers as touring artists, several of these musicians played important roles as teachers, composers, publishers, and organizers of tamburitza activities, and several found new roles in the evolving entertainment industry.

Peter Savich and John Plasay, veterans of the Zvonimir group, settled in Chicago after ceasing touring. In 1929 they established an ensemble, Javor, which performed folk and popular music for social events; the two men also continued to use their show business acumen to "uplift" the Slavic immigrants' culture. Javor also assisted Chicago-area Croatian and Serbian amateur singing societies to develop productions of operettas and served as the operetta's pit orchestra (Hlad 1977). In February 1937 Javor recorded several selections for Columbia Records, alternating between familiar folk songs like "Crven fesić" and well-known classical pieces like "U boj, u boj" from Ivan Zajc's opera *Nikola Šubić Zrinjski* (Spottswood 1990, 946).

In 1938 John Plasay played a key role in establishing and serving as conductor for a tamburitza group of symphonic proportions called the Chicago Tamburitza Club. The core of the orchestra (twenty-five or thirty musicians) consisted of the members of several Chicago-area professional combos: the Popovich Brothers, Jadran, Javor, and Šar Planina (Hlad 1977).

Rudolph Cernkovich (Crnković) was another important veteran of the Zvonimir ensemble. He was very influential through his composing, arranging, and music publishing efforts. Born in Brod Moravica in the Croatian region of Gorski kotar in 1889, Cernkovich immigrated to Pennsylvania in 1905, initially intending to stay only a few years. As a young man, he used his musical abilities to teach and direct local amateur choirs and tamburitza orchestras. He joined Zvonimir in 1913, touring with the group for five years. After leaving Zvonimir, Cernkovich married and settled in Chicago. He studied harmony, counterpoint, and orchestration through the extension program of the Chicago Conservatory of Music. For a while he manufactured tamburitza instruments, but because of health problems, he sold the instrument-making business to a cousin and devoted his time to arranging and publishing tamburitza music.

In 1933 Cernkovich obtained the position of postmaster in the small town of Bradley, Michigan—a secure government job when the US economy was suffering through the Great Depression. Although he was geographically isolated from other *tamburaši*, Cernkovich nonetheless continued his music publishing business from this rural location in central Michigan. He published several folios of sheet music and a number of pamphlets on tamburitza-related topics, using a modest mimeographed format and marketing his publications by mail order. He reached his customers by word of mouth in the tamburitza network and by advertising in Croatian and Serbian ethnic newspapers. His arrangements included simple song arrangements suitable for children and other beginners, as well as more complex material, including renderings for tamburitza of operatic arias and other classical music (http://www.tamburitza.org/TAA/hof.html [hereafter cited as TAA], accessed 2011).

The example of the nationwide and international touring by groups like Zvonimir, coupled with the educational emphasis of the Elias Serenaders, provided an inspiration for the formation in 1937 of the Duquesne University Tamburitzans that became the American flagship ensemble for validating the beauty of eastern European folk culture. The Tamburitzans were initially a twelve-member ensemble directed by Matt L. Gouze, a Croatian American from Ely, a town on the Iron Range in northeastern Minnesota. The student musicians received college scholarships to Duquesne University, a Jesuit-founded institution in Pittsburgh, in return for serving as ambassadors for the university in nationwide performances. The ensemble eventually grew to more than thirty members and included in its repertoire music and dance from all of the eastern European countries. In addition to the touring student ensemble, the Tamburitzans operated a Cultural Center, an archive and museum of eastern European music, dance, and costume (Kolar 1975).

After fifteen years of leading the Tamburitzans, in 1952 Matt Gouze was followed as director by Walter W. Kolar, a Croatian American born in Ambridge, Pennsylvania, a former Tamburitzans ensemble member who became a leading authority on tamburitza music. Kolar brought in the choreographer Nicholas Jordanoff, a Bulgarian American, so that

The Duquesne University Tamburitzans, 1941–42. (Courtesy of Duquesne University Tamburitzans)

an emphasis on choreographed folk dances from several eastern European countries ultimately replaced static orchestral presentations in the Tamburitzans' performance repertoire.

Since the 1960s, the Tamburitzans have been selected by the U.S. State Department to represent the United States on several international tours, something that might have seemed impossible to the marginalized Slavic immigrants in the 1920s. Another former Tamburitzans ensemble member, Paul Stafura, who grew up steeped in the tamburitza tradition of western Pennsylvania, succeeded Kolar as director in 1988 and remains in that post.

Although all the performers are full-time college students, the ensemble continues to perform an average of eighty performances annually. The Tamburitzans perform for general audiences, but in those locations where there is a large Slavic community, their performances often become an important ethnic community event, sponsored by organizations such as the local Croatian Fraternal Union lodges. Following the formal concert in an auditorium, the ethnic lodges often sponsor a dinner/dance in a church or fraternal hall. Ensemble members play for social dancing, mingle with the audience, and usually join in the festivities (Jordanoff 1988; Kolar 1988; Stafura 1999).

TAMBURAŠI AS RECORDING ARTISTS

Culture change is often stimulated by technological change. Edison's invention of the phonograph had far-reaching consequences for musical cultures everywhere, and the United States was a country where this impact had been felt early in the twentieth century. In the first years of the recording industry, national companies like Columbia and Victor sent representatives into the field in urban and rural America, as well as elsewhere around the world, to determine who were the popular musicians in a particular area. The companies recorded these musicians, sometimes in rather improvised studios, and produced a relatively small number of copies of records, which then were sold primarily to local markets by local retailers (Malone 1968, 38–46).

In the 1920s, a major portion of the population of the United States was foreign born. The immigrants brought musical tastes and preferences from their homelands. In order to sell records to this large immigrant market, the record companies followed their conventional practice of seeking out and recording the music ensembles indigenous to the immigrant communities. These efforts produced the great era of ethnic recording (Gronow 1982).

Dozens of tamburitza ensembles made recordings from the early years of the twentieth century until the early 1940s; space permits the mention of only a few of the most influential musicians and groups. Vaso Bukvić was an early recording artist who immigrated from San Petru Mare, a culturally Serbian village in the Rumanian section of Banat province, an ethnically mixed area in the Danube River valley. In 1912, in Elizabeth, New Jersey, he and his brother Mirko, along with three others from their home village, established a tamburitza combo called Banat, named for their home region. In June 1916 Vaso and Mirko recorded several songs for Columbia Records in New York; in 1917, after the United States had entered World War I, Vaso and other Banat members stressed that they belonged to an allied nation, using the group name Srpski muški kvintet (Serbian Male Quintet) when they recorded for Victor Records such bellicose anthems as "Napred stupaj!" (Advance forward!) and "Rado ide Srbin u vojnike," translated on the label as "With Joy the Serbian Enters the Army" (Spottswood 1990, 939–40).

Vaso left the East Coast, settling in the Chicago area in the 1920s. Nonetheless, the Banat orchestra had a long, continued existence, without the Bukvić brothers. With core members from the Jezdimir family, Zdravko, Milutin, and Walter, the ensemble lasted into the 1970s making numerous recordings, which emphasized music for kolo dancing (TAA).

In the Midwest, Vaso found a larger community of *tamburaši* than in New Jersey. In that milieu he became a very influential musician, a renowned *primaš*, playing with noted *tamburaši* like Djoko Dokić, John Krilčić, Peter Savich, and John Plasay as well as mentoring emerging future celebrated musicians like the Kapugi Brothers, Vasil Crljenica, Steve Vučinić, and Marko Popovich. Vaso had an important role in establishing the improvisational Banat style of *prima* playing in the Midwest, but because he tended to move from group to group and did not consistently maintain his own ensemble, his recording career waned (Hlad 1977). In 1924, in Richmond, Indiana, Vaso recorded seventeen numbers for his own short-lived Jugoslavia record label at the Gennett Records studio operated by the Starr Piano Company. He recorded only two more sides for Columbia in 1928 (Spottswood 1990, 940).

Another outstanding *primaš*, also from the culturally diverse Banat region, who had an amazing if tragically curtailed recording career was Dušan Jovanović. Jovanović, based in Philadelphia, toured much of the eastern United States with his Orao (Eagle) orchestra, performing for the Rumanian and Hungarian as well as the Serbian and Croatian ethnic communities (Opacich 2005, 154–55). From August 1924 to March 1929 Jovanović and his orchestra were involved in fifteen recording sessions for both Columbia and Victor, ultimately recording eighty-seven sides for Columbia and forty-four for Victor. Of the 131 total recorded tunes, 18 were Rumanian and 6 Hungarian, including several with vocal parts in those languages. On some of these records, Columbia listed the name of the group as Delmagyar Tamburicasok (Magyar tamburitza band) in Hungarian or stated in Rumanian, Cantat de Dan Joan din Temisoara, cu Orchestra lui Tamburice (Song of Mr. John from Timesoara and his tamburitza orchestra), which hints that Dušan Jovanović may have come from the vicinity of that very ethnically diverse city in Banat.

Beginning in July 1927 until his last recording session in March 1929, Jovanović recorded sixteen comic sketches in Serbian, punctuated with music and singing, which are highly reflective of the way of life of his generation of Slavic immigrants. The following are a few titles of the sketches followed by the English translations as shown on the record labels: "Prosidba u Ameriki (Engagement in America)," "Svadba u Ameriki (A wedding in America)," "Amerikanac putuje za stari kraj (An American Croat goes to Europe)," "U kraju ću malo bit, povrati ću se u Detroit (Won't be long in the Old Country, Will be back soon in Detroit)," "Razvenčanje (Divorce)," "Mainerska krčma kod lepe Mare (In the miner's inn with Mary)" (Spottswood 1990, 949–53).

A frequent theme in these comedy sketches recorded by Jovanović and also those recorded by other *tamburaši* of that era, such as Adamov and Company, include Prohibition and bootlegging. To the immigrant *tamburaši*, the laws prohibiting alcohol that were in effect in the 1920s must have seemed particularly preposterous. Most frequently, though, the skits concerned male-female relationships, with the male musicians often criticizing the supposedly overly assertive ways that many immigrant women adopted after coming to America.

Although I have been unable to locate historical documentation for the incident, legend has it that Dušan and his entire band were killed in a car-train collision while they were driving to an engagement in 1929, ending his phenomenal career (Opacich 2005, 155).

Due to the influence of Bukvić, Jovanović, and the Banat orchestra, music of the Banat region became influential in the music of American *tamburaši*—even though immigrants from that fertile, relatively rich Danube River valley were vastly outnumbered by immigrants who had their origins in other regions, especially poor mountainous or rocky coastal regions like Lika, Dalmatia, or Gorski kotar. Compared to many of the musical traditions from those regions, the Banat music was sophisticated and urbane. Even vernacular musicians lacking formal training from Banat and its neighboring regions of Bačka and Srem seemed to arrive in America with highly developed tamburitza-playing skills. Their obvious virtuosity and the fact that their music possibly could appeal to a number of different ethnic groups no doubt facilitated their ability to be recorded: once recorded, the record sales themselves further spread this musical influence.

Throughout the 1920s a highly influential group of tamburitza musicians was actively making recordings in various combinations, under varying ensemble names. The violinist Stevan Zerbes was among the earliest to record, in 1918 and 1919, under his own name or as the Royal Serbian Tamburitza Orchestra. His violin playing is said to have so influenced another key *tamburaš*, Djoko Dokich, that he prevailed upon his son Milovan to study violin. Milovan (Mel) Dokich became the outstanding violinist on the tamburitza scene from the 1940s through the 1970s. Very little is known of Zerbes. He may have started the prac- tice among *tamburaši* of recording for various record companies in quick succession. Between March 29 and May 1918 he recorded in at least five sessions in New York: three for Columbia and two for Victor including some of the same titles for both companies (Spottswood 1990, 976). Zerbes's reputation is besmirched by a particularly outrageous legend that circulates among *tamburaši*. According to the story, while in a drunken state, Zerbes desecrated the holy water in a church with his urine. He had to flee to the Old Country where the legend has it that he died of venereal disease—perhaps a divine retribution.

Ilija Miškovich, Nikola Plavšić, Sandor Huszar, Mirko Kolesar, Djoko Dokich, and Joe Radich were also members of the core group of musicians who made dozens of influential recordings on Columbia and Victor under such names as the Jorgovan Tamburitza Orchestra, Huszar-Miškovich Tamburica Orchestra, M. Kolesar Tamburaški zbor, Miškovic Tamburitza Orchestra, and Tamburaški zbor "Balkan." Most likely, many of these musicians were from the Danube region. Djoko Dokich hailed from Selo Tuk in Srem, and Sandor Huszar was most likely a Hungarian, a major component of the population of that area. Some *tamburaši* stated that Mirko Kolesar was a Russian, but it may be more likely that he was a Rusin or Ruthenian, an ethnic group from the western Ukraine that colonized the Danube region during the eighteenth century.

In June 1926 Jorgovan recorded what may be the biggest tamburitza hit of the 78 rpm disc era, "Mladi Doktore" (The young doctor). The Jorgovan member Joe Radich claims to have written the "Mladi Doktore" lyrics using the tune of an old Slavonian song, "Ajd na rogalj momče," and indeed, on the hit recording, Jorgovan ends up the song by singing the first verse of that song. Like many of the humorous sketches, "Mladi Doktore" is a comedic song with plenty of sexual innuendo, concerning a young doctor's examination of a youthful female patient. As is also the case in many of the recorded humorous sketches of that era, the jesting seems to be grounded in male concern about the more independent and assertive role of women in modern American society, which the *tamburaši* contrasted with their idealized memory of more submissive Old Country village women.

Milan Verni was another major recording artist. Verni, who had shortened his last name from Vraničević, led an orchestra called the Balkan Mountain Men, which toured on the Lyceum and Chautauqua circuits, and regularly entertained during the late 1920s and 1930s at the Dubrovnik Restaurant in New York City. The band featured such outstanding *tamburaši* as Jim Kovachevich, Frank Toplak, and Matt Vidak. In the 1930s and 1940s Verni recorded more than fifty sides for Columbia and Victor. Verni's recorded versions of such well-liked songs as "Čuješ mala" and "Kolika je Javorina planina" influenced many American *tamburaši*, helping to make a significant part of Verni's recorded repertoire into standard tunes. In the 1940s Verni relocated to Pittsburgh, where he resided until the early 1970s when he died. For many years he entertained at his own restaurant, the Balkan Café (TAA).

Edo Ljubić, a singer born in Donji Vakuf, Bosnia, in 1912, was already a well-known radio and recording artist in Yugoslavia when in 1939 he was engaged to sing for the music program presented at the Yugoslav exhibit at the New York World's Fair. When World War II broke out in Europe later that year, Ljubić opted to remain in the United States, where he continued his successful musical career, ultimately becoming the American tamburitza scene's first true singing star. A gifted vocalist and a dashingly handsome figure, he usually performed in formal attire. Ljubić was equally adept singing light opera arias, French and German cabaret songs, Hungarian romances, as well as the *sevdalinka* (unrequited love songs) of his Bosnian homeland. The strength of his singing voice is attested to in an anecdote that still circulates. While he was performing in National Hall in Chicago in the 1940s, a thunderstorm blew up, knocking out the electricity in the large hall. Edo kept the audience calm and entertained by continuing to sing in the dark, quite audibly, without the aid of a microphone (T. March 2009; Daniels 1982).

In March 1940 he recorded six songs in New York for the Victor Company, accompanied by Milan Verni's tamburitza ensemble. One of those songs, the *sevdalinka* "Oj kaduno," became a signature tune of his repertoire. Between November 1941 and February 1942, in Chicago, Ljubić made several more notable recordings, an additional twenty-four songs, also for Victor, backed by the strong Kapugi Brothers tamburitza orchestra, which included Djoko Dokić and Djoko's teen-aged son Milovan (Mel) Dokić. From these sessions, Ljubić's virtuoso vocal performances on the romances "Nekad svale bjele ruže" and "Slomljena nada" as well as the *sevdalinka* "U Stambolu" consolidated his reputation as arguably the most outstanding singer in the American tamburitza world (Spottswood 1990, 958–59).

Edo served in the American armed forces, and after World War II, he resumed his singing career, recording several songs on Continental Records, a small East Coast label that specialized in ethnic recordings. He was accompanied by the members of the Banat Orchestra of New Jersey. He also studied hotel and restaurant management, ultimately settling in Los Angeles, where he was the proprietor of (and sometimes entertainer in) a continental-style restaurant, La Place. He made a few self-produced records, but his restaurateur occupation henceforth largely supplanted his musical career (Daniels 1982).

The Kapugi Brothers had their own illustrious career beyond backing up noted singers like Edo Ljubić, Vinka Ellisen, and Uroš Seferović. Four of the eight children of Adam and Milka Kapudjija were active for decades in the Kapugi Brother's Šar Planina Orchestra, named for the most famous mountain in their father's home region of western Macedonia. Martin and Frank Kapugi (using the shortened version of their name that the family members used in America) were born in Chicago in 1910 and 1912 respectively, prior to the family's 1913 return to Milka's

Edo Ljubić (1912–93) sheet music album, 1944. (Richard March Collection)

native Lika region of Croatia. In 1925 the Kapugis all returned to Chicago, but the experience of living twelve formative years in Lika deeply imbued their souls with the music and culture of the Old Country. They settled in Chicago's Pilsen neighborhood, an area with a diverse population of Eastern European immigrants and which became an incubator for Slavic ethnic traditions.

In 1929 brothers Martin, Frank, Louis, and Adam began a decades-long career of performing professionally, often including in their ensemble outstanding *tamburaši* like Vaso Bukvić, Djoko and Mel Dokić, Bela Balog, and Steve Makarewitch. The eldest brother, Martin, known to everyone as Marty, was the leader, arranger, and most outstanding musician. Though he was completely self-taught, in 1928, at the age of eighteen, Marty instructed his brothers in tambura playing. Teaching his brothers foreshadowed his long career, from the 1950s through the

1970s, of organizing and instructing Chicago-area youth tamburitza orchestras. Marty played *brač* and *čelo brač* and was a passionate singer with an unmistakable tenor voice (M. Kapugi 1977; TAA).

Marty pieced together a livelihood in various music-related pursuits. He was a musician, of course, but also worked for many years as an instrument maker at the Harmony Guitar Company. Predictably, he also used those same woodworking skills to build *tambure*. From 1946 to 1952 the Kapugi Brothers operated and performed in their own tavern, the Tamburitza Café, at the corner of Seventeenth and Laflin Streets in the heart of the Pilsen neighborhood. Marty was proud that musicians from the Chicago Symphony Orchestra frequented the tavern and expressed appreciation for his ensemble (M. Kapugi 1977).

The Kapugi's and their Tamburitza Café became part of the cultural synergy of Pilsen. A short distance away, on Eighteenth Street, Pilsen's main business thoroughfare, was the Balkan Music Store, established by Slavco Hlad. The Hlad family hailed from the vicinity of Veliko Trgovišće in northwestern Croatia, near the Slovenian border. Moreover, they happened to be of Czech ethnicity, a minority in the area. Thus Slavco could speak Croatian, Czech, and Slovenian, and was able to orient his music business toward satisfying the ethnic music interests of Serbs, Croats, Czechs, and Slovenes. Nonetheless, his first love was tamburitza. Slavco was a *prima* and *brač* player who gigged with several bands, especially John Plasay's Javor Orchestra, and he was the son of Ivan Hlad, a noted *tamburica* maker. For a while in the 1930s he himself worked at making the instruments (S. Hlad 1977).

In 1940, as the major labels were beginning to move away from ethnic recordings, Slavco established Balkan Records, with a studio located right in his music shop. Marty Kapugi was a key musician in the Balkan Recording Orchestra, the "house band" associated with the Balkan record label. The band was a fluid aggregation featuring some of the finest *tamburaši* of the era: John Krilčić (Slavco's partner in the record business), Steve Vučinić, Vaso Bukvić, Tony Markulin, and Balkan's singing star and *bugarija* player Dave Zupkovich.

Meanwhile, Rudy Orisek, a young man of Slovak descent born in 1924 in the Pilsen neighborhood, had returned from serving in Europe in World War II and was trying to break into the radio business. Rudy described his early experiences that fostered an interest in ethnic traditions: "It was a poor neighborhood—only none of us knew we were poor at the time. There were Serbs, Slovaks, Hungarians, Blacks, you name the nationally and we had it there. It was just like a little Europe. In school, we were all in there together, in the same classes. . . . As a teenager we had taverns all up and down the neighborhood each offering a different type of ethnic entertainment for their patronage. So you had a German tavern and a Polish tavern and a Czech and an Irish. And they all had different types of music" (qtd. in O'Dell n.d.).

Rejected by the major stations because he lacked the sonorous type of voice expected for commercial announcers, Rudy thought of another approach. Although foreign-language programs playing ethnic music flourished on local radio, they were slowly losing their audience as America's English-speaking second generation came of age. Rudy's idea was to create a multiethnic music radio show announced in English: "I knew the kids liked their parents' music but because they didn't speak their parents' language they couldn't really relate to it. I wanted to become the bridge between them and the music of their heritage" (ibid.).

Rudy started a program on WTAQ, a small station, and sought commercial sponsorship from "every butcher shop, clothing store, and bookstore that I could call upon." Then he found Slavco Hlad:

> [Slavco had] a tiny, local music store that produced its own records for the Croatian and Serbian community and he sponsored my show for fifteen minutes on a Sunday and he did it purely out of the kindness of his heart. He couldn't afford it but I didn't know he couldn't afford it. Nevertheless he bought the time for me. . . . Well, after four weeks, he found he had a response out of the show, the community was talking about the show and his records. . . . I was on the air with him as a sponsor, for ten years. Even after I had moved to other stations, I continued to do that show for him out of loyalty for what he did for me. (Ibid.)

The weekly show was called *The Balkan Musical Caravan* and featured Mary Kapugi's orchestra in live performance.

Beginning in 1953 Rudy added a program titled *International Café* to the variety of shows he produced on several Chicago-area stations. In 1956 he successfully proposed a television version of that show to WGN, the largest independent television station in Chicago. The hour-long show aired on Saturdays and proved to be very popular. It continued until 1970, with the Marty Kapugi band as the house band for most of the programs. They accompanied well-known guest artists like the Yiddish singer Martha Schlamme, the folksinger Judy Henske, and the so-called Gypsy violinist David Romaine; the Kapugi band performed their own material as well. These regular appearances on *International Café* by the Kapugi ensemble constitute the most prominent and lasting American broadcast media presence achieved by a tamburitza ensemble (ibid.).

The post–World War II trend away from recording ethnic music by the major labels had a notable exception. A tamburitza ensemble, the Skertich Brothers, hailed from the Calumet Region, the steel-mill section of South Chicago and northwestern Indiana, another area with significant Serbian and Croatian ethnic communities. Unlike most ethnic recording acts, which after 1945 were ignored by the major labels, the Skertich Brothers continued to record for Columbia Records for more than a decade after World War II. The Skertich Brothers George, Joseph, John, Nicholas, and Peter Skertich were five of the nine children born in the southern Illinois coal-mining town of Gillespie to immigrants from the Gorski Kotar region of Croatia. They were encouraged to take up music by their father, Janko, who himself was a left-handed fiddler in tamburitza combos (N. Skertich 1996; TAA).

The Skertich Brothers learned on Farkaš tamburitzas and remained faithful to that type of instrument long after most combos had switched to Srijemski-system *tambure*. Incidentally, the two fine *brač tambure* used in the combo by brothers John and George were made by Ivan Hlad. Though the Skertiches moved from southern Illinois to the Chicago area, their style of playing had none of the Banat-Bačka influence that was prevalent in other Chicago combos. Their musical aesthetics were decidedly Western, and indeed such musical preferences prevail in their ancestral home region, Gorski Kotar, which is located in western Croatia, adjoining Slovenia. They played mostly in major keys, in regular waltz, polka, and fox-trot tempos.

The Skertich Brothers had five recording sessions for Columbia between November 1940 and July 1942. Following World War II the Skertich Brothers continued to record for Columbia. They benefited from a wave of popular enthusiasm in the United States for polka music. Frankie Yankovic, a Slovenian American from Cleveland, had created an appealing sound combining Slovenian folk music with American country music and jazz. He also was a Columbia recording artist, and his 1946 polka-style rendition of "Just Because," a country song, was a big national hit. Although the Skertich's *tambure* sounded nothing like Yankovic's accordion, polka enthusiasts could dance to and enjoyed their music. In 1942 the Skertiches had begun the practice of recording an instrumental dance tune, a polka or a waltz, on one side of a 78 rpm disc, with a Croatian song on the other side. The danceable polka and waltz melodies with no "foreign" lyrics had an appeal to a broader audience, so Columbia kept on making and marketing Skertich Brothers recordings (N. Skertich 1996).

The Popovich Brothers of South Chicago was yet another brother-based tamburitza combo in the Calumet Region whose experience parallels yet contrasts with that of the Skertich Brothers. The Popovich brothers, Eli, Adam, Ted, Marko, and Pete, whose parents, Nikola and Ljubica, were Serbian-ethnic immigrants from the Croatian province of Lika, were born and grew up in mining towns in Nevada and Colorado. (They also had five sisters.) The musically talented boys received instructions from George Kachar in Pictou, Colorado, beginning in 1924; they began performing in 1926 for the Slavic miners and their families in the scattered mining-camp settlements across the West. They purchased a trailer for their instruments and equipment, and set out by automobile on an extensive musical tour of the West Coast and the Rocky Mountains. When they returned home, their mother encouraged them to advance their musical ambitions by touring eastward to the midwestern Slavic communities. In the Midwest, the brothers were so impressed with the large appreciative audience of Serbian and Croatian Americans that they found in South Chicago, along with the industrial employment opportunities there, they sent for their parents and sisters to join them. All relocated to Chicago in 1929 (A. Popovich 1976; T. Popovich 1976; TAA).

Though they frequently performed in the same venues as the Skertich Brothers, the two ensembles' styles and repertoires could hardly have been more dissimilar. The Popovich Brothers' music was strongly Banat-Bačka influenced. They also punctuated their live performances with an occasional a capella *lički ojkan*, an old type of song from their parents' home region, and they played a lot of Bosnian *sevdalinka* numbers as well, albeit usually sung by them in an *ojkan*-like group vocal. The group was renowned for the virtuoso *prima* playing of Marko, the youngest brother, and for the full-throated vocals of Ted and the all-around musical leadership of brother Adam. In addition to performing in the tamburitza combo, Adam Popovich was the director of Sloboda, the choir of the St. Archangel Michael Serbian Orthodox Church, and he also taught a youth tamburitza orchestra there.

They played extensively at community events, and in the postwar years they operated and performed in their own tavern, Club Selo, during the 1930s and 1940s. At this time the Popoviches did very little recording. They cut a few 78 rpm discs for small labels, Lira and Balkan Records, often as accompanists for other Serbian singers. Then in the 1960s, as early exponents of a burgeoning trend among ethnic musicians, they began recording and selling their own self-produced LP albums without the involvement of a record company. By 1976 they had produced six LPs (T. Popovich 1976). Their recording efforts ended after the sudden death of Marko in 1976 at age sixty. After a short hiatus, Adam and Ted (Eli and Pete had left the combo several years earlier) brought in some younger sidemen, and the combo resumed playing until the early 1990s (Opacich 2005, 56–57).

The Popovich Brothers attained national recognition thanks to the work of the New York folklorists Martin Koenig and Ethel Raim, who recommended them for the program of the Smithsonian Institution's Festival of American Folklife in 1973. Koenig and Raim's further efforts prompted the filmmaker Joan Godmillow to make *The Popovich Brothers of South Chicago*, an hour-long documentary film, released in

1978, about the band and their community. In 1982 Adam Popovich was a recipient of the National Heritage Fellowship from the National Endowment for the Arts.

The Crljenica Brothers, a tamburitza ensemble that had the most extensive career in the American entertainment industry, especially in Hollywood films, is almost totally unknown outside of tamburitza enthusiasts in the American Croatian and Serbian communities. Jovo Crljenica was born in the vicinity of Sisak, Croatia, in 1875. He began to play tambura in 1893 and immigrated to the United States in 1906, settling in Gary, Indiana. Jovo found opportunities to tour, playing on the vaudeville and Chautauqua circuits with a band called Gorski Vijenac. After completing a tour in 1910, Jovo sent for his wife, Mara, and two sons George (b. 1902) and Vaso (b. 1906) to join him in Gary. By the 1920s, Jovo formed a family band with George and Vaso plus younger siblings Steve, Paul, and Mildred, and their cousin Mary. The Crljenica family had a long-term musical engagement playing at a hotel in the famous spa resort town of Hot Springs, Arkansas.

George Crljenica was a promising young violinist and had begun teaching at the South Bend (Indiana) Conservatory of Music when he died suddenly in 1924 at the age of only twenty-two. Jovo and Mara were heartbroken at the loss of their eldest son and wanted to make a complete change. They moved from Gary to California that same year, initially to Fontana, a steel-mill town near Los Angeles, that was attracting steel workers from places like Gary. Vaso stayed in the Midwest for nearly eight more years, but when he joined the rest of the family in California in 1932, as the band's *primaš*, he seems to have provided the needed spark to launch their career (TAA).

In 1933 Warner Bros. studio was making *Storm at Daybreak*, a film based on a play by Sándor Hunyady. Set in Sarajevo in the World War I era, the Crljenica's music seemed a perfect fit and was selected for the film. The next year, 1934, Metro Goldwyn Mayer (MGM) made a film version of Franz Lehar's operetta *The Merry Widow* starring Jeanette MacDonald, and again the Crljenicas were hired to provide music. There followed a long string of movie credits for the band, on the sound track and occasionally playing on screen, whenever Slavic or Eastern European music was required for a movie. They played to accompany the singing of Nelson Eddy in *Balalaika* (1939) and in *The Chocolate Soldier* (1941). They played the famous Russian song "Shining Moon" to accompany a Fred Astaire song-and-dance routine in the movie *Second Chorus* (1942).

Sometimes their music showed up in odd cinematic places. They played for a Western movie, *Ride a Crooked Mile* (1938), in which the actor Akim Tamiroff played a Cossack from Russia who became a cattle rustler in the States. Even more bizarre was the horror movie *The Cat People* (1942), concerning a woman descended from Serbian devil-worshipers who could supernaturally transform herself into a vicious panther.

Jovo retired in 1937 and the Crljenica brothers had a break from movie work during World War II. Steve and Paul joined the US Army Band and participated in performances for General Eisenhower as well as for presidents Roosevelt and Truman.

After the war the band resumed as the Crljenica Brothers Continental Five and made a number of their best-known singles, such as "Hora Staccato" and "Shining Moon." Steve composed a bilingual parody song, "Tamburitza Boogie," recorded in 1949. It is amusing that the jazz bandleader Louis Jordan also recorded a bluesy version of "Tamburitza Boogie" in 1950, and the song became one of Jordan's bigger hits, spending ten weeks on the R&B charts.

More work in the movies followed, with the Crljenicas providing music for *Taras Bulba* (1962) starring Yul Brynner, and *Lawrence of Arabia* (1962) starring Peter O'Toole, but their most famous soundtrack item was Vaso playing "Lara's Theme" for the film *Dr. Zhivago* (1965) backed by a 150-piece orchestra. Their last movie credit was a return to the ludicrous—the 1976 Walt Disney Studios film *Gus* concerning a Yugoslav mule that became a placekicker for a California football team (Opacich 2005, 54–56).

The *tamburaši* who immigrated to the United States—their progeny as well as the children and grandchildren of immigrants who took up the instrument in their American ethnic communities—infiltrated the tamburitza tradition into American culture, albeit marginally. They toured the country as exotic acts in vaudeville and Chautauqua circuits, playing for both ethnic and mainstream audiences. Duquesne University still supports a tamburitza troupe as performing ambassadors for their institution. *Tamburaši* became recording artists in the era when the fledgling American record industry was inviting into the studio any sort of musician who seemed to have an audience. They squeezed their way into broadcast media, obtaining a toehold in radio, and made a foray into television. A few of them became recognized by American learned institutions, and the music of one tamburitza ensemble improbably was captured on the soundtracks of several Hollywood movies. Although it remains nearly unknown and invisible to most Americans, time and experiences in America resulted in the development of an American tamburitza tradition.

CHAPTER 6

The Soloistic Tambura

With the strap of my Uher tape recorder over one shoulder and the strap of my Pentax camera over the other, I waited on the asphalt parking lot in front of my apartment building in Velika Gorica, Croatia, one early morning in spring 1978 as my colleague from the Ethnology and Folklore Institute Dr. Jerko Bezić pulled up in his car. Dr. Bezić, a small, bespectacled, studious-looking man with curly hair, was taking me on a folklore fieldwork expedition to the Papuk mountain region of Western Slavonia. Dr. Bezić's studious appearance was no illusion. He was an immensely knowledgeable ethnomusicologist who at the institute offices was always generously willing to answer my questions and refer pertinent literature to me. Now he was going to devote a long day to assisting my research project. Thanks to Dr. Bezić's acquaintance with the local *tamburaši*, we were going directly to their homes to record and photograph them, saving me a lot of preliminary scouting.

Dr. Bezić opened the car trunk and placed my equipment and briefcase inside. Then he paused, and with a note of formality in his voice said, "There's one thing we have to do before we set out. When we go into the field as colleagues, we have to be '*na ti*,'" referring to the familiar form of address in Croatian. "And you have to call me Jerko." He was nearly twenty years my senior and a scholar whom I had admired for years. It was a little jarring to contemplate addressing him now just as I

Author (*left*)
recording a *samica*
player in Otočac,
Croatia, April 1978.
(Photo by Jerko
Bezić; Richard
March Collection)

did my school chums and family members. Nonetheless, I stammered,
"OK, može. Hvala . . . tebi . . . Jerko" [OK, all right. Thank . . . you
(familiar) . . . Jerko].

It was an important moment, a rite of passage in my relationship
with Jerko that English speakers have trouble appreciating unless we
also speak another language. It is indicative, too, of the great importance
of fieldwork to our discipline and of the comradeship engendered while
engaging in team fieldwork. Thus it is an appropriate moment to make
it clear that from this point on, the material presented in this work is
based on my own fieldwork, solo or team, which I conducted formally
in the period from 1975 to 1983; I have continued the fieldwork as a
participant-observer up to the present. So in a sense, from here on, I
need to be "*na ti*" with the reader. I will be describing my personal
experiences, frequently in the first person. There will be long passages
without citations describing field experiences as well as generalizations

based on my long-term participation in the tamburitza tradition. My knowledge has been informed by conversations, many fleeting and informal, with scores of people, mostly musicians but also a few scholars. Because thirty years have passed since the completion of the original version of this book, I shifted from the present to the past tense wherever feasible, and added many updates about subsequent changes in the tradition and additions to my knowledge, which needed to be injected into the narrative.

Any contemporary description of a cultural tradition can be at best fragmentary. Unlike a historical study where the data is automatically limited to that which has been preserved from an earlier time, in a contemporary study the data potentially available could be infinite. My survey of the current tamburitza tradition as I researched it in the 1970s and early 1980s focused on the various types of ensembles then active, emphasizing the geographic zones of the wider areas of Zagreb and Chicago. Deliberate choices and accidental happenstance brought me into contact with particular tamburitza musicians and the subculture groups in which they functioned. With the advice of knowledgeable senior scholars like Jerko Bezić and my own general knowledge of the tamburitza world, I developed a research plan that aimed to document a characteristic sampling of the tradition.

The hundreds of tamburitza ensembles are ever in a state of flux, a continual process through which old groups break up and new ones form. Most of the groups I researched three decades ago no longer exist. Many excellent musicians have died, and new generations of *tamburaši* have formed. The contemporary tamburitza tradition, as it was thirty years ago and still is today, is the legacy of a complex historical process. Both in North America and in some republics of the former Yugoslavia, there continue to be large orchestral ensembles, small combos, and folk dance troupes that feature the tamburitza. And music making on various types of the soloistic tambura, the root of all the later forms, continues as well.

⤳

In the United States and Canada a significant number of immigrants, especially from the Lika and Kordun regions of Croatia, still actively play the small soloistic tambura (or *samica*) that is prevalent in their home regions. And many Bosnians, scattered across North America and Europe, play the ever-popular *šargija* in their new homes.

In Cleveland where there is a community of Croatian Kordunaši from the vicinity of Cetingrad, a few young men like Mato Cvitković and Tomo Jurčević, factory workers in Cleveland, amused themselves and their families with their *samice*, which in their dialect they call by the name *kozarice*. When I met the men in 1979, they had been in the United States only a few years. Their music was identical to that which they played in Europe with no appreciable Americanisms. The *kozarice* brought from Kordun were quite similar in shape and décor to the Bosnian *šargija*—not surprising because Bosnia is only a few miles from Cetingrad. The instruments are more Asian in style. There were several small sound holes in the top, which also featured burned-on decorations characteristic of Middle Eastern instruments. Like most *samice* players, Cvitković and Jurčević arranged the four strings in two courses of two identical notes: on the higher course they played a melody while on the lower course they strummed a drone tuned a fourth below the upper strings. Playing with a long, flexible pick, they would strike all four strings with each stroke. They did not attempt to pick out single notes on one course of strings. Their repertoire consisted mainly of dance music—Sremica, Vrtikolo, Milica. They played a couple of tunes from other regions, "Bećarac" from Slavonia and "Kad si bila mala Mara" from Dalmatia, which in their original versions are song melodies, not associated with dance music. But to these Kordunaši, the tunes are to accompany a specific form of couple's dance (Cvitković and Jurčević 1979).

They played strictly for the narrow circle of family and for friends from their home region—never in public performance. In 1979 they did not seem to attach great symbolic importance to the *kozarica* or its persistence in their traditions. In fact they seemed to be somewhat ashamed of this so-called primitive instrument. Mato Cvitković stated that his son "won't play this" despite the fact that the little boy seemed rather fascinated by the *kozarica*. They just seemed to enjoy playing the music as a reminder of their home region, associating it with personal nostalgia rather than national or ethnic pride, and playing the *kozarica* exclusively in private (ibid.).

Twenty-five years later, the situation had changed considerably. In
Pittsburgh, in May 2004 at TamFest, a festival of adult amateur tamburitza orchestras organized by the Croatian Fraternal Union, a group of
Kordunaši from Cleveland, consisting of about thirty members, displayed the traditions of their home region using *kozarice* as the featured
instruments. The music of Zvuci Domovine's presentation, under the
leadership of Kata Stepić, differed markedly from the other orchestras
participating in the festival. Most of the other groups presented orchestral performances, and a few groups performed choreographed dances
in the manner of Lado, the Croatian folk dance company. The Kordunaši, however, performed in the manner of a village group at the Zagreb
Smotra folklora. While the other orchestras used Srijemski instruments to play arrangements learned from sheet music, the Kordunaši,
wearing their local folk costumes, enacted a dramatization of an encounter on their village street. (Male friends meet, shout greetings, and
sing *ojkan*, their local form of singing two-line *deseterac* verses to the
strumming of *kozarice*. Then the women enter, engage in a singing

Members of the adult ensemble KUD Kordun from Cleveland, performing
at TamFest in Pittsburgh, 2003. (Photo by author)

"contest" with the men, and ultimately dance a few of the local types of kolo to *kozarica* accompaniment.)

While the membership of the other adult tamburitza orchestras was comprised mostly of American-born descendants of early twentieth-century Croatian immigrants, the Cleveland Kordunaši performance group was comprised of recent immigrants. The number of Kordunaši in Cleveland increased significantly in the 1990s when Kordun was subjected to "ethnic cleansing" during the Homeland War. Their zeal to preserve their local traditions in exile, combined with the presence among their numbers of experienced participants in regional *smotre* in Croatia, have made it possible for them to enact this type of performance. The Zvuci Domovine performances have tremendously enhanced public visibility of their type of soloistic tambura in North America (Stepić 2004).

While there are a number of immigrants who play soloistic tambura in the United States, there are very few American-born players. Also in 1979 in Cleveland I met Michael Svilar, the son of a Serbian immigrant from Lika, who enjoyed playing song and dance tunes on his father's *samica*. Unlike the Kordunaši who brought the *kozarice* with them when they immigrated, the senior Svilar did not have a *samica* when he arrived in America after World War II. In the 1950s he obtained the instrument as a gift from a relative who came to visit him (Svilar 1979). Judging by its size, shape, and décor, this instrument appears to have been made in Kuterevo, a village in the northern part of Lika where several craftsmen specialized in producing *samice* as a cottage industry, a sideline to their main occupations as woodcutters, herders, and farmers. These instruments, sold on the marketplaces of towns in Lika and neighboring regions, have been so valued among the local populace that many Ličani name the instrument itself after the town—they call it a *kuterevka*. *Kuterevke*, more Western in décor than the Cetingrad *kozarice*, feature a single central sound hole and are decorated with a pick guard of darkly stained inlaid wood.

The Kuterevo *samica* craftsman that I documented in April 1978 was Pajo Sporčić, a craggy-faced man whose wispy white hair wreathed his face beneath a shapeless dark felt hat. Pajo was seventy-eight when I met him. On Wednesday mornings he sold his instruments at the marketplace in Otočac, the nearest larger market town, a couple hours' hike down the mountain from Kuterevo.

Jerko Bezić picked me up in his car once again and we headed for the Wednesday market in Otočac. Also in the car was Branko Kostelac, a Zagreb resident whose family roots go back to Lika. Branko was the artistic director of Vinko Jeđut, a railway employees' amateur folk dance ensemble. We were on a quest to find *kuterevke*.

We reached mountainous Lika and the town of Otočac after a few hours. The market was thronged with local townspeople buying spring vegetables from villagers. Sellers stood behind long tables, their wares spread before them. They were mostly women wearing kerchiefs and homemade dresses, with fringed shawls draped over their shoulders and tied around the waist against the chilly mountain air. I bought a pair of knitted woolen slippers from one woman, then we found, off to one side of the square, a purveyor of wooden objects—barrels, butter churns, taps for wine barrels—who included among his wares a couple of *kuterevke*. The seller was not the maker of the instruments and, hoping for a greater selection and a chance to meet the instrument maker himself, we asked him where the artisan might be found. The vender gestured toward the Generalturist office, where one can book accommodations in private homes, and indeed there were two *kuterevke* in the office, for sale on consignment—but no artisan. We examined them and noticed on the back of the peg head, stamped in blue ink, there was a trademark reading "Made by Pajo Sporčić, Kuterevo." Now we knew the maker's name.

Outside again on the street, we finally spotted the elusive Pajo Sporčić himself. He was striding away from us, moving toward the livestock market from the town square, a *kuterevka* in one hand proffered to prospective buyers, peg heads of others protruding from the top of the khaki rucksack he was wearing. As we hurried to catch up with him we watched the sales routine. A young man was having a go at one of Pajo's instruments. The potential buyer strummed the strings, seemed to praise and/or criticize its qualities, seemed to dicker about the price, but finally handed it back to Pajo and left.

We caught up, greeted Pajo, and in a flash he had whipped several *kuterevke* from his pack. All three of us had now at least one instrument in hand. The instruments were quite reasonable, depending on their size, 100 to 200 Yugoslav dinars (the equivalent of six to twelve dollars in U.S. currency at that time). We assured Pajo that we wanted to buy some of his wares but also wanted to visit his workshop and to record an interview with him. We agreed to meet after lunch, when he would be finished selling and ready to return home.

With Pajo now on board, Jerko crept up a barely passable rocky road to Kuterevo. The village is but a few clusters of houses in the mountains. Pajo's "shop" was actually in his spotless bedroom. Beside the bed was a knee-high wooden workbench with a pedal-controlled vise. He called it his *kuja* (bitch) because, he said, she barks (he pushed the pedal and it squeaked) and will bite you (he snapped the vise shut).

Pajo Sporčić (*right*) selling his *kuterevke* on market day in Otočac, Croatia, April 1978. (Photo by author)

Pajo's tool inventory was meager. It included only an ordinary wood saw, a chisel, a gouge, a drawknife, and an ordinary kitchen knife. He cut suitably sized maple trees, split the trunk into quarters with an ax, and then carved large spoon-shaped *samica* necks and bodies from the maple quarters. These were dried for a few days, leaning behind the wood stove in his kitchen or hanging from nails in the ceiling beams. Once dried, the "spoon's" cavity was fitted with a top, a thin spruce board inlaid with a dark plum-wood pickguard. Pajo bought coils of ordinary wire for frets and spools of thin steel wire for strings. He used no sandpaper but smoothed the wood using a piece of broken glass. Because there was no separate fingerboard, Pajo stained the light maple neck a reddish brown, stamped it with his trademark, and lacquered the whole instrument.

Pajo kept paperboard templates for the shapes of the instruments and a special template for the distances between frets for the various sizes of *samice* that he made. He also had a separate fret template for the *šargije* he produced to sell to Bosnians. In outward appearance, Pajo's *šargije* are exactly the same as his *samice,* including the paisley-shaped peg head, which imitates that of a *brač* tamburitza and which Pajo demonstrated "will hang on any nail."

Jerko bought a *samica* for the institute, I bought one just to play, and Branko bought two large ones for his folk dance ensemble. We asked Pajo about tunings, and he described a few different ways to tune the instrument—two courses of two strings tuned a fourth apart or a fifth apart, three strings identical with the last a fourth lower, or all four strings identical. The choice of preferred tuning is idiosyncratic to the individual player, but Pajo thought that the fifth tuning was more common in Slavonia than in Lika where the fourth tuning prevailed (Sporčić 1978).

After downing a shot of his homemade plum brandy to finalize our deal, Pajo grabbed a chunk of cow horn and whittled off a few picks for us. Shavings from a horn, a horse's hoof, a large feather quill, or cherry bark traditionally were used for picks. By the late 1970s, plastic picks bought at the music store or cut from a plastic container had become common.

Samice are very rarely made in North America. The only American-made *samica* I ever encountered was owned by another of the rare

American-born players, Tom Marincel, a postal worker who was born in the 1930s in Ashland, Wisconsin. Ashland is a small city in a relatively isolated area, located on the shore of Lake Superior at the northern tip of Wisconsin. A considerable number of Croatians, Serbs, and Slovenians immigrated to the area in the early twentieth century to work as lumberjacks or in the iron and copper mines. Some Croatian miners and loggers, mostly from Gorski Kotar and Lika, were able to buy cutover land near Ashland where they established a farming community. It is difficult farmland—rocky, originally covered with tree stumps, and a short growing season.

Marincel calls his instrument a *danguba*, a term commonly used in Europe as well—literally meaning a "day-waster," a pastime. In a number of folk songs the phrase "tamburica moja dangubica" (tamburitza, my little day-waster) appears. The instrument was made by a boarder named Mato, an immigrant from Lika, who lived in his family's house when Tom was a boy. In most respects it was identical to the European-made instruments but with some notable exceptions. The peg head has geared machine tuning pegs like modern tamburitzas instead of wooden pegs held in their holes only by friction. The back of the pear-shaped resonator is not as round as the European *samice* but is flattened off quite a bit to reduce sliding against the player's body. There is no pick guard of dark hardwood. The instrument features a remarkable unique decoration. Carved in relief on the spruce top of the *danguba* is the profile of a sitting dog modeled after Nipper, the dog depicted in the famed RCA Victor trademark.

I learned that Tom Marincel's father was born in Kuterevo, the *samica*-making center of Lika. Although Tom was not sure, it seems likely that Mato the boarder was also from Kuterevo since boarders commonly stayed with their landsmen. Thus it also is likely that Mato learned to craft *samice* from the Kuterevo artisans.

Although his instrument is like the Lika *samice*, Marincel's music is not in the Lika style. His mother, from whom he learned most of the Croatian songs he knows, was from Gorski Kotar, along whose northern border the Kupa River adjoins Slovenia. In many respects, the dialects, customs, and folk arts of Gorski Kotar are transitional between Slovenian and Croatian culture. The Croatian song repertoire Marincel learned from his mother, like Slovenian folk music, is mainly in waltz and polka tempo. Moreover, there are also Slovenian influences on Marincel's music in his American community. There are many people of Slovenian descent in the Lake Superior area; his wife is Slovenian, and one of Tom's musical heroes, the famed Slovenian American accordionist Frankie Yankovic (1915–98), was one of the most popular musicians in the Ashland area.

Like other American *samica* players, Tom Marincel also tends to play his *danguba* exclusively at home only to entertain his family and friends. Although it was more frequent when his parents were living, friends and relatives still gather around a table at the Marincel house to eat, to drink, and to sing old favorite Croatian songs like "Poletile bijele vile," "Ti neznaš što je ljubav," "Samo nemoj ti," and "Sinoć si meni rekla." Though this sort of singing and repertoire is quite common among Croatian and Serbian Americans, it is unusual for the *samica* to be used to back up such songs. Marincel had to devise an idiosyncratic style of play, often having to work against the limitations of his *danguba*'s seven-tone diatonic scale in order to achieve a satisfactory accompaniment. Nevertheless, Tom likes the *danguba* because the other two instruments he plays, the diatonic button accordion and the piano accordion, are loud and tend to drown out the singers' voices. Because of Tom's creativity, the *danguba* has retained at least a toehold in his locality's traditional music, whereas elsewhere, a guitar might commonly be used to back up this sort of singing.

Marincel also is proficient on the three-row button accordion and on the piano accordion that he plays professionally in his small dance band, Tom's Trio, which plays for weddings, anniversaries, and other festive occasions in his area. His button accordion, affectionately called a "button box," was crafted in the 1920s in Cleveland by Anton Mervar, a legendary Slovenian American accordion maker. Tom plays a repertoire of Croatian and Slovenian waltzes and polkas on the button box, as is typical of Gorski Kotar's musical traditions. He plays some of the same songs on button accordion that he plays on *danguba*, but also he can perform more musically complex tunes like "Kukavica," which modulates from the G major on the verse to C major on the chorus, which would scarcely be possible on *danguba*.

At the public dances, his typical audiences include members of the various ethnic groups in the Ashland area—Czechs, Finns, other Scandinavians, Poles, Germans, as well as Croatians, Serbs, and Slovenians. Audience members often request the music of their own nationalities or perhaps American jazz and popular music numbers. Marincel can perform this eclectic repertoire using his versatile 120-bass piano accordion. To fulfill requests for an "old time" tune, Tom brings his Mervar button box to dances, but the *danguba* always stays at home (Marincel 1977).

In America there is little evidence that interest in playing the *samica* extends beyond the immigrant generation, with rare exceptions. For example, Tom Marincel's son plays rock music on electric bass guitar and sometimes accompanies Tom at polka dances, but in 1979, he had no inclination to take up the *danguba*. The exceptions have been American-born musicians involved with folk dance ensembles who learned to play *samice* in choreographies of dances from Slavonia or Lika. In the 1970s Keith Papalko of the Živili kolo ensemble, and Kenny Herak and Frank Maydak of the Duquesne University Tamburitzans were a few such players. American-born musicians have continued playing *samice* in this context into the twenty-first century. However, even in Lika and Slavonia choreographies, because *samice* are rare in America, many groups will have a *tamburaš* strum a Srijemski *prim* in the manner of *samica* playing to approximate its sound.

If *samica* playing is rare in North America and only continues to exist in a narrow context, a different situation prevails in some Croatian regions. In Lika, Kordun, and Banija it was common in the 1970s for young men to carry a *samica* when socializing with friends, and the practice has not entirely died out. Singing is still a frequent part of the social activities of young people in these regions. They may sing some of the recent hits heard on the radio, although singing a type of traditional song, often called *ojkan*, also remains popular. Like the related genre of Slavonian *na bas* singing, *ojkan* features two lines of *deseterac*, usually rhymed, ending on a strong, sustained dominant fifth chord. Singing these songs remains a popular activity in rural taverns, at indoor or outdoor festivities, or at the custom of communal work bee (*sijelo* or *prelo*), still common in the 1970s but rare today. According to custom, young unmarried men and women gather, usually at the home of one of the women, to carry out some sort of repetitive manual task like cleaning feathers for pillows, cracking nuts, or carding wool. They pass the time singing traditional improvised songs in the *ojkan* form. There are certain forms of *ojkan*, which according to tradition only women or only men are supposed to sing, but nowadays, males and females also frequently join voices on the same songs. The strumming of a *samica* may provide a typical accompaniment, but the singing can go on in the absence of any instrumental music. The songs are expressive of an immense range of topics—sometimes witty, sometimes serious, occasionally downright lewd with sexual double entendre lyrics. In my 1970s fieldwork, I found it interesting that the young women at these events enthusiastically sang lewd lyrics to tease the young men just as often as the men sang them.

Although there are fewer occasions that require the repetitive hand labor that was the original reason for the *prelo* or *sijelo*, the name of the custom continues for a type of party or a symbolic name for a folk-themed event, especially in Lika, Kordun, and Slavonia. For example, the Cleveland Zvuci Domovine group of Kordunaši has named their annual winter concert/dinner/dance party Prelo, and a festival in Županje in Slavonia, the Šokačko sijelo, has been going on for many years (Stepić 2004; http://www.zupanja.hr/, accessed 2011).

Though singing *ojkan* at a *prelo* or other festive occasion generally is viewed positively, that view is not unanimous. In the 1970s fieldwork I saw a young woman, a member of a Lika folk dance ensemble, make a wry face when a few of the men from her group began to sing *ojkan*. When I asked her why she looked so sour, she replied, "Oh, to you this is interesting, but we have it all day. My father's friends come over and right away he says, 'Bring some wine, bring some ham, serve the guests!' And they sit there all night and make that racket and get drunk like asses" (Petrović 1978). In any case, good fellowship, strong voices, and traditional songs to the tinkling notes of the *samica* are still an important part of the culture of several Croatian regions.

The *samica* is also played in the public performances of "authentic folklore" groups from Lika, Kordun, Banija, and Slavonia. At a regional *smotra* in Slunj in 1978, folk dance groups from Cvitanović, Rakovica,

Krnjak, Kordunski Leskovac, and Crevarska Strana all used *samice* as their major instrumental accompaniment for songs and dances. The last group plus their fellow Banijci from Graberje included the tambura *dvožice*—the two-stringed tambura—which produces an archaic pentatonic scale rather than a diatonic scale like most *samice*. The *dvožica* players were all elderly men, so it made me wonder if any of the younger musicians would take up the *dvožica* to preserve that part of the folk dance group's repertoire.

The *samica* players in these groups were young men, although the group from Rakovica featured one very proficient, middle-aged female *samica* player. Some of the groups featured two or more *samica* players who took turns playing as soloists. The group from Kordunski Leskovac seemed to be replicating the early nineteenth-century process of tamburitza ensemble formation by utilizing a larger and a smaller *samica* played together in a rudimentary combo. The group from Krnjak was also taking up the same process in a different way. They formed an ensemble of a *samica*, a guitar, and a *berde* (March fieldwork notes 1978).

In my 1978 work in Slavonia, at the regional *smotra* Đakovački Vezovi, I only saw one group rely exclusively on the *samica* for accompaniment, the group from Vetravo. All the other groups had ensembles of four to eight *srijemske tambure* (ibid.).

While this situation in the 1970s might have represented a decline of interest in the *samica*, since that time, cultural organizations have undertaken efforts to promote and perpetuate the instrument. Most notable is the Smotra svirača na tamburi samici (Tambura *samica* players' festival) held annually in December since 1998 in the Slavonian village of Donji Andrijevci. In a statement on the December 10, 2009, *Dobro Jutro Hrvatska* (Good Morning Croatia) program of Croatian Television, when asked by the hostess if *samica* players were scarce and whether Antun Božić and Tomislav Vučković, the two young men who had just performed, were rarities, the president of the festival's sponsoring organization, Josip Perčević, said, "Not a rarity now, maybe ten years ago when we introduced this program. . . . It is a traditional instrument and we got into the situation that mainly older people played it; we wanted to rejuvenate the team, and now we are satisfied

because we have more and more young tambura *samica* players" (http:
//www.youtube.com/watch?v=nJfP3gjSmG0, accessed 2011).

The 2009 festival was successful despite the deficiencies of the dete-
riorating local Dom Kulture (Culture Hall). According to a report on
the Donji Andrijevci municipal website, 350 people turned out on a
stormy December Saturday to enjoy the program. (The reporter complained that a piece of the rain-soaked ceiling above the stage crashed
to the floor, nearly missing the mayor!)

It is evident from the 2010 program that the festival's organizers
have had considerable success in helping stimulate young boys and
men to become *samičari* and may have even speeded the development of better cultural infrastructure. The 2010 festival was held in the
"newly opened school auditorium. Of the 27 *samičari* performing, 24
were young men including twelve boys aged 12–15 years. There were
two older men in their fifties and one sole *samičarka*, Katarina Hasilo,
a 17-year-old-girl from Retkovci. Also on the program was a group of
three boys from Bosanska Posavina playing *šargije*" (http://ww2.donji
-andrijevci.net/, accessed 2011).

SAZ AND SEVDALINKA

Samica playing in Croatia represents Westernized styles of soloistic tambura, but the Eastern style remains very active in Bosnia-Herzegovina,
and among Albanians both in Albania and Kosova. The Eastern tradition may be divided into urban and rural components: the rural
tradition of *šargija*, and the urban tradition of *sevdalinka* singing to *saz*
accompaniment.

As previously mentioned, the urban tambura tradition of the Bosnian Moslems (now usually called Bošnjaci) and Albanians may be
the oldest form of tambura playing in the Balkans. The instruments
themselves have remained stable in form, retaining their original shape,
while the musical tradition with which they are associated is improvisational and adaptive. To the strum of the *saz* or *šargija* (or more
recently to the accordion or synthesizer) musicians may sing historical
songs that are centuries old or they might sing recently composed hits
with verses reflecting modern-day concerns. The tradition is fluid; the

same songs may be sung to numerous melodies, or certain melodies may be applied to many different texts.

The most common term for the Bosnian urban singing tradition is *sevdalinka*. The origin of the term is not known, but writing in 1954, Bosnian ethnomusicologist Vlado Milošević mentioned that "the oldest singers and connoisseurs of Bosnian singing with whom I am acquainted did not use the term *sevdalinka* in their youth" (early in the twentieth century). Milošević suggests that the term probably was originated by professional singers (Milošević 1954, 16).

The word *sevdalinka* is derived from *sevdah*, a concept crucial to the musical style and indeed to Bošnjak culture in general. *Sevdah* is the Turkish word for love, but in Bosnian it has other connotations. The definition of *sevdah* in Bratoljub Klaić's dictionary of foreign words and expressions is "love, caressing, yearning, longing, delight, fiery desire, deep urge, burning addiction, suffering from love, sighing" (Klaić 1958, 453). The term embraces a broad range of passionate feelings.

Late one evening in July 1976, in Philadelphia, I was sharing a bottle of *rakija* (plum brandy) with *sevdalinka* singer and *saz* player Ćamil Metiljević. We were on a coast-to-coast performing tour of the United States organized by the Smithsonian Folklife Festival. Ćamil tried to explain to me the meaning of *sevdah* and the ambience necessary for its performance and appreciation. Ćamil is from Bunički Potok, a village near Sarajevo, close to the once-sumptuous Austrian-built spa at Ilidža. In a pensive mood, Ćamil spoke slowly and deliberately but with great eloquence. Perhaps he had spoken these words before:

> Come visit me at home and you'll see what the *saz* really is. What I'm playing here is only a shadow. What you need, what there has to be is *beram* and *merak* and *sevdah*—Turkish words, you coastal people don't know them. *Beram* is in the late spring, when spring is over-ripe already. The spring is dying and becoming summer. You're sitting under a cherry tree in the *bašta* [a garden, usually enclosed] and petals, cherry blossoms, fall into your glass. That's *beram*. Then *merak*, *merak* comes when you have been drinking but you now are sobering up. Maybe you were loud before. Now you are peaceful. You see things in a new light.

And *sevdah, sevdah* is what you feel then and you can only release it with the *saz* and a song. (Metiljević 1976)

Ćamil described how *sevdah* can lead a person into self-destructive behavior and illustrated the point with examples from his own experience and that of his friends. *Sevdalinka* and the ethos of *sevdah* can transport a man into an altered state of consciousness where, carried away by the music and emotion, he may deliberately mutilate his hands with a broken wine glass, or might even violently bash his own head with a bottle. This behavior is depicted in the 1985 Yugoslav film *Otac na službenom putu* (When father was away on business) by director Emir Kusturica.

Sevdalinka has been commonly performed either as musical entertainment in coffeehouses or among secluded Moslem women, a context in which it has never been researched. Traditional songs and tales mention women, virtually prisoners in the *haremluk*, the female quarters in the traditional Turkish house, who sat in a *demirli pendžer*, a bay window screened with wooden lathing to obstruct the view from without, who sang *sevdalinka* while doing needlework (Hormann 1933, 6).

In the coffeehouse, traditional *sevdalinka* may be performed by a male singer who accompanies himself on *saz*, or by a female or male vocalist with the assistance of accompanists. Traditionally, females did not play instruments in public and few do so even today. The vocalist typically sings solo. Traditional *sevdalinka* seldom makes use of vocal harmony parts. When other voices occasionally join in, it is often in unison. The singing style is characterized by a wide range of dynamics, from a near whisper to a full voice. There is extensive use of melismatic ornamentation of the melody (Milošević 1963, 19). The precise pitch of the melody or grace notes may not be easy to distinguish because glissando is frequent. There is no rigid metrical structure. Tempo is often so free that Milošević characterized *sevdalinka* as a "type of melodic recitation" (ibid.). Time values of particular notes may not be stable. The singer may change them each time the melody is repeated during a song performance improvising freely both melody and tempo.

The *saz*, the largest of the Middle Eastern type of tambura in the Balkans, is the favored instrument to accompany "classical" *sevdalinka*.

While I was doing fieldwork in the 1970s, I gained the impression that *saz* playing was becoming rare in Bosnia, that it had largely been replaced in the coffeehouses by modern instruments. In 1976 Emina Ahmethodžić-Zečaj, the Sarajevo *sevdalinka* singer who favors *saz* accompaniment to her singing, was one of the performers who toured the United States as a part of the Yugoslav program organized by the Smithsonian Folklife Festival. Emina complained to me then that it was becoming ever more difficult for her to find accomplished *saz* players (*sazlije* as they are called in Bosnia). Her usual accompanist, Hašim Muharemović, a medical doctor from Srebrenik, was not available to make the tour, and it was only with great difficulty that she managed to find Ćamil Metiljević to fill in for Muharemović (Ahmethodžić-Zečaj 1976). Ćamil himself informed me that he was acquainted with only three other accomplished *saz* players in Bosnia (Metiljević 1976). While I assumed there must be more *sazlije* than three, it seemed that they were indeed becoming scarce.

If my impression from the 1970s had any merit, there certainly has been a considerable change. In a few minutes of searching the Internet, I identified more than two dozen Bosnian *sazlije*, Avdaga Vrabac, Avdo Lemeš, Rajko Simeunović, Husein Belkić, Ahmet Hogić-Ahmo, and Dr. Mehmet Gribajčević to name just a few who seem to be current residents of Bosnia. Some fine Bosnian *sazlije* are now also living abroad, such as in Australia, Kadir Djulović, and in France, a *sazlije* who identifies himself on YouTube only as MessudO.

In the United States a very active musician is Mirsad Zulić. Zulić was born in 1952 in Brđani near Kozara in western Bosnia, the son of Zulfo Zulić, a noted *saz* maker. Mirsad began learning to play *saz* from his father when still only a small boy. Mirsad also credits encouragement from his mother, Hatidža, who said to him, "Sine ne ima sevdalinke bez saza" (Son, there is no *sevdalinka* without the *saz*). In 1974 Mirsad and his father performed for the first time on Sarajevo television. Having had to flee the 1992–95 war in Bosnia-Herzegovina, Mirsad settled in Chicago, where he has continued his musical pursuits, frequently performing, often for humanitarian causes, releasing five CDs of his songs, and placing videos of his performances on the Internet (Zulić 2010).

Perhaps the Bosnian *saz* player in the most unexpected location is Jadranka Stojaković, born in Sarajevo in 1950 and a well-known singer of folk and popular music in 1980s Yugoslavia. She includes some *sevdalinka* in her repertoire, often in a form influenced by jazz or electronic music, and accompanies herself on *saz* on some of her songs. Jadranka has been a resident of Tokyo since 1988.

Moreover, northeastern Bosnia is a hotbed of *saz* activity. Just as *samica* playing is promoted by the festival in Donji Andrijevci, lately in Srebrenik and Lukavac, two towns in the Tuzla county area, there are at least three events organized for the purpose of preserving and promoting *saz* playing. Srebrenički dani saza (*Srebrenik saz* days) and Veče saza (An evening of *saz*) are both in Srebrenik. Festival saza i sedalinke (*Saz* and *sevdalinka* festival) is in Lukavac. In June 2009, fourteen *sazlije* competed for prizes, participating in the very first run of the Lukavac festival (Srebrenički dani saza and Festival saza i sedalinke websites, accessed 2011, no longer accessible).

The future of *saz* in Bosnia seems secure. Zanin Berbić is a promising young *saz* player and singer from Gračanica (northeastern Bosnia). Born in 1996, Zanin's musical ability has already received considerable notice, winning first prize at the First International Youth Festival of Islamic Spiritual Songs (1. Internacionalni Omladinski Festival Ilahija i Kasida) (1. Internacionalni Omladinski Festival Ilahija i Kasida website, accessed 2011, no longer accessible).

The *saz* carries a social connotation of a refined Middle Eastern urban musical instrument; the music itself is a sophisticated Bošnjak art form. The ornate improvised melodies and the lyric poetry of the *sevdalinka* songs are highly esteemed for beauty and understated artistry. In the intimate environment of the traditional coffeehouse, the guests sit around low tables, pouring thick Turkish coffee from small copper *džezvice* (coffee pots in the shape of a truncated cone) into small *fildžan* cups set on large, round, etched brass trays. Typically alcoholic beverages are also served because the Islamic prohibition of alcohol never was widely accepted among the general Moslem population of Bosnia-Herzegovina. In this setting, *sevdalinka* may provide an elegant background to conversation or it may be the intense focus of attention. It is a music that is at once calm and full of strong feeling.

Sevdah is expressed in the music; the singer, like an overheated boiler, seems to be releasing intense emotional pressure through a tiny valve. The melodic line may be light, lilting, and unhurried, yet the singer's feathery voice quality is pervaded by a taught strain of yearning and pain.

The audience may react to a performance in a number of ways. A patron may "pay for" a certain song (i.e., make a request along with a substantial tip). Audience members typically listen quietly but, inspired by intense feelings of *sevdah*, sometimes a listener may stand up, wave his arms, toss money at the musicians, and generally engage in extravagant behavior, even smashing drinking glasses. In fact, in the 1970s I observed signs posted in coffeehouses, "For every deliberately broken glass, 50 dinars charge."

Audience members are seldom sole individuals but mixed groups of friends. They interact with each other at the same time as listening to the music, sometimes singing part of the songs, gesturing to each other, indicating perhaps that they feel the sentiments expressed in the songs. The American anthropologist Andrei Simic studied coffeehouse behavior in Bosnia and Serbia (Simic 1973), and Mark Forry studied the phenomenon among Serbian immigrants in Los Angeles. Forry characterized coffeehouse behavior as involving "drinking, conspicuous spending of money, and a display of good fellowship" (Forry 1977).

While *saz* accompaniment of *sevdalinka* has certainly not become extinct, nonetheless, various modern musical instruments have replaced *saz* in most entertainment venues. Small tamburitza ensembles have been used to accompany *sevdalinka* since the early decades of the twentieth century, and numerous *sevdalinka* songs were recorded by *tamburaši* in the United States in the 1920s and 1930s. *Sevdalinka* performed to tamburitza combo accompaniment is less improvised and musically more Western than the *saz*-accompanied style. Minor keys and Oriental-sounding musical clichés replaced the true Middle Eastern sound of the *saz*.

In addition to the noted Bosnian-born singer Edo Ljubić, Vinka Ellesin, a Serbian American from Detroit, performed to tamburitza accompaniment. Vinka was active from the 1930s to the 1970s and was publicized as "the queen of *sevdalinka*." Accompanied by the combo of the tamburitza virtuoso Steve Pavlekovich, she made recordings of such classic *sevdah* songs as "Bul bul mi poje," "Na Bembašu," and "Proplakala zumbul Ajsa"; she is best remembered for her signature song "Mili Bože, a što mi ga nema" (Opacich 2005, 80).

Around 2004, singer Sonya Kosovec, a member of a musically talented Croatian American family from Detroit, began to perform *sevdalinka*. The daughter and granddaughter of noted *tamburaši* from Detroit, Sonya, like her brother Peter and cousin David, had been a member of the Duquesne University Tamburitzans. She had moved to Chicago, where she met Adis Sirbubalo, a skilled accordionist from the large community of Bosnian refugees who had come to Chicago in the 1990s. In 2008 Sonya and Adis recorded such classic *sevdah* songs as "Zapjevala sojka ptica," "Moj beharu," and "Stade se cvijeće rosom kititi" with brother Peter on *kontra* and her then future husband Robert Sestili on *basprim* (S. Kosovec 2008).

In Bosnia, from the 1960s through the 1980s, noted *sevdalinka* singers such as Zora Dubljević, Zehra Deović, Safet Isović, Vejsil Hadžibegić, and Zaim Imamović frequently performed and recorded to the accompaniment of the Radio Sarajevo tamburitza ensemble. Nonetheless, in the same time period, these singers and others were accompanied even more frequently by the *narodni orkestar* or folk orchestra (Vrdoljak 1978). The folk orchestra had rapidly developed and spread since World War II, largely supplanting the *saz* and tamburitza combo as the most frequent accompaniment to sevdalinka and the newer *narodnjak* popular songs that followed. A *narodni orkestar* typically has at least one accordion, perhaps two or more, and a rhythm section consisting in its complete form of an electric guitar, an electric bass guitar, and a drum set. Sometimes one or more of the rhythm instruments might not be present. The accordions are piano keyboard accordions or chromatic button accordions, never the diatonic button accordions of the type frequently used in Slovenian, Dalmatian, and northern Croatian folk music. Additional melody instruments often include clarinet, violin, or saxophone.

Since the 1990s, the *narodni orkestar* increasingly has become supplanted in its turn by the electronic keyboard synthesizer with a drum machine. Just as in its original form, to the accompaniment of a lone *sazlije,* now a single musician is able to provide a loud, complex accompaniment to Bosnian singing or dancing, using one or two Korg synthesizers mounted on a stand. The music references the original *narodni orkestar* insofar as it is an electronic approximation of the sounds of an accordion, drums, a clarinet, or violin. As a term for this music, English-derived words "folk" or "turbo-folk" are supplanting *narodnjak* when designating the newer electronic style.

The *narodnjak*/turbo-folk music is an important commercial music idiom in the former Yugoslav republics, especially in Bosnia, Serbia, and Croatia. The best-known singers become celebrities in the mass media. The recently composed songs performed to the accompaniment of modern instruments are generally condemned by the intelligentsia as *Kitsch* or *šund,* cheap maudlin creations without artistic merit. Nonetheless, the musical genre is very popular with rural residents and working-class urbanites. In the 1970s, the Croatian music critic Dražen Vrdoljak informed me that a *narodnjak* hit record might sell 100,000 copies, and 500,000 copies of a few of the very biggest hits have been sold, quite remarkable considering that the population of Yugoslavia at that time was about 20 million and a *narodnjak* singer could not have hoped to appeal to the entire Yugoslav population due to the language and cultural differences (ibid.)

In an article that was a pioneering study of Yugoslavia's music industry, the musicologist Koraljka Kos presented sales figures for several of the big hits of 1970 and 1971. Kos listed six newly composed *narodnjak* hits that altogether sold more than a million copies during that period, with "Majko majko" by Meho Puzić leading with 400,000 copies sold, followed by "Što će mi život" by Silvana Armenulić selling 260,000. Kos noted that in the "category of popular music too, the tunes most readily accepted by the audience are those which are simply modernized versions of songs which enjoyed popularity some thirty years ago or the folk songs of urban type" (Kos 1972, 69).

Thus, a musical idiom that in its origins is associated with types of the tambura has evolved into a popular music idiom that continues to be spread by a commercial music industry, through records, television, radio, and concert performances. The geographic region in which the music is popular has increased, especially to the north and west into areas where this Oriental-style music was not part of the local folk tradition. Thus the performances of the *narodnjak* singers are responsible for spreading an Eastern musical influence, albeit in a modern Westernized form, farther into Central Europe. This influence runs counter to the opposing trend: the "Europeanization" of the Ottoman musical legacy ever since the Austrian occupation of Bosnia in 1878 (Kos 1972, 67).

The replacement of the *saz* with Western instruments in *sevdalinka* has necessitated important modifications in the musical style. Melodic and rhythmic improvisation cannot be as free in ensemble play as when a singer is accompanied by a solo *sazlije* who can readily respond to the visual and aural cues of the singer. With ensembles, then, the freest improvisation occurs at defined moments of the song, often just before the final chord when the instruments pause, allowing the singer to perform something like a cadenza during which he or she can display a powerful blast of melismatic riffs. Also, the singers' melismatic articulation of the melody, as long as it does not break out of the regular rhythm, is quite feasible and is a burgeoning element of vocal style in modern *sevdalinka*.

The *saz*, once the most important instrument in *sevdalinka*, now has been overshadowed by other instruments. Its decline is the result of several factors. First, the *saz*, with its thin tone, is not a loud instrument. Conditioned by the sounds of international popular music, the modern audience expects loud music with heavy bass and rhythm. Second, the *saz* has certain musical limitations. In order to change the key in which a song is to be sung, all the strings need to be retuned, because the same fingering positions must be used. For example, when Ćamil Metiljević was accompanying Emina Zečaj in 1976, when he acceded to repeated requests that he sing at a particular performance, he needed several minutes to accurately retune all ten strings to a key that suited his voice.

Third, the placement of the frets on the *saz* neck does not produce the Western chromatic scale, so it cannot play the more Westernized elements that have become stylish in *sevdalinka*. Furthermore, for a considerable period of time, the instrument was not promoted by cultural revivalists, a situation that changed recently.

Because it is an urban instrument, and folk traditions have been widely associated with the peasants, the *saz* was not always recognized as an indigenous element of Bosnian folk culture. Most of the instruments are imported, manufactured in Turkey and Syria, and seldom the products of local artisans. Moreover, as an urban tradition, it has to appeal to urbanites, who as a general rule have been more influenced by changing fashions and receptive to new technologies, including new musical instruments.

Unlike the tamburitza tradition, which is defined specifically by the instruments played, *sevdalinka* is a vocal tradition, a singing style, not necessarily linked to any particular accompanying musical instrument; it refers to a feeling, not an instrument. As in the case of the American folk music blues, the genre is named for its predominant underlying emotion, *sevdah*. If the music retains the feeling of *sevdah*, it is *sevdalinka* without regard to particular instrumentation.

In these days *sevdalinka* retains a relatively small degree of connection to the tambura, which serves as an important comparison to the development of other urban aspects of the tamburitza tradition. With the tamburitza, the instrument has been preserved in gradually updated forms, while the range of musical styles played on it have expanded and changed. *Sevdalinka* preserves the basic feeling behind the music and the singing style, and allows all else to freely change.

THE ŠARGIJA

Besides the urban *sevdalinka* and *saz*, the *šargija*, another Oriental tambura continues to play a very vital role in the folk music of Bosnian villagers, especially in the Sava and Drina River valleys. The *šargija* is undoubtedly the most common Oriental-type tambura in the geographic area of former Yugoslavia. It is played by Bosnians of all three major religious groups—Moslems, Catholics, and Orthodox Christians. Also, Albanians from Kosova play a practically identical tambura known in Albanian as *šarkija*, linguistically the same name.

The *šargija* is similar in shape to the *saz*, but smaller. Instead of a pieced back, a *šargija* is typically carved out of a quarter section of a tree trunk. Like the *samica* or *saz*, the *šargija* player mostly strums across all of the instrument's five to seven metal strings. There are three courses of strings, either in a double-single-double pattern or all double strings or occasionally with a triple course of low strings. As is true also of the *saz*, melodies on the *šargija* are played primarily on the highest string or double course of strings, the remaining strings serving as a drone. By itself the instrument is sufficient to accompany singing or to provide music for dancing. In Bosnia, however, the *šargija* is often combined with the violin in a typical ensemble of those two instruments. The violin provides a melody line while the *šargija* mainly provides rhythmic accompaniment. Occasionally the *šargija* is used to accompany kolo dance tunes performed on the *frula*, an end-blown wooden flute. Among the Kosova Albanians, the *ćitelija*, a small two-stringed tambura, is the most frequent lead melodic instrument.

In northern and eastern Bosnia, the *šargija* or the violin and *šargija* ensembles are important in the village singing tradition. In these regions, solo singing exists, but the use of two or more voices singing together is more frequent. Normally, one singer begins a song or verse, and then the other voice joins in following him or her at a predefined moment. The accompanying voice may begin on the same pitch as the leader, or a major second below. The singing of the verse may end with unison, a major second, or, more recently, a fifth—the last being an influence of *na bas* singing (Bezić 1976, 199). Bosnian village singing may be performed with or without instrumental accompaniment. Because they play traditional acoustic instruments and sing in an old traditional style, the musicians in *šargija* ensembles are known by the term *izvornjaci* (from *izvorni* "wellsprings" folklore).

A *šargija* player usually begins a song with a characteristic introduction, which is repeated with slight variation between each of the song's verses. During the singing, the *šargijaš* and violinist may cease playing entirely, or the *šargijaš* may restrict himself to percussive rhythmic effects. Sometimes the instrumental music seems almost irrelevant to the singing.

Songs of both an epic and lyric nature may be performed to this kind of accompaniment. Matije Murko, the Prague-based scholar of Slovenian background, who thoroughly researched the South Slavic epic during the early decades of the twentieth century, and whose ideas and concepts were crucial to the well-known work on South Slavic epics of Milman Parry and Albert B. Lord, commented, "It was long believed that the *gusle* is the only instrument which serves to accompany epic singing. This viewpoint was disproven by Matica Hrvatska when they published the Moslem epic songs from Bosanska Krajina which are exclusively sung to the tambura or the *tamburica* with two strings" (Murko 1951, 335).

According to some of Murko's respondents in Bosanska Krajina, "the Orthodox [Serbian] does not like to listen to the Turkish tambura, nor does the Moslem care for 'the shepherd's [*vlaška*] *gusle*'" (ibid., 337). This statement by Murko's interviewee is hardly applicable to the situation I encountered in the 1970s and observe today. There were skilled Moslem *guslari*, and, as mentioned, when it comes to lyric songs, all three religious groups play the *šargija*. Since the 1990s wars, though, more Bošnjak Moslems express an antipathy for the *gusle*, characterizing it as a Serbian instrument, and it seems to be true that exclusively Bošnjaks and Kosovars use *tambure* to accompany epic songs.

The lyric songs of Bosnian villagers are quite varied. The most common form is *deseterac dvostih*, with its two lines of ten syllables, often rhyming. Some of the current lyrics were originally collected as early as the nineteenth century, while others may have been improvised on the spot. During the 1970s I encountered songs dealing with the plight of the *gastarbajter*, the Yugoslav "guest workers" who, beginning in the 1960s, began to support their families by taking jobs in Germany and other Western European countries. The most common theme is loneliness for the family, friends, and homeland.

The following two songs were performed at the 1978 Smotra folklora in Zagreb by young men from the village of Bunar near Derventa in north-central Bosnia. The first is a *gastarbajter*'s lament; the second discusses how suitable men of various occupations would be as husbands.

Ti si brate u tuđini bio
Daj mi pričaj šta si zapazio.
Ima l'igdje kao Jugoslavija

Da se pjeva uživa i pije?
Dragi brate, kad me pitaš tako
Kazat ću ti nije bilo lako.
Ima hrane kao i kod nas ovdje
Ima piće kao hladne vode
Al' kad nemaš svoga potkraj sebe
U grudima srce ti ozebe.
Tko god nije u tuđini bio
I zavačaj rodni ostavio
Taj ne znade niti može znati
Kako srce u tuđini pati.
Nema seje, nema malog brata
Nema majke da otvara vrata.
Nemaš svoga voljenoga druga
Da ti srce obavi od tuge.
Nema drage da joj ljubiš lice
Zemljo tuđa, gore od groznice
Zemljo tuđa gore od groznice!
Nema nigdje naših običaja
Domovina ljepše si od raja.
Ova pjesma za vas je zemljaci
Vratiti se domovini majci.

[Brother, you were in foreign parts / Please tell me what you saw. /
Is there anywhere like Yugoslavia / For one to sing, enjoy and drink? /
Dear brother, since you ask me / I'll tell you, it wasn't easy / There is
food as we have here / There is drink like cold water / But when you
don't have your own people beside you / Your heart aches in your
breast. / Whoever hasn't been in foreign parts / Knows not nor can he
know / How the heart suffers in foreign lands. / There's no sister or
dear brother / There's no mother to open the door. / You don't have
your beloved comrade / To save your heart from sorrow. / There's no
sweetheart's face to kiss. / Foreign land, worse than a fever / Foreign
land, worse than a fever! / Our customs are not present there /
Homeland, you're more lovely than heaven. / This song is for you,
countrymen / Return to your mother homeland.]

Dušo Marice, bi li htijela za zidara?
Neću majko neću mila, za zidara neću živa!
Zidar zida na visoko a na druge baca oko.
Oj majko za Boga, ja ne mogu poć za toga.
Dušo Marice, bi li htjela za šofera
Neću majko, neću mila, za šofera neću živa!
Šofer vozi drumovima, hvati cure na brzine
Oj majko za Boga, ja ne mogu poć za toga.
Dušo Marice, bi li htjela za bećara?
Hoću majko, hoću mila, za bećara hoću živa!
Oj majko za Boga, ja ću poći za toga.

[Mary, my soul, do you want to marry a bricklayer? / Mother dear, I
really don't want to marry a bricklayer. / A bricklayer builds a wall up
high and casts his eye on other girls. / Oh mother, for God's sake, I
can't go with him. / Mary, my soul, do you want to marry a truck
driver? / Mother dear, I really don't want to marry a truck driver! /
A truck driver drives the roads and catches girls with all his speeds. /
Oh mother, for God's sake, I can't go with him. / Mary, my soul, do
you want to marry a rake? / Mother dear, I really do want to marry a
rake. / Oh mother, for God's sake, I will go with him.]

CHAPTER 7

Tamburitza Combos

In 2009, on a blustery fall day in early October, I made the two-and-a-half-hour drive from my home in Madison, Wisconsin, to the Chicago suburb of Lombard, Illinois, to attend the 2009 Tamburitza Extravaganza. In a land of urban sprawl, curving residential streets, and strip malls, the Westin Hotel in Lombard, venue of the event, towers above a glistening shopping mall where it is situated. It is an appropriate setting. A majority of the Croatian and Serbian Americans, who flock to this annual event held in a different American city each year, reside in middle-class suburbs like Lombard, having largely deserted the old industrial urban neighborhoods of their parents and grandparents. Since the end of World War II, these descendants of the Slavic immigrant laborers are now economically middle class thanks to much better educational opportunities in the rapidly expanded community colleges and state universities, many taking advantage of the GI Bill.

The Tamburitza Association of America (TAA) has organized the festival annually since 1971, although some older TAA members argue that antecedent events were held at least since 1968 (Opacich 1975). The TAA, a grassroots organization, is governed by a board of a dozen or so officers and members, mostly themselves tamburitza combo musicians. Their main mission is to organize the annual gathering.

The 2009 Extravaganza followed the model for the event that has been established over the years. Twenty to twenty-five professional combos and their fans assemble from across the United States and Canada. Friday and Saturday concert programs each featuring short performances by twelve or more combos take place in a large ballroom set up with a stage and chairs. But for *tamburaši* that's just the beginning of music making. After the formal banquet and the presentation of awards and inductions into the TAA's Tamburitza Hall of Fame, the festivities continue until late in the evening. In the early years of the festival, all-night jam sessions in hotel rooms used to disturb other guests and brought on the wrath of hotel staff. In more recent years the TAA has booked "*bećari* suites," convention meeting rooms in or attached to the hotel for informal performances and jams. Those who prefer dancing assemble in the ballroom for hours of kolo dancing to a live band. Although kolo is technically the name for only one type of Balkan line dance, American Croatians and Serbs use the term generically to mean any Balkan line or circle dance, including kolo, *drmeš*, and *oro* (Werner 1980).

On Sunday morning, the event's program informs those interested that they may attend a Serbian Orthodox liturgy at a nearby church or a Catholic Tamburitza Mass, which is celebrated in the hotel. That the program lists both Orthodox and Catholic observance opportunities for Extravaganza festival participants is an indication of the TAA's clear intent that the event welcomes both Serbians and Croatians.

I arrived at the hotel about noon and noticed that several of the cars in the parking lot had Croatian, Serbian, or tamburitza-related bumper stickers, decal emblems, or vanity license plates. This must be the right place! Passing through a revolving door into the lobby, I entered a beehive of activity. In different parts of the lobby and connecting hallways two or three combos, consisting of young musicians, were playing to clusters of surrounding listeners. Heart of Croatia, the pop-up version of an otherwise online gift shop selling Croatian products, had their wares hung on racks and spread over several folding tables. The proprietors, Pam Kelly and Melissa Obenauf, formerly directors of Živili Kolo, an Ohio-based folk dance troupe, now make the rounds to sell at all the bigger tamburitza events. John Filcich, an amazingly spry nonagenarian, had a smaller but nonetheless extensive display of Balkan recordings, videos, and dance instructions.

It's a very sociable crowd. Every few steps through the lobby I paused to exchange greetings with numerous friends and acquaintances. I joined the crowd filtering through the ballroom's double doors in order to secure a seat for the Saturday afternoon concert. Some of the Chicago *tamburaši*, as hosts of the event, were scurrying to finalize the setup. Two large video monitors flanked the stage, as has become conventional at rock concerts, and were used to give close-up camera shots during the performances. To keep the assembling crowd amused until the concert began, a humorous video played, apparently prepared by Joe and Nick Gornick of Chicago's Sinovi ensemble. It was "in-joke" humor. The video was not funny unless you knew the personalities of the *tamburaši* who were being parodied.

Just before each band performed, a short video profile about each band showed up on the monitors. Much of the video footage obviously was shot in the bands' home towns and emailed to the event organizers.

The videos bring to mind that a pronounced sense of modernity pervades the tamburitza combo tradition. The performers don't wear folk costumes. A few of the eldest *tamburaši* wear vests that seem vaguely ethnic but are actually more like a band uniform. The middle-aged and younger musicians wear stylish clothes, casual or slightly dressy; or they might wear matching shirts, sometimes with the band's logo; black dress shirts with black slacks have been popular in recent years; or in many cases the musicians' clothes choices may be totally individualistic. Combo *tamburaši*, like rock musicians, abandoned wearing band uniforms long ago.

When it comes to repertoire, the combo musicians know a lot of songs that are eighty to a hundred years old or more. But they also follow the latest hit songs from former Yugoslav countries, searching for suitable numbers to include in their performances.

Modernity is restrained only in one crucial factor—the tamburitza instruments. The vast majority of the combos use acoustic tamburitzas. Some combos augment their sound with accordions, violins, or use a string bass instead of a *berde*. But it is abundantly clear that this is the Tamburitza Extravaganza because it is tamburitzas that are making the music.

Small instrumental combos are widespread in North America as well as in Croatia and northern Serbia. The term "combo" became prevalent among American *tamburaši* in the 1940s, referent to the popular jazz combos of that era. In jazz of that era, a "band" likely was a "big band" of a dozen or more musicians, while a combo typically had fewer than ten players. While use of the term "combo" may be fading among younger, post–jazz age *tamburaši*, it is still quite frequently used by tambura players in the American Midwest. European *tamburaši* do not use the term. A small group is likely to be called a *sastav* (a put-together), *zbor* (choir), or an *ansambl* (from the French word *ensemble*), or even an *orkestar* (orchestra), although that designation does not distinguish a small group from a large one.

The importance of combos to the American tamburitza scene is greater than in Europe. In Europe the role of small-group musician does not confer the high status of serious musician as does being an orchestra leader, a composer, or the main *primaš* of a large tamburitza orchestra. In Europe small group music is generally viewed as a pleasant but trivial activity compared to the so-called serious music of a classical orchestra.

On the other hand, in the United States, being the leader of a semi-professional tamburitza combo is one of the most important musical roles to which one can aspire in the ethnic communities. The members of combos often cross over into roles the Europeans consider more important. They might become the teaching music directors/conductors of junior tamburitza orchestras like Steve Makarewitch in the Calumet Region, Tony Muselin, Marty Kapugi, and Roko Abramovich in Chicago, Ken Kosovec in Detroit, and Charles Elias Jr. in Milwaukee. Adam Popovich of South Chicago was the director of the Serbian choir Sloboda in addition to playing in the famous Popovich Brothers combo.

If a combo is in consistent demand to play jobs, its members may significantly supplement their incomes, although American tamburitza combo musicians nearly always have to have a day job to support themselves. In 1978, while trying to recruit a young musician to join up, a member of a popular Chicago combo asserted that he could make more than $6,000 per year, about half of an average annual salary at that time. The musicians usually are paid a fixed fee for playing in such venues as a wedding, a picnic, in a restaurant or tavern, plus they may receive even more money in the form of generous tips from their audience. Conspicuous spending, which includes lavishly rewarding musicians to play a requested song, is a long-established custom in the South Slavic communities, especially pronounced among the Serbians. To enhance status before one's colleagues, a big tipper feigns nonchalance about passing a large-denomination bill to the musicians. The nonchalance is feigned in the sense that the tipper usually makes sure everyone notices the tip. It is rare for someone to inconspicuously slip money in a musician's pocket. Typically the spender strides dramatically up to the band, may request a particular number out loud, and linger a moment to tear a small hole in the center of a large-denomination bill in order to hang it on one of the tuning pegs of a tamburitza. The bill remains on display on the tuning peg, often joined by several more bills, until the musician finds a convenient moment to remove them. Sometimes it seems the musicians display the bills as an encouragement for additional tips.

Another even more conspicuous manner of putting one's tip on display is to plaster the bill on the forehead of a *tamburaš* where it sticks to the musician's perspiration. Sometimes the tipper slops beer or wine on the bill to enhance adhesion. This form of tipping is distasteful to many musicians who find it degrading (Opacich 1975). The attitude about taking tips or requests varies quite a bit among combo musicians. Some *tamburaši* are anxious to do whatever is necessary to maximize tips. In restaurants they encourage tips by surrounding the tables of high-tipping parties; in taverns they play alongside the bar, mingling with their drinking, tipping audience. An experienced *tamburaš* related how at community events where there may be music for kolo dancing, an activity that seldom generates tips, he encourages the youthful players in a new or impromptu combo to play for the dancing so his own combo can concentrate on playing alongside the bar to rake in tips. Another combo musician termed this behavior "money hungry," saying he would rather receive fewer tips but retain more dignity and have more independence in the choice of music. "When they lay that money on you, it's usually 'Marijana' or 'Suze liju' that they're asking for. I get so sick of playing those songs, I'll never play 'em unless they're paid for" (Vučinić 1977).

Some *tamburaši* view the compulsion to tip as an addictive vice like reckless gambling or excessive drinking. They may be concerned about the welfare of the family whose income provider is throwing money at them. One young musician told me how he would surreptitiously give the money back to the wife of a reckless tipper because he knew the family could not afford to do without the sums he was sticking on the instruments (Tarailo 1977).

A Predominantly Male Realm

American tamburitza combo membership is mostly male. From perusing the bands' photographs in past program books of the Tamburitza Extravaganza and reading the names in the TAA's Tamburitza Hall of Fame, it is clear that more than 90 percent of combo musicians are men. In the twenty-one combos that participated in the 2009 Tamburitza Extravaganza, there were 105 male band members and only seven females—the five members of Šarena, an all-female combo, and Veseli's two female members, Rose Puskarich-Husnick and her sister Marilyn "Chee Chee" Repasky. As of 2009, only 10 of the 148 musicians in the Hall of Fame were females. This imbalance might be surprising because a lot of women do learn to play tamburitza. Females frequently comprise a majority of the members of junior tamburitza groups or of amateur adult orchestras, and they are exactly half of the collegiate troupe the Duquesne University Tamburitzans.

Nonetheless, the professional combo scene remains largely male. It is indicative that a frequent casual term for a combo musician is *bećar*. There always seems to be at least one active combo named Bećari. Currently a group from St. Louis is so named. In the 1970s and 1980s there was another Bećari group in Pittsburgh. In its Turkish origins the word simply means a young man, but in tamburitza culture it connotes a wild, merrymaking, free-spirited fellow, who nonetheless has a sensitive and poetic side to his nature. A *bećar* group's rehearsals and performances constitute a gendered space, a domain in which male bonding takes place much like on a sports team or in fishing and hunting parties. It is seldom within the men's culturally defined concept to be comfortable including a female in this setting on an equal basis.

There are two main pathways to becoming a combo member. Either you are invited to join an existing ensemble, or you originate a new combo with friends and/or relatives. Ties to a musical family can provide the path for a woman musician as it did for Rose Husnick and for Patsy Jurkovich-Lucas of the erstwhile Milwaukee combo Zagreb. A *tamburašica* might be a daughter, sister, or wife of a combo member or may be included in the origination of a family-based group. It is rare that the youthful combo Do Zore, with members living near both sides of the Illinois-Wisconsin border, has an unrelated female leader, Julie Rukstales Hughes, who handles the bookings and other band business. Julie acknowledged to me that it is indeed rare to be a female bandleader of an otherwise male band. She asserted that it is probably because she is a little older than the men in the combo who are mostly of college age (Rukstales Hughes 2011).

There are a few all-female combos comprised of friends and relatives. Since the late 1950s the most established female combos on the American tamburitza scene have been the creations of either Ljubica Fill of Youngstown, Ohio, or Honey Zimmerman and Miki Arandjelovich, two sisters who were key musicians in the Trivanovich Sisters of Chicago, a group active until 1968. During the past half century, "Libby," as Ljubica Fill is known, has trained dozens of women musicians for her all-female combo, including her own daughter Stacey. Honey has played a similar mentor role to wannabe *tamburašice*. After the disbanding of the Trivanovich Sisters she formed her own group, Šećeri, in Cleveland in the 1970s, which included two of her nieces. Later on, in the 1990s, Honey and her sister Miki formed Šarena.

There have also been a few all-female combos that originated in the ranks of junior tamburitza groups, but most of these have been short-lived. In Pennsylvania in the 1980s, Bijela Zvijezda, Ljubav, and Danice were three all-female combos that lasted for a few years. In most cases it is difficult for a woman as she matures, marries, and has children to continue to play in a combo. She typically faces community and family pressures to cease playing or to move into a socially approved role such as the teacher in a junior tamburitza group.

Libby Fill and her combo. (Richard March Collection)

Moreover, a tamburitza combo's gigs often are at taverns that most "respectable" mature women are expected to avoid. The musician is immersed in a realm of festive and sometimes excessive behavior. Drinking alcohol is the rule at virtually all of a combo's performance venues. Wedding receptions and the summertime lamb-roast picnics at ethnic lodges and churches are more family friendly, but the tavern jobs take place in a male-dominated world where women have to be tough, careful, or both.

Operating in a predominantly male domain, the female tamburitza combo musicians, like Libby and Honey, adopted an assertive manner. They are strong women, unsurprised and unflustered by the sometimes crude behavior of men and who can compete with men on equal terms.

In the spring of 1979 I had the opportunity to observe an all-day rehearsal of the all-female combo Šečeri. The bandleader Honey Zimmerman was breaking in a new member, Annette Nikoloff, a violin player who was a recent graduate of the Duquesne University Tamburitzans. The marathon rehearsal began in the late morning in the kitchen of Honey's west-side Cleveland home and lasted until late evening. While male family members and their friends sat in the next room, watching a basketball tournament on television, the women were preparing for an upcoming gig at a local Croatian tavern. On the Formica kitchen table in front of Honey there laid a bulging notebook, crammed with hundreds of song lyrics, printed, typed, or handwritten on various-sized sheets of paper, arranged alphabetically by the songs' titles. There were almost no pages with musical notes; there were lyrics only. Honey stood, leaning over the table, paging through the notebook with her *bugarija* strapped on. She would pause on a song that struck her fancy, slap out a few chords on the well-worn instrument, at first alone, to determine the key that would suit her singing voice, then shout to the others something like, "Hey, you guys, did you ever hear this one? It goes like this; it's got three parts and they all sound the same, but they don't." She would play the rhythm and chords beginning at an easy tempo, start to sing the lyrics to the verse, the chorus, then "the bridge," the short melodic passage played between verses. The other women would join in, quickly figuring out what were the possibilities of the song for their instruments or finding a vocal harmony part for the verse or chorus. They sang based on rote memorization of the lyrics. Except for a few novelty numbers in English—the Crljenicas' "Hey Tambu-re-bop," Ray Charles's "What'd I Say," and Buck Owens's "Act Naturally"—all their songs were in Serbian or Croatian, with also a few in Macedonian. Despite the fact that none of them fluently spoke a Slavic language, they generally pronounced the words well with very few language errors.

The rehearsal continued without any recognizable break for more than ten hours. Hunger was assuaged by cans of beer and snacks from the nearby refrigerator while the other family members and friends passed the hours watching basketball, also unavoidably listening to the music as well as caring for the babies who crawled about the floor. At one point, probably while thinking about food, the women sang an English parody of "Ne luduj Leno." In place of the lyrics "Čini se čini, po mjesečini" they instead sang:

"Chili some chili, bring us some chili,
Bring us some crackers to go with the chili."

SERBIAN AND CROATIAN TAMBURA STYLES

Honey is Serbian, and although she has had Croatian and Macedonian band members, her repertoire has tended toward what would be called "Serbian" numbers—like "Daskalice" from the operetta *Koštana*, "Čifte cifte," a Macedonian gypsy song, and "Mujo kuje konja po mjesecu," a Bosnian *sevdalinka*. This repertoire tends to feature irregular rhythms, minor keys, and Middle Eastern musical phrases. The band was preparing for a gig at the Croatian-frequented Two Crows Bar on Cleveland's east side, so Šečeri practiced several Croatian songs as well—"Marijana," "Da nije ljubavi," and "Samo nemoj ti" among others—in foxtrot, polka, and waltz tempo. It is notable, though, that their style of play remained consistent in the Serbian manner—a violin lead ornamented with many grace notes. Whether the structure of the song was conducive to it, Annette inserted a maximum of Oriental or Hungarian Gypsy-style ornamentations—even where they didn't fit, for example on Dalmatian songs. Šečeri gravitated to an up-tempo, all stops out, breakneck style, and they disparaged the soft and sweet style of play as "boring."

The distinction between "Serbian" and "Croatian" styles of American tamburitza combo playing does not neatly correspond to the national background of the musicians. Indeed, quite a number of the most significant musicians—Martin Kapugi, Milovan Dokich, Ljubica Fill, Milan Opacich, and others—were of mixed Serbian and Croatian background. In the 1970s and 1980s the Serbian/Croatian distinction generally referred to the amount of Eastern influences in the style of play—Serbian having more southeastern European sounds and Croatian more central European.

Changes in cultural and political conditions have made the distinction more complex. During the period of the Homeland War and the breakup of Yugoslavia in the first half of the 1990s, it became difficult to sustain the combined Serbian/Croatian nature of the tamburitza scene because of strong feelings on both sides. Some bands, like the

Lira Orchestra of Detroit, which had mixed membership and played a varied repertoire, found it difficult to get bookings. They broke up, reforming into two ethnically specific bands. The Drina Orchestra of the Calumet Region retained their mixed nationality membership (indeed the leader Milan Opacich was of mixed parentage, so the band couldn't become ethnically "pure"), but nonetheless they emphasized playing for Serbian venues.

In a shocking departure from their past practice, in the run-up to the war, one ethnically mixed combo released a cassette titled *Patriotic Songs of the Serbs*, which included the most provocative Četnik songs like "Ko to kaže, ko to laže" and "Sprem'te se sprem'te Četnici." The Četniks were Serbian Royalist fighters during World War II, celebrated by Serbian nationalists but despised by many Serbs and the non-Serbs of the Balkans as war criminals. At the same time, some Croatian combos began to perform openly pro-Ustaši songs. The Ustaši were an elite military force of the quisling Croatian state established by the Axis. Like the Četniks, the Ustaši are admired by extreme Croatian nationalists but reviled by most Croatians and by the other Balkan nationalities for their war crimes.

Prior to the war, there existed a few Serbian and Croatian bands that catered to the tastes of strongly nationalist audiences, but these were most often "electric" bands—not tamburitza combos. Most *tamburaši* were second- and third-generation Americans who did not follow Yugoslav politics and who wanted to avoid controversial songs. In the 1970s and 1980s, several musicians expressed to me their discomfort having to fend off requests to play openly chauvinistic songs because it is in the musical culture to satisfy the tipping customer. If they refused to play the songs, they would anger the customer. On the other hand, if they did play them, everyone would hear about it. It would be reported on in the community's active gossip network and would surely alienate the part of the community that didn't approve of such songs' sentiments. For the *tamburaš* there was no easy solution.

In the fall of 1991, a wedding in Chicago brought public attention to the tensions between the local Serbian and Croatian ethnic communities that had been engendered by the outbreak of the Homeland War in the old country, but simultaneously it demonstrated the continuing cross-ethnic ties that managed to weather the strains of that conflict. Mike Royko, a renowned local newspaper columnist for the *Chicago Daily News* who often wrote about community happenings, noted in a column that he had been contacted by a Croatian American bride-to-be from South Chicago. She bemoaned that the *tamburaši* hired to play at her long-planned wedding to a Serbian American groom had cancelled the booking, indicating that they feared they would lose business as a result of playing for the "mixed wedding." Having seen Royko's column, several friends, Serbian American and Croatian American *tamburaši*, agreed to form an ad hoc ensemble, and they played for the wedding—gratis. Royko noted this happy outcome in a later column.

Even though the Homeland War resulted in an outburst of songs expressing Croatian and Serbian nationalist sentiments in the repertoires of several combos, the musical style of *tamburaši* was evolving in ways that obscured a clear distinction between Croatian American and Serbian American tamburitza music. Ever since the mid-1970s, the Croatian bands' repertoire and style became increasingly influenced by the Vojvodina Romani style of Janika Balaž (1925–88), Momčilo Nikolić, and Milan Marković. This music is considered a Serbian style because of its sound and the fact that the city of Novi Sad in Vojvodina is the epicenter of that style. The Pennsylvania Croatian American tamburitza virtuoso Jerry Grcevich, who mastered playing in the style of Janika Balaž, has had a huge influence since the early 1980s. He inspired a generation of highly skilled young *tamburaši* who have emulated Grcevich and generally raised the musical standards in the American tamburitza combo idiom.

BEĆARI

Combo musicians are an essential element in the most festive and bacchanalian events in the ethnic communities' culture. Thus the notion has evolved that a combo *tamburaš* is most likely a *bećar*. As stated earlier, the term generally implies the darker side of *bećar* behavior— hard drinking, womanizing, reckless disregard for one's health, and general instability. A more positive view of the same sort of behavior was presented by Rudy Orisek, the host of Chicago's *International Café* television program in his comments as MC at a 1969 event, which was a precursor of the Tamburitza Extravaganza, the first "Tamburitza Testimonial Banquet and Dance." Speaking at a hotel in the industrial suburb Dolton, Illinois, Rudy waxed eloquent:

> What is a *tamburaš*: Well, first of all . . . he's a lover; he loves his people and his land and most of all . . . his mistress, the music of each. He is admired by women, respected by men and followed by children. He has a memory that is unlimited . . . almost an Eighth Wonder of the World. He can remember hundreds of songs . . . but often forgets to come home. He has hands that are strong and fingers that are gentle . . . he will hold the tamburitza like a child he loves and yet in his fashion can make it heard loudly. He is a vagabond . . . a restless soul always on the go. He is a ham and he'll break his heart to please anyone who will listen. A *tamburaš* is not made . . . he is born under a special spell . . . a fortunate child who can hear the echoes of the wind sing the sad song . . . a happy song . . . the love songs of his people. That's a *tamburaš*. (Tamburitza Association of America 1970)

A prize example of a hard-living, hell-for-leather *bećar* is the legendary Dave Zupkovich (1920–63) of Youngstown, Ohio, who died at age forty-three in 1963. Zupkovich was an extraordinarily charismatic performer. He recorded prolifically, primarily for Slavco Hlad's Balkan Records label. Featured in his bands were many of the most talented musicians of his era: Martin Kapugi, John Krilcich, Joe Matacic, Tony Markulin, and George Skrbina. His appeal was not limited to his musical gifts nor to his ability to project the image of a tortured artist, burning himself out in a blaze of creative agony—akin to Hank Williams or Jimi Hendrix. Zupkovich is remembered in anecdotes concerning his music making but also his prodigious drinking and ability to do without sleep. Certain songs, like "Leti leti pjesmo moja" and "Jel' ti žao," though previously and subsequently performed by others, became associated with him as "Zupkovich numbers" for decades after his death. In 1977 I saw Steve Paulich of the Dunav combo do a convincing impersonation of Zupkovich singing "Leti leti." Thus, fifteen years after his death, his persona and style were still well known, imitated, and recognized.

Although the wild *bećar* has been a stereotype of a typical combo musician, at no time did all combo players live out this role. There has always been a range in the personalities and behavior of *tamburaši* from wild and carousing to sedate and dignified. Jim Kovacevic of Cleveland, John Plasay of Chicago, Steve Jurkovich of Milwaukee, and Charles Elias Jr. of Kenosha are but a few among the many names that could be mentioned as good examples of dignified, polite combo musicians.

COMBO INSTRUMENTATION

The instruments utilized in American tamburitza combos vary extensively. Many combos rely only on instruments from the tamburitza family, the *prim, brač, čelo brač, bugarija,* and *berde.* Quite a few combos include other, non-tamburitza instruments in their lineups. In the 1970s and 1980s, the string bass was actually more frequent than the *berde* in American combos. Proponents of the string bass mention that it is a more versatile instrument, easier to maintain and repair, easier to obtain strings, not as physically demanding to play, and on occasional songs the bass player can use the bow for sustained notes. Nonetheless, since the 1990s, there has been resurgence in the use of the *berde.* Combo members who use *berde* stress that the unique metallic ring of the steel strings on the frets is specific to and important to tambura music. The *berde's* tone is described as having more "punch" than the string bass. In recent years the *berde* is favored by most of the younger *tamburaši* (David Kosovec 2004).

The violin is used as the lead instrument in a number of combos. Use of the violin was considered one of the characteristics of the Serbian style in American tamburitza—although it is interesting that the most influential violinists on the tamburitza scene have been of other nationalities. Bela Nagy, John Halik, and Julius Peškan were Romani violinists; Tony Markulin was Croatian; George "Whitey" Halasz was Hungarian; and Milovan "Mel" Dokich, perhaps the most influential of all, had a Serbian father and a Croatian mother. Annette Nikoloff, a Macedonian American (and the young violinist joining

Honey Zimmerman's Sečeri combo in 1979), candidly acknowledged to me that Peškan, Markulin, and especially Dokich were her musical models (Nikoloff 1979). Walter Pravica of South Bend, Indiana, Joe Peretin of Chicago, and Mel Evanovich of Youngstown, Ohio, are three more important tamburitza combo violinists. Tamburitza violinists emulate the Hungarian and Rumanian Romani style of violin playing. For the older violinists, the early twentieth-century recordings of Vojvodina Romani violinist Joca Mimika were influential.

It is not uncommon to find the accordion in tamburitza combos both in Europe and in North America. While in Europe various types of accordions are used—diatonic button, chromatic button, and piano keyboard—in America only the piano accordion, the standard 120 bass model, is used. In the 1970s and 1980s, some of the American combos using accordions were the Plavi Dunav Orchestra of Mount Olive, Illinois, near St. Louis; Lira of Detroit; Mirko Roknich of Ohio; and Sloboda and Veseljaci of Chicago. Currently, the Yeseta Brothers of Los Angeles are a combo featuring Tom Yeseta on accordion. Different combinations of tamburitza instruments have been used in the various combos. Plavi Dunav used two *brač*es: *bugarija* and string bass. Supporting their accordionist Sanda Pavlovic, Lira had a violin lead, *čelo brač*, *bugarija*, and string bass. Veseljaci's accordionist Mickey Kusecek, the rare Slovenian American to play in a tamburitza combo, was joined by the band's leader Nick Skertich on *čelo brač*, Roko Abramovich on *brač*, and Ray Jankovic on string bass.

Use of the accordion is controversial among *tamburaši* because some claim it is too loud, drowns out the other instruments, and destroys the unique tamburitza sound of an all-strings orchestra. Indeed, the loud volume of the accordion has led some groups to become accordion-dominated, like Mirko Roknich's band, which sounds more like a Bosnian or Serbian *narodni orkestar*. Veseljaci amplified the *brač*es with contact microphones so that the *brač* lead is fully audible, and Lira strived to maintain an even mix of the other instruments with the accordion.

Since the early 2000s, the recent Bosnian immigrant Adis Sirbubalo has frequently performed on accordion in the characteristic *sevdalinka* style with Chicago's Tamburitza Rroma group. Adis also provided the main melodic backup on a CD of *sevdalinka* songs recorded by Sonya Kosovec (see chap. 6).

The most controversial bands in the 1970s and 1980s were the fully electric combos, although over time their role as a part of the tamburitza scene has become accepted, especially as groups to play for social dancing. There were two degrees of electrification. Tony Muselin's Continentals and Veseljaci represented a less radical departure. They amplified their original acoustic tamburitzas with contact microphones, playing them in the same manner as before. The amplification allowed Muselin to reduce his band's size to a trio—*brač, bugarija*, and string bass. To vary the sound of the sole lead instrument, curiously, he resorted to using a wah-wah pedal on his *brač* for some of the instrumental numbers. Since its invention in 1966, the wah-wah has become a popular device for electric guitar sound effects in rock and fusion bands.

In the 1970s in Pennsylvania, three bands made a more complete transformation from a tamburitza combo to become tamburitza-flavored rock bands: the Trubaduri and Bećari of Pittsburgh, and also Johnny Krizancich and his Internationals of Sharon, Pennsylvania. The two Pittsburgh bands utilized a modern drum kit, electric guitar, and bass guitar with lead parts played on an amplified *brač* or *prim*. The Krizancich group featured an accordion lead with *bugarija*, electric bass guitar, and drums. The Bećari and especially the Trubaduri were influenced by late 1960s and 1970s Yugoslav rock bands, from whose records they learned a good portion of their repertoire. Indeed, the name of the Trubaduri is patterned after the long-popular Yugoslav-era rock band Dubrovački Trubaduri. These Pittsburgh groups represented a synthesis of Yugoslav and American rock with tamburitza music while the Krizancich group has had the same influences plus a strong influence of Slovenian American polka music. These bands omnivorously combined musical influences from their cultural environment. Rather than seeking to preserve older forms of the ethnic heritage, their main impulse was to launch fully modern ensembles to play popular Croatian-associated music for their ethnic community with a minimum of cultural conservatism.

A parallel tradition of modern music with a Croatian ethnic connection also developed in Europe among Gradišćanski Hrvati, the

Croatian minority living in Austria's Burgenland region. In 1980 during the first recording session of Bruji, the genre's pioneering band, an Austrian sound engineer called their music *Krowodnrock* (*Krowodn* is the local German dialect word for Croatian), and the term has been embraced by the musicians and their community. Typical rock band instruments predominate, but Bruji uses also accordion and *prim* on numbers that retain musical similarities to Croatian folk songs. Initially Bruji's songs were overtly assertive of Croatian minority rights in Austria, but over the three decades that have passed, political issues have become overshadowed by typical rock music themes in the repertoire of Bruji and the new generation of *Krowodnrock* bands like Elektrikeri and Kacavida (YouTube videos of Bruji).

In Pittsburgh, the Bećari have disbanded, but the Trubaduri have continued to perform in essentially the same style for more than thirty years. Their performances alternate American popular songs with old-time *starogradske pjesme* and recent Croatian popular hits. We should note that the electric instruments are not mandatory for playing pop music in English and Croatian. The Sinovi orchestra of Chicago, using acoustic tamburitzas only, has a considerable repertoire of American and Croatian popular songs along with their more traditional tamburitza material.

Other electric bands have emerged, such as the Majstori, who promote themselves as "Chicago's finest TambuRok Band," and Ludi Ritam (crazy rhythm), also from Chicago. They have been influenced by Croatian groups like Gazde, which play in a similar style to the Trubaduri, with similar instrumentation. *Tamburaši* recognize that the electric ensembles represent a separate category from acoustic tambura combos; sometimes they are characterized pejoratively as "boom boom groups" (Lacko-Kelly 2004). Nonetheless, the electric bands have established a niche in the tamburitza tradition. Many young people, raised with rock music, expect to hear and dance to a loud rhythm section made up of a drum kit and bass guitar . . . and they get it from these bands.

American Musical Influences on Tamburitza

In the early twentieth century. a significant number of Croatians and Serbs settled in the mining towns of the western United States, often comprising a significant percentage of the population of the small towns. In these communities a different process of modernization and Americanization of their traditional music took place. These communities generally did not maintain as extensive contact with the old homeland as have the larger urban ethnic communities. The South Slavic residents of the Western mining towns are almost exclusively the descendants of pre–World War I immigrants. Unlike the urban American Croatian and Serbian communities, there has been practically no new immigration to mining towns like Anaconda, Montana; Bisbee, Arizona; Ely, Nevada; Helper, Utah; or Rock Springs, Wyoming. Indeed, in their area these people still are generally called "Austrians" since their forebears emigrated from Austria-Hungary.

The small ethnic communities lacked institutions such as ethnic stores selling imported records or ethnic radio programs featuring music from their European homeland. Thus the folk and popular songs that were current in the home regions of their ancestors in the period when they immigrated, from the 1890s to the 1910s, dominate the music repertoire they associate with their ethnic identity. Living in small towns in the Intermountain West, the American music to which they had the greatest exposure has been country and western. Musicians in these small Serbian and Croatian ethnic communities have taken to singing the old Slavic songs learned from their parents in a country music style.

Working as a public folklorist organizing a local folk festival, in 1979 I had the opportunity to spend a few weeks in Ely, Nevada, a copper mining town. I fell in with an informal group of local country musicians led by the Slavic brothers Joe and "Bonny" Mesich, both of whom played electric guitars. In addition to their repertoire of country songs sung in English, they sang several songs in Croatian—"Mladi Kapetane," a song that refers to the 1912 Balkan Wars, "Kukavica," a popular waltz tune with risqué lyrics, and their favorite, "Ja sam sirota," an old sentimental song. When singing these songs, they did not change their style in the slightest, strumming the guitar rhythms and singing the Slavic words in the nasal tones typical of country-western music. Moreover, they rendered the songs closer to country style by omitting the repetition of the final two lines of each stanza, which is typical of South Slavic songs but not of country music.

Indicative of the ethnic diversity of the mining towns, a third member of this informal group of country singers was Fook Quong, born and raised in Ely and the descendant of Chinese immigrant miners. Fook enthusiastically sang the old Slavic songs in a nasal country style while sporting a large white cowboy hat, his wide, tooled leather guitar strap prominently emblazoned with his Chinese name in Latin letters.

The inclusion of guitars and mandolins in tamburitza groups is not uncommon, especially in the cases of more informal groups. These fretted string instruments have a similar sound and playing technique to tamburitzas, and are much more readily available in the United States. For example, the Velebit Orchestra of Chicago featured an electric mandolin and the Dobar Dan Tamburitzans of Seattle used two guitars in the roles of *bugarija* and *čelo brač*. Devotees of the *prim* contend, however, that the mellow tone of the mandolin is not as bright and piercing as the *prim*, and *bugarija* players assert that chording on guitar cannot duplicate the ringing tones of the *bugarija*.

Aside from the inclusion of non-tambura instruments in some combos, variety in combo instrumentation is also present even among those combos that use only instruments of the tamburitza family. The number and type of melodic instruments varies considerably although nearly every combo has a *berde/bugarija* rhythm section. The *berde* hits the downbeats while the *bugarija* emphasizes the weak beats. Often the melodic instruments drop out and only these two rhythm instruments play while the group is singing. Therefore a good *berde/bugarija* rhythm section is essential to a quality combo.

When it came to the melodic instruments, in the United States there was significant regional variation, which has diminished considerably since the 1970s and 1980s. In Chicago and northwestern Indiana, four-piece groups often featured *prim* and *čelo brač* in addition to the rhythm section, while in Ohio and western Pennsylvania two *brač* players typically filled the melodic roles. In five-piece groups, one may find one of each melodic instrument, *prim*, *brač*, and *čelo brač*, or alternatively, two *bračes* and a *čelo*. In America, combos rarely feature more than one *prim*, although in Europe, first and second *prim* parts are common especially in Slavonian combos (see also chap. 3).

The greater emphasis upon *prim* in the Chicago area in the 1970s was in large part a result of the influence of Marko Popovich and Steve Makarewitch, two gifted *primaši* from that region. Marko played for more than fifty years with his brothers in the Popovich Brothers Orchestra until his death in 1976. Steve played in various groups including Dunav and the Marty Kapugi Orchestra. Steve was also the music director of Croatian and Serbian youth orchestras in the Gary, Indiana, area until his death in 1978.

Both of these musicians exhibited a complete mastery of the *prim* in a fluid and improvisational style and were equally comfortable playing a fast intricate kolo dance or a slow sentimental melody, decorating the tune with a series of delicate grace notes and arpeggios. Marko's music has been preserved for younger aspiring *primaši* on the six LP records made by the Popovich Brothers. Although Steve did not make many recordings, he had a direct influence upon young players through his extensive teaching efforts.

It is interesting to note that Steve was not of Serbian or Croatian background but hailed from the small Ruthenian (western Ukrainian) ethnic group in northwestern Indiana. According to Steve, his family always associated with the more numerous Croatians and Serbs in his neighborhood with whom they share a Slavic heritage. Steve began to play tamburitza while still a small boy and was completely at home with South Slavic music. To pay tribute to his Ruthenian background, Steve liked to perform wearing a satin Cossack-style shirt, and he always taught his tamburitza students a few well-known Russian songs such as "Two Guitars" or "Kalinka."

MILAN OPACICH

An important combo musician, tamburitza maker, and the writer of a column in *Serb World* magazine about tamburitza, Milan Opacich (1928–2013) lived in northwest Indiana. He and his wife Rose proved to be crucial informants to this study. When I was doing fieldwork in the Chicago–Gary area, I frequently drove north from Bloomington, Indiana, where I was a graduate student at Indiana University. Milan's tamburitza-making shop, which completely filled his two-car garage in

Schererville, Indiana, was usually my first stop. Milan introduced me
to numerous *tamburaši*, often in chance meetings when the musicians
happened to come into his shop while I was there, perhaps to have
an instrument repaired, or maybe just to chat. His shop was a *tamburaši* hangout, sometimes to Milan's chagrin, when he had a lot of
work to do.

Like a surprising number of excellent *tamburaši*, Milan was of mixed
Serbian and Croatian heritage, his mother a Croatian from Lika, his
father a Serb from the Croatian province Banija. They met and married in America. Such mixed marriages were far from uncommon in
the period before World War II. Born in Gary in 1928, Milan grew
up in the close-knit Serbian and Croatian community of that steel-
mill town. He experienced the hardships of the Great Depression as a
boy when mill work became scarce. But according to Milan, during
the hard times, the ethnic community ties were strong. Neighbors relied
upon each other for mutual support and for shared amusements. Living a stone's throw from the old Serbian Hall in Gary, Milan remem-
bers his magnetic attraction to the tamburitza music he heard there
while still very young. He listened to the Popovich Brothers, the Skertich Brothers, the Crljenica Brothers, and other area groups performing at picnics and dances. Then as now, it was the custom for parents to
bring their children to ethnic community events, thus exposure to live
tamburitza music comes practically from infancy.

Milan's desire to play was so great that while still a small child, his
father made him a toy tambura out of a piece of plywood and strung it
with rubber bands. Milan's desire didn't abate, so his father had to make
sure that his son acquired a real instrument. Milan learned to play on
his own. He did not belong to a youth orchestra, did not learn to read
notes, and played entirely by ear (Opacich 1975).

As a teenager during World War II, Milan also was attracted to
country music, and he learned to play guitar. The possessor of a deep
mellifluous voice, he performed popular Western songs for his schoolmates at Lew Wallace High School in Gary. They nicknamed him "the
Yugoslavian Cowboy."

As a young man he formed a combo, The Continentals, with a few
of his friends. Milan played *prim* at their jobs in and around Gary. On

one occasion, the combo ventured all the way to the Iron Range of northern Minnesota, more than five hundred miles, to play a gig. Although music was his first love, Milan, like nearly all other *tamburaši*, couldn't manage to make a living solely as a tamburitza musician. The music remained a part-time pursuit. Milan married a local girl, Rose Nikolich; they soon had a daughter, Karen. To support his young family Milan used his excellent manual skills to learn to be a tool and die maker, working in several area factories and machine shops.

His mechanical and musical interests combined in an interest in tamburitza making. Milan heard that a *prim* could be fashioned with a turtle shell serving as the instrument's back. In the 1950s, the turtle-shell *prim* became his first attempt to make a tamburitza. In order to obtain a large turtle shell, he enlisted the help of his brother Robert, who had been a Marine sharp-shooter in World War II. Together they made their way to a swamp near Lake Michigan, looking for a big snapping turtle. They spotted a turtle, and Robert, the sure shot, bagged it through the neck. Robert had the hunter's ethic that he must eat what he has killed, so they prepared turtle soup. Milan was unnerved by the dead turtle's reflexive movements and declined to eat any of the soup.

Milan sold the turtle-shell *prim* but after decades of passing through the hands of different owners, Milan finally had a chance to buy it back from Larry Regan, the proprietor of Jenny's Restaurant, where he frequently performed. He considered his rookie work on the turtle-shell *prim* too crude to play at all, so it hung on a pegboard above his workbench, without strings, a treasured souvenir.

In the 1950s, during a slow period in tool and die work, Milan managed to obtain a position as firefighter for the City of Gary, a job he held for twenty-five years. His work hours as a firefighter were twenty-four hours on-duty, then forty-eight hours off. Milan's instrument-making skills increased because this schedule allowed him time to work on making and repairing tamburitzas in his home workshop during his two consecutive days off. He sometimes had a chance to make minor repairs to *tambure* on a workbench at the firehouse.

When the Chicago tamburitza maker Ivan Hlad retired, he sold his tools and patterns to Milan, who continued to use them to make some of the distinctive Hlad-designed *tambure*. Most notable was Hlad's unique *prim*, which, like the f-style mandolins made by the Gibson Company of Kalamazoo, featured an ornamental scroll on the upper side where the neck joins the body. There was also a cut-away on the opposite side of the neck to facilitate reaching the highest frets.

Milan's instrument-making business burgeoned over the years. With his tool-and-die-making skills, Milan fashioned his own templates and forms to speed and improve his processes. Soon tools, materials, and instruments overflowed the basement of his Glen Park neighborhood home in Gary. In the mid-1970s he moved his family to a suburban house with a very large garage, now well-filled with hand and power tools, stacks of lumber, the walls adorned with hanging instruments and photographs of vintage tamburitza groups. As he worked, a couple of speakers tinkled with taped music from his collection of 78 rpm tamburitza recordings from the 1920s through the 1940s. Milan also collected fine examples of the work of noted American tambura makers

Milan Opacich
(1928–2013).
(Photo by author)

of the past. He has, for example, a superbly inlaid *brač* made by John Bencic of Cleveland and f-hole-style *bugarija* by Andrew Groeschl of Chicago.

After twenty-five years as a firefighter, Milan retired from that job in the late 1970s to devote himself full time to tamburitza, as an artisan, a musician, and a community scholar. He also accepted an offer to write a regular feature in every issue of *Serb World*, a periodical published in Arizona six times a year. Drawing on his extensive collection of historical photographs of *tamburaši*, he wrote profiles of musicians of the past, accounts of recent conversations with tamburitza figures, or thoughts on issues and developments in the world of tamburitza. In 2007 the publisher of *Serb World* released *Tamburitza America*, a compilation of dozens of Milan's best columns along with their accompanying photographs. At the same time, Frank Valentich of Pittsburgh was the only other full-time tamburitza maker in the United States, and even part-time tamburitza craftsmen were rare. Peter Zugcic of Youngstown, Nick Vukusich of Milwaukee, and Steve Aleksich of Los Angeles were among the few such artisans who were active in the 1970s.

With more time to devote to craftsmanship, Milan taught a class in guitar making at the Indiana-Purdue University campus in Hammond, Indiana, and taught instrument-making skills through the Folk Arts Apprenticeship program of the Indiana Arts Commission. A full-time artisan, Milan was able to take on bigger jobs. He outfitted not only individuals but also entire youth orchestras.

As a 1970s musician, Milan was a member of a circle of about a dozen *tamburaši* of his generation who combined, broke up, and recombined into various combos. Milan once stated, "We get into an argument every five years or so and switch bands." Milan could play all the tambura instruments. In the late 1950s he shifted from performing as a *primaš* to emphasizing *čelo brač* and singing. For nearly forty years he was a leading member of a combo called Drina. Milan asserted that the name was appropriate because the Drina River (despite some geographic inaccuracy to the idea) serves as a metaphor for the border between Serbia and Bosnia or Croatia, and the band had always been comprised of both Serbs and Croats, or, as in the cases of Milan and Mel Dokich, of "half-breeds." As *čelo* player and lead singer, Milan was a mainstay of the group along with his close friend, the bassist Jack Tomlin. Drina made two self-produced LP albums: the first in 1971 with Julius Peškan and Horace Mamula, and the other in 1977 with Mel Dokich and Matt Jurich.

As some of the musicians of Milan's generation passed away or ceased to be active, Milan recruited younger musicians, George Ivancevich, Nick Rakich, and the Brajac brothers Steve and Moe. Drina's lead violinist Mel Dokich died of cancer in 1978. Milan tried out some potential new lead players. Dissatisfied with the available players, with some trepidation, Milan returned to the role of *primaš* in 1980, carrying on the tradition of the fine midwestern *primaši* until he finally retired from the band in 2009 and died in 2013.

In recognition of his outstanding contributions to his tradition, in 2004 Milan received the National Heritage Fellowship from the National Endowment for the Arts. He was the second of three *tamburaši* ever to receive the award. Previously, in 1982 Adam Popovich, a member of the Popovich Brothers Orchestra, and subsequently in 2006 Jerry Grcevich, the outstanding *tamburaš* from Pittsburgh, received this recognition.

Combo Repertoire, Music, Politics, and Nationalism

In the early twentieth century, Farkaš instruments were the main type available to American *tamburaši*. In the second half of the 1920s, most players switched to the Srijemski system. Musicians from Srijem and Vojvodina, where the instruments originated, played them even earlier. There were a few groups like the Skertich Brothers who had invested in Farkaš instruments and continued to play them for several more years, but by the end of the 1930s, Farkaš ensembles became rare. In the 1970s and 1980s there were still two combos in the Chicago area that continued to use Farkaš instruments, the Star Serenaders of Highland, Indiana, and the Orao Orchestra of Chicago.

The Star Serenaders played regularly for many years at the Golden Shell, a popular Croatian restaurant in South Chicago. They played an eclectic repertoire including much modern music, despite their archaic instruments. A typical forty-five-minute set might have included a couple of jazzy Mills Brothers tunes, a rock number like "Hang on Sloopy," along with a sentimental Dalmatian air like "Adio Mare" and an upbeat tamburitza standard, the Bosnian song "Kolika je Javorina planina."

The Orao group was not professionally oriented. For the most part, they played the older well-known songs for social events at the Holy Trinity Croatian Catholic Church in Chicago's Pilsen neighborhood, the area where Ivan Hlad had his tamburitza workshop, where Slavco Hlad started his Balkan Record Company, and where Rudy Orisek encountered the Kapugi brothers, playing in their tavern. The church and its hall remained a gathering place for Croatian Americans for many years even after the businesses disappeared and the residents of the neighborhood were primarily Mexican Americans.

When it came to repertoire, in the 1970s and 1980s American *tamburaši* had less knowledge of the particular European regional associations of specific songs and tended to think of their material in chronological terms: they were either new songs or old songs. In Europe most musicians knew the regional provenance of a song, for example, from Međimurje, Podravina, or Slavonia. They knew the musical stylistic traits associated with those regions and recognized the dialect of the lyrics. Although such awareness has been increasing in America in recent years, due to more contact with homeland musicians, fewer of the American *tamburaši* have the level of knowledge or are as concerned with the issue as were the Europeans. Currently, the outstanding young American *tamburaš* Peter Kosovec frequently performs and has recorded a medley combining "Sremačko je selo moje" and "Sajo sarajlije." The two songs work together musically, which is Peter's criterion. It would have been unlikely that European *tamburaši* might have connected these two songs in a medley because the first is from Srijem, a province in the Croatian-Serbian border region, and the latter is from Sarajevo, the capitol city of Bosnia.

American *tamburaši*, especially the older musicians, have an idea of when a particular song entered the generally known repertoire of combos. The oldest "old time" numbers are the pre-1900 folksongs or *starogradske pjesme*, most common in the community's oral tradition such as "Ja sam sirota" or "Tiho noći." Other songs, perhaps equally old but which the *tamburaši* learned later through hearing a recording, are considered newer.

During and immediately following World War II, several of the old patriotic songs like "Vilo Velebita" or "Čuj Dušane" were played frequently and new war-related songs emerged like the Četnik song "Sprem'te se Četnici" or the Partisan tune "Domovina zovi nas." Since these songs reflected political differences that became ever more intense as the war went on, the *tamburaši* had to take care to perform them only for an audience that supported the causes they symbolized.

Such songs could evoke a big reaction, even decades later, in the communities of political refugees who arrived in the United States in the later 1940s and early 1950s as "displaced persons." Many of them had had an association, often only slight, with the defeated sides in Yugoslavia during World War II. Their political leaders fostered a continuing dedication to their causes, such as the Četniks (Serbian Royalist Guerillas), the Nedići (Serbian quislings), or the Ustaši (Croatian quislings). Some of them had narrowly escaped death at the hands of the war's victorious partisans, led by Marshal Tito. Many had spent months or years in refugee camps in Italy or Germany, and they tended to be fiercely anticommunist and also hostile to their "enemy" nationality, Croatians or Serbians, as the case might be.

By the end of the war in 1945, there had been a hiatus of more than twenty years in new immigration to the United States from former Yugoslavia. The National Origins and Quota Act of 1924 reduced immigration from a stream to barely a trickle. By the time the post–World War II refugees were allowed into the United States, there had developed a substantial difference between the lived experience of the so-called *starosjedioci* (old settlers) and the "displaced persons," as they were referred to pejoratively by the earlier immigrants and their descendants. The *starosjedioci* and their progeny descended from impoverished villagers in the homeland who went "trbuhom za kruhom" (by stomach after bread) to America, taking difficult ocean voyages to become exploited toilers in the mines and heavy industries of the United States. Most of these immigrants, both Serbian and Croatian, departed from the ethnically diverse Austro-Hungarian Empire in the period from 1890 to 1918. Far fewer came from the more homogeneous

kingdom of Serbia. Mostly they were Croatians from Croatia and Bosnia, and Serbians from Croatia and Bosnia, often from the very same
regions. In the pre–World War II ethnic communities, especially in the
smaller ones, the Serbian and Croatian immigrants had close and usually harmonious social interactions.

But even here there was no ethnic-relations utopia. The communities were not completely free of the inter-religious/inter-ethnic antag-
onisms, such as were portrayed in a best-selling 1929 recording of a
humorous skit titled "Maksa trazi burt" (Max seeks a boardinghouse)
(Columbia 1124-F). The protagonist Maksim Prdić (his last name
means "little fart") arrives in Pittsburgh looking for a room in a boardinghouse. The owner, Gazdarica Kata (Landlady Kate), is a Kajkavian-
dialect speaker whose parlance pegs her as hailing from northern Croatia. Hearing Maksa's Serbian accent, Kata calls him a "Vlach" (which
to Maksa meant a shepherd from a small minority group, but to Kata
it was a pejorative term for a Serbian). Maksa replies that he's no *Vlah*
but rather a "regular Serbian." Kata counters that it's all the same to her,
you're all *Vlasi*. Nonetheless they become friends, enjoy singing together, and eventually become lovers. But Maksa has to flee to Detroit
when Kata's dangerous husband, Štef, another Kajkavian speaker, comes
home after his release from prison. The record remained popular for
decades, and four skits continuing the story were released from 1929 to
1931 (Spottswood 1990, 964–65).

The free and mostly positive interactions of earlier Serbian and Croatian American immigrants contrasted sharply with the inter-ethnic
hostility of the post–World War II refugees. Moreover, because of their
anticommunism, the refugees identified with the political Right in
America. On the other hand, in the post–World War II era, the earlier
immigrants had a tendency to be politically left of center. They had
been exploited industrial workers, many of whom had participated in
the 1930s in difficult and sometimes bloody struggles to organize the
left-leaning CIO unions: the United Steelworkers, the United Packing-
house Workers, United Auto Workers, and the United Mineworkers
of America. They revered Franklin Delano Roosevelt as a heroic leader
because of his administration's support of the right of workers to organize and as a key world leader in the just-ended war to defeat the Axis.

These stark cleavages in and between the ethnic communities, engendered by the arrival of the refugees, led to conflicts, occasionally violent, over the control of ethnic parishes and lodges, radio programs, and newspapers. It could hardly be expected that these conflicts would leave the tamburitza tradition unaffected. Because many of the Serbian Četnik and Nedići refugees hailed from the lands of the former Serbian kingdom where tamburitza was practically unknown, they objected to the very existence of the tamburitza combos and youth orchestras that were associated with Serbian churches and lodges. "That is Croatian," they insisted (Opacich 1975).

On the Croatian side, the Ustaši had absorbed the Nazi nationalist ideology of a "pure" Aryan culture, and during the war, in their Independent Croatian State (NDH), they had tried to purge the Croatian language of foreign words, much as they tried to purge their territory of religious and ethnic minorities. In America, the former Ustaši refugees strenuously objected to anything they perceived to be a Serbian influence on Croatian culture. In that effort, they endeavored to eliminate the song repertoire of tamburitza combos and youth orchestras of any Serbian or pro-Yugoslav material. It is ironic that few of these critics had much knowledge of South Slavic folksongs and their origins, so in practice, unless there was a direct reference in a song to a Serbian geographic location or a Serbian historic figure, Serbian love songs like "Ima dana" or "Koliko te srce moje voli" typically passed unnoticed. The nationalist critics launched particular venom at Serbian dances that had become common at Croatian social dance parties. Kolo dancers enjoyed the rhythm of *Žikino* kolo, and good dancers could show off their fast footwork on *Čačačko* kolo, but Žika is a common Serbian name, and Čačak is a town in central Serbia, so bands could be blackballed by the parishes and lodges that the Croatian nationalists controlled if they dared to respond to the dancers' requests to play such tunes.

Here is an illustrative example of what could happen to a band that violated the nationalists' criteria: In 1976 Michael Bilandic (Bilandžić), a Croatian American, was campaigning to be elected mayor of Chicago. The Drina orchestra was hired to play at a "Croatians for Bilandic" fund-raising dinner at St. Jerome's church hall in Bilandic's home area, the Bridgeport neighborhood of Chicago. The members of Drina at that time were Milan Opacich and Mel Dokich (mixed-breeds), and Matt Jurisich and Jack Tomlin (Croatians). The Drina members knew that they had to play Croatian repertoire at this event for there were sure to be a number of passionate nationalists in attendance. However, Drina never played with prearranged set lists. At the end of a song, a band member would suggest the next song. Milan acknowledged that he made "a bad call" when he suggested, and the band started to play, "Oj Šumadijo." Milan didn't realize that the mere mention of Šumadija, a region of central Serbia, would elicit such a reaction. Several seconds into the song they were greeted with a chorus of boos and shouted threats from the nationalist faction in the crowd. Soon a shower of cups, glasses, and silverware was tossed in their direction. The music was over. Fortunately, the band quickly managed to retreat to a small room and weren't hit by any flying objects. The Bilandic campaign staff who had organized the event apologized to the Drina members and formed a group to escort them safely to their cars in the church parking lot (Opacich 1976).

For decades, tamburitza combos have had to navigate a minefield of potential objections, usually not as dramatic or violent as that experienced by Drina. The American-born musicians often have not known the political/ethnic/religious symbolism of a particular song and might be unsure about which songs a particular audience might object to. There can be, however, a joking and playful aspect to this generally difficult issue. For example, in 1981 at a social event in the hall of St. Augustine Catholic Church in Milwaukee, I saw Mickey Crnojevich, a Serbian American, the *primaš* of the Sarajevo Tamburitzans, attach a large tip on the tuning peg of the *brač* of Steve Jurkovich, the Croatian American leader of Tamburitza Orchestra Zagreb. Mickey and Steve were friends, but they seemed to be arguing, so I moved closer to listen in. "There's your money, so you've got to play it," Mickey insisted. "You know I can't play it here," Steve countered. Mickey kept insisting. Steve looked furtively to the left and right. "Let me see if that Ustaša is still here," Steve muttered. Apparently not seeing whoever he was looking for, Steve said, "OK, here you go," and quietly began playing "Marširala Kralja Petra garda" ("King Peter's Guard Marched"—a Serbian nationalist song). I asked Mickey what was going on. He said, "This is to pay Steve back. He tipped me and made me play 'Vilo Velebita' (The Velebit Mountain Fairy"—a Croatian nationalist song) at Serb Hall last month."

By the 1950s a noticeable influence of American musical styles could be detected in the music of American tamburitza combos. The Crljenica Brothers recorded a novelty song, "Tamburitza Boogie," in 1950. The tune featured a basic twelve-bar blues chord progression and a shuffle beat. A solo on an amplified *brač* imitated the sound of an electric guitar. The song lyrics are inane, what blues players term "throwaway" lyrics:

Sviram žicu G, onda žicu D,
Žicu A, žicu E, sviram sve do dalnjie
Tamburica boogie, tamburica boogie
Prosli stari dani kad su sviral' za bećare
It's the Tamburica *boogie,* ludi *boogie woogie.*

[I play the G string, then the D string, / the A string, the E string,
I play on and on. / Tamburitza boogie, tamburitza boogie, / the days
are gone when they played for *bećari*.]

Surprisingly, the next year the tune was "covered" by the well-known jazz bandleader Louis Jordan. Jordan's version of "Tamburitza Boogie" emphasized electric organ and had unrelated vocals about drinking beer and wine, in English, except for one word: Jordan sings "*ludi* (crazy) boogie woogie."

In the mid-1950s Dave Zupkovich recorded another tamburitza blues, "Hey Tambu-re-bop," a rockabilly-style tune. The lyrics are a Slavic-English patois:

Ja sam kazao, *"I go,"* Mama kaže, *"No!"*
Ja sam išao svirat, Mama kaže, *"Get out!"*
Hej tambu-re-bop . . .

[I said, "I go," Mama says, "No!" / I went to play music, Mama says,
"Get out!"]

A jazzy touch was provided to the song by an African American saxophonist whose band was waiting its turn to use the Balkan Records recording studio and who offered to add a saxophone solo to the number.

Playing a few rock or pop novelty numbers has remained a feature of the repertoire of many American tamburitza combos. Such well-known blues and rock tunes as "What'd I Say," "Proud Mary," and "Brown-Eyed Girl" are now performed frequently.

As mentioned earlier in connection with the Slavic musicians in Western mining towns, country music is another American idiom that has had a considerable impact on tamburitza combos. Many country songs are easily adaptable to tamburitza because that genre has a number of musical similarities to a significant portion of the original tamburitza repertoire, especially Dalmatian and *starogradske pjesme*. Both the country and tamburitza idioms feature waltz tunes in triple meter, as well as songs in duple meter. Like country, much tamburitza repertoire is in major keys with three-chord (tonic, subdominant, and dominant seventh) chord progressions.

Many *tamburaši* appreciate country music. Milan Opacich, for example, having acquired the nickname "the Yugoslavian Cowboy," pondered becoming a country musician but went into tamburitza instead, mainly because at that time (during World War II) in Gary, Indiana, the so-called hillbilly bands received only beer and liquor as compensation, while the *tamburaši* received generous monetary payment. Nonetheless, Milan's appreciation of country music never ceased. With a little coaxing he would launch into a Marty Robbins gunfighter ballad. He did repair work on an expensive guitar belonging to the legendary country guitarist Chet Atkins, and in his workshop there was an autographed photo of Atkins thanking Milan for his fine craftsmanship. Milan even had the opportunity to meet the country music legend Roy Acuff in Nashville (Opacich 1977).

The country song "Blue Eyes Crying in the Rain," written by the Nashville songwriter Fred Rose and originally recorded by Roy Acuff in 1945, became popular with *tamburaši* who sang it in translation as "Suze liju plavi oči." The song became such an accustomed part of tamburitza repertoire that when Willie Nelson made a new recording of the song in 1975, some thirty years after Acuff's version, the original recording was no longer remembered. Thus, in the mid-1970s I often heard *tamburaši* assert that Nelson had "stolen" the old tamburitza song (Jurisich 1976). There is even another, poetically weaker English version of the song, "Tears Are Falling from Your Blue Eyes," translated back from the Croatian by someone obviously not familiar with the English original.

Influenced by the singing of the country music legend Jimmie Rodgers, a *tamburaš* from Cleveland, Nick Tarach, promoted himself as "the Tamburitza Yodeler." His trademark style featured yodeling that was a cross between the Rodgers-style yodel and Alpine yodeling.

Recently recorded country hits sometimes enter tamburitza combo repertoire, are played for a short while, and dropped after the song's popularity fades. For example, in the 1970s a number of combos played the Kenny Rogers song "You Picked a Fine Time to Leave Me, Lucille," but by the early 1980s, it was rarely heard anymore.

Most tamburitza combos play a variety of melodious international numbers—especially from Italy, Greece, the Middle East, or Russia. The Neopolitan song "O Sole Mio" (often sung with the English lyrics popularized by Elvis Presley) is often attempted by combos with a strong singer. "Lara's Theme" from the soundtrack of the 1965 film *Doctor Zhivago* became popular with *tamburaši*, especially because the tinkling of the *prim* played by their colleague tamburaš Vaso Crljenica is audible amid the lush music of the 101 Strings Orchestra of Hamburg, Germany. *Tamburaši* also took an immediate liking to another film song, the theme from the 1960 film *Never on Sunday*, composed by Manos Hatzidakis. The tune is in the style of traditional Greek music and was played on the tambura-like bouzouki. Another very popular Greek tune, "Miserlou," has been known to *tamburaši* since the 1940s. A longtime favorite has been the Hebrew song "Hava Nagila." Also popular are the Russian Jewish themed songs from the Broadway musical *Fiddler on the Roof*, which opened in 1964, and the film version released in 1971. Combos that manage to get bookings to play for a general audience outside the ethnic communities often rely on this "international" repertoire.

Some combos have developed a following among international folk dance enthusiasts. Dances from the Balkans are among the favorites of these folk dancers, most of whom do not have any ethnic connection with Balkan cultures. The combos play dance tunes, some directly associated with a certain dance step or motions, "Niška banja," "Makedonska devojče," "Miserlou," or "Kolo u šest" for example.

In the 1960s American tamburitza repertoire was affected by a marked increase in the amount of contact with the Old Country where a new wave of migration from Yugoslavia to Western Europe and North America began. In 1962 the Yugoslav government took measures to allow their citizens to work abroad. For many years there had been few new arrivals in the American South Slavic ethnic communities. But now these new economic migrants were anxious to obtain newspapers, magazines, records, food items, and other reminders of their homeland. Enterprising businessmen opened ethnic stores to supply these needs.

At the same time, charter flights began to provide cheaper air travel between Europe and North America. Currency exchange rates were favorable to the dollar. It became affordable for many older immigrants and their descendants, who previously had only sporadic correspondence with their European relatives, to visit Yugoslavia. The vacationers returned to America with enthusiastic stories of the warm hospitality they experienced. They hosted house parties to show the home movies, slides, and souvenirs from their travels. Among the souvenirs were Yugoslav folk and popular music records. Many encouraged their friends to sign up for charter flights the following summer. A much more active and intense communication between Yugoslavia and the immigrants and their descendants blossomed during the 1960s.

At this time the Yugoslav recording industry was maturing. In its early years, the Jugoton record company, established in Zagreb in 1947, was virtually the only company, and they put out relatively few releases. By the later 1950s, however, Yugoslavia was emerging from its postwar reconstruction. Material conditions had improved for the Yugoslav public. People had some disposable income to buy records. In 1958 RTB (Radio Televizije Beograd) established a records division, which competed with Jugoton. Much of the potential market consisted of recently urbanized peasants eager for the music that recalled their village roots, yet seemed modern and up to date. Thus the best-selling domestic artists performed in a modern but folk-influenced genre known as *narodnjak*. The two companies rushed to record and promote the *narodnjak* singers (Kos 1972). The newly arrived immigrants to America were especially eager for these records to remind them of their homeland. The music of the American *tamburaši* seemed too old-fashioned and the American elements in the tamburitza music sounded foreign to them.

To serve the new immigrants, and also the longer-established ethnic communities, Yugoslav ethnic stores began to proliferate. In the 1960s and 1970s such stores opened in nearly every city with a significant South Slavic community. Many of them were run by travel agents with whom one could book a flight to the homeland or arrange for relatives to travel to America. The stores typically sold a selection of current Yugoslav newspapers and magazines and often some specialty food items: bags of coffee from the familiar Yugoslav companies, jars of *ajvar*, a red pepper relish, raspberry, or cherry syrups, jams, pickled peppers, and bottles of mineral water from well-known springs in Yugoslavia. In the 1970s I was amused to find that the store in Gary, Indiana, run by Ljubo Stojanovski, a Macedonian immigrant, carried "muška voda," spring water reputed to cure impotence in men. By the later 1990s the number of these stores had decreased. Now, because of access to the Internet, immigrants read the homeland's news online, book flights at travel websites, and watch videos of their favorite singers on YouTube. The surviving stores emphasize selling food specialties.

The items in these stores that had the biggest impact on the tamburitza tradition were the records—small 45 rpm discs, LPs, cassettes, and CDs, mostly Jugoton and RTB releases, costing about the same as American records at the time. The majority of the records were *narodnjak* along with some urban popular music (*zabavna glazba*). Through these records *tamburaši* became acquainted with recent Yugoslav hits. And they could pick the songs they liked. Following the conventional practice in Yugoslav music stores, the store clerk would play some of the record for a customer deciding on a purchase. Another place to hear the current hits from Europe was on weekly ethnic radio programs. Some *tamburaši* recorded the radio broadcasts in order to learn the songs (Tarailo 1977).

The accompaniment to most of the *narodnjak* hits was an accordion-dominated *narodni orkestar*. The *tamburaši* needed to rework the song's arrangement for their instruments. *Narodnjak* hits that became tamburitza standards included "Jeremija" by Tozovac, "Sliku tvoju ljubim" by Tomo Zdravković, and "Kafu mi draga ispeci" by Predrag Gojković. Two American combos made an able synthesis of tamburitza combo and *narodni orkestar* styles: Mirko Roknich of Ohio, and Lira of Detroit. Both combos had immigrant and American-born members and included *narodnjak* songs in their repertoires.

The search for new tamburitza material can be intense. Competing with the other combos, *tamburaši* try to be the first in their community to perform a new hit song. American-born *tamburaši* rarely compose new songs, although some make up additional, often humorous verses, to existing songs. Few of the American *tamburaši* were educated in Serbian or Croatian, and most tamburitza repertoire is in those languages; the limits on their language ability thus handicap them in writing lyrics. An unusual original composition was an English-language song paying homage to Chicago's Popovich Brothers, written by members of the Knez Jakovac Orchestra of St. Louis. In the 1990s Vjeko Dimter, a talented *tamburaš* and outstanding songwriter, emigrated from Slavonia to the United States to perform as a member of the Duquesne University Tamburitzans. His original songs are a mainstay of the repertoire of Otrov, the combo in which he plays *bugarija*.

Dance music is an important part of the repertoire of tamburitza combos. Although playing for dancing does not generate many tips, in order to get bookings it is important also to satisfy the dance enthusiasts. At many community events a combo will first play non-dance vocal selections, and then finish off with several dance tunes. The tunes are associated with a particular dance step and are typically played as instrumental music without singing, even though many of the tunes like "Milica," "Seljančica," "Zaplet," and "Šetano kolo" do have lyrics that the combos occasionally sing. The combo tries to maintain the momentum of the dancing by picking tunes that will keep dancers on the floor. After a fast kolo or *drmeš*, for instance, they might pick a slow Macedonian *oro* to allow the dancers to continue dancing but also to catch their breath. Line dances predominate at the ethnic events, but

Vjeko Dimter (1969–) (*third from right*) jamming with members of Otrov at TamFest, Pittsburgh, 2003. (Photo by author)

combos will typically include a few couples' dances in polka and waltz tempo. "Vatrugasna polka" or "Kada čujem tambure" are popular polkas. "Kukavica" and "Samo nemoj ti" are well-known songs in waltz tempo. They might do a swing jazz tune like "In the Mood" or a rock number at or near the end of a set.

JANIKA, ZVONKO, AND KIČO

It is impossible to overestimate the influence of two outstanding ensembles from Yugoslavia that, beginning in the 1970s, enthralled the world of tambura: Janika Balaž with the singer Zvonko Bogdan, and Krunoslav "Kičo" Slabinac and the Slavonski Bećari. Janika Balaž was born in 1925 to a Hungarian-speaking Romani family in the vicinity of Zrenjanin in Vojvodina. He began to play violin in coffeehouses at the age of ten. He soon switched to tambura, specializing in the *prim*, an instrument seldom used in the Vojvodina Romani tambura ensembles. As a young man, he led a combo in Subotica, and then from 1948 to 1951 he held a position in the orchestra of Radio Titograd in Montenegro. When Radio Novi Sad formed in 1951, Janika returned to his native Vojvodina, by day playing the lead *prim* in the radio tamburitza orchestra directed by Sava Vukosavljev, a job that he held until his death in 1988. At night, he played with his own eight-man tamburitza ensemble that had a long engagement across the Danube from Novi Sad in the restaurant in the Petrovaradin Fortress (Klajić 2004).

Zvonko Bogdan, a member of the Bunjevac ethnic group, Croatians from the Dinaric Mountains who settled in Vojvodina in the eighteenth century, is an accomplished singer and talented composer of original songs. Born in 1942 in the Vojvodina town of Sombor, he spent much of his childhood on the farm (*salaš*) of his maternal grandfather. At age nineteen he went to Belgrade to study drama. He took singing jobs to support his studies, but his singing sideline soon overtook his school work. Zvonko's steady singing engagement at Belgrade's Hotel Union lasted nearly thirty years. Zvonko also began to perform regularly to the accompaniment of the eight-man ensemble of Janika Balaž. The Balaž-Bogdan combination has produced some of the most outstanding tamburitza music of all time (Panović 2006). I was fortunate to have several occasions to attend performances, both at the Hotel Union, where tambura instruments were not used, and at Petrovaradin.

Janika's orchestra of Romani musicians played in a highly improvisational and intricate style. Although the players seemed to be in a constant simultaneous improvisation, they were nevertheless able to attain unity even when playing in very free rubato tempos. Sometimes they seemed to be able to read each other's minds.

Born to Romani families with generations of musicians, their musical spontaneity was part of their heritage. Moreover, their daily life was full of music; as members of the Radio Novi Sad orchestra they practiced five mornings a week, and then they played six evenings a week in the Petrovaradin restaurant.

Zvonko's singing style was obviously influenced by his dramatic training. He still has a commanding, dignified stage presence and sings with

Zvonko Bogdan (*left*) with the Janika Balaž tamburitza orchestra. (Photo by author)

immaculate diction and understated emotion. His live and recorded performances not only revitalized interest in the traditional folk and *starogradske pjesme*, but some of his most successful songs are original compositions in the traditional style. "Ej salaši na severu Bačke," "Govori se da me varaš," "Kraj jezera jedna kuća mala," "Bunjevačko prelo," and "Već odavno spremam mog mrkoga" are five of his most famous compositions. So fully has Zvonko remained faithful to the traditional song style that many people take his originals for old folk songs. Many of his songs draw on nostalgia for his rural upbringing on the *salaš*.

Zvonko raises horses for harness racing and a number of his songs ("Odsedlaću moga vranog ždrebca," "Do dva konja a obadva vrana") deal with love of horses. *Zvonko Bogdan peva za vas*, perhaps his most influential LP album, is known among American *tamburaši* as "the horse-head album" owing to the cover photograph of Zvonko patting the neck of a favorite black horse. Zvonko is obviously very passionate about his racing endeavors as two more of his albums feature photographs of him with horses. On the album simply titled *Zvonko Bogdan* there is a cover photo of him driving a racing sulky pulled by his beloved horse Diktat. The inner fold of this gateleg album features Zvonko's writings: a biography of Diktat and a short article about another hobby of his, racing carrier pigeons.

During the 1990s, dismayed by the wartime conditions in his home region, Zvonko spent a few years working with thoroughbred horses at the Arlington Park race track near Chicago. In that period he also made several singing appearances, usually accompanied by Chicago's Slanina tamburitza orchestra.

By the mid-1970s most American combos were eagerly learning numbers from the "horse-head album." A group of young men, members of the Duquesne University Tamburitzans, formed a combo called Cigani (the Gypsies), and they tried to replicate the style of Janika's orchestra.

Janika's influence in America was achieved despite minimal performances in America. In 1973 the Balaž orchestra was brought to the United States to appear at the Smithsonian Folklife Festival (without Zvonko), but despite numerous inquiries about booking an American tour of Zvonko with Janika, their regular playing gigs in Yugoslavia made it difficult. It was not until the summer of 1980 that the Balaž-Bogdan combination managed to make its sole tour to the States and Canada for several performances.

After Janika's death, several members of the original eight-man ensemble continued to play under the leadership of Mile Nikolić. This ensemble performed in the United States in the summer of 2004, notably at the Tamburaland festival in Pittsburgh.

In 1979, as a part of the observance of the eighty-fifth anniversary of their founding, the Croatian Fraternal Union (CFU) organized a marathon musical tour. The program featured the tamburitza orchestra from Osijek's cultural and artistic society (kulturno i umjetničko društvo, KUD) Pajo Kolarić along with Krunoslav "Kičo" Slabinac and the Slavonski Bećari. More than twenty concerts were scheduled in most of the larger Croatian ethnic communities in Canada and in the eastern and midwestern states—in Pittsburgh and several smaller cities in western Pennsylvania, in Youngstown, Cleveland, Akron, Detroit, Chicago, Milwaukee, Whiting, Indiana, St. Louis, and Kansas City. Kičo, with his booming voice and emotive singing, turned out to be the star of the show. Born in Osijek in 1944, Kičo was a well-known popular singer in Yugoslavia for songs like his 1972 hit "Zbog jedne divne crne žene." In 1971 he represented Yugoslavia in the Eurovision popular song contest. In the mid-1970s Kičo began to emphasize his Slavonian Croatian heritage by performing folk songs, dressed in traditional village costume, accompanied by the tamburitza combo Slavonski Bećari, directed by *primaš* Antun "Tuca" Nikolić. In 1975 *Hej bećari*, his first *tamburica* LP, was released followed by *Seoska sam lola* in 1979. He also teamed up with the established Slavonian folk singer Vera Svoboda on duet recordings. A few American *tamburaši* already had been aware of his records, but the 1979 tour made Kičo's Slavonian songs and the Slavonski Bećari's tight, transparent music all the rage. Rabid fans drove hundreds of miles from concert to concert to see the show again and again. Kičo's records and cassettes hawked at the concerts were eagerly snatched up.

In contrast to Janika's Romani style, which is more flowing, overwhelming the listener with a wall of endlessly intercascading improvisational parts, Tuca Nikolić's Croatian style seems tight, clear, and

Krunoslav "Kičo" Slabinac (1944–). (Courtesy of Croatia Records d.d.)

precise. Like Janika, they are playing intricate melodies, countermelodies, and obbligatos, much of it improvised; the overall impression they give is of a complex, well-oiled machine, functioning like clockwork. The musicians in Janika's band were so skilled that their virtuoso playing seemed effortless. I was amazed that the free improvisations of those nonchalant, almost bored-looking Romani musicians managed to fit together so beautifully.

The songs on the Bogdan and Slabinac LPs became "the latest" style and immensely influential on American *tamburaši*.

Awareness of the Old Country culture had declined over a long period of lessened contact between North America and the former-Yugoslav lands. By the 1970s, there were very few active *tamburaši* who were themselves immigrants and therefore had firsthand knowledge of the homeland. There were a few exceptions—Julius Peškan, a Romani violinist, and Ivo Kućan, a *berde* player, were immigrants. A few important *tamburaši*, the Kapugi brothers and Steve Jurkovich, were born in America, but their parents had taken them, when they were children, back to Europe. They returned to America as young men. With few exceptions, by the 1970s most of the *tamburaši* in the States were American-born children or grandchildren of South Slavic immigrants who came to this country in the period between 1890 and 1924. The immigrants' descendants, often of mixed ethnic parentage, had diminishing knowledge of the languages and general culture of the European homeland, despite their love of tamburitza music. At Indiana University in the mid-1970s, I had a visit from a Croatian American college student, Tom Glibota, a *tamburaš*. I asked him if he could speak Croatian. "No, but I can sing it," he replied cheerfully, and to prove it he launched into "Čuješ mala."

If *tamburaši* had been members of junior tamburitza groups or the Duquesne University Tamburitzans, their awareness of Old World culture might have been enhanced. The suites of songs and dances performed by these groups and the costumes worn were, and still are, regionally defined—songs and dances from Slavonia, from Lika, or Posavina. This awareness tends to be limited to the specific material in the choreography. As a result of the fading awareness of Old World regional distinctions, it was possible to hear combo musicians playing a song from one region in a style of another. I heard a young violinist playing the Dalmatian song "Da nije ljubavi" in a fast Rumanian-influenced style typical of the Banat region. Sometimes lyrics were sung in a dialect inappropriate to the song's origins. For example, a combo of young brothers whose grandparents came from Gorski Kotar in western Croatia sang the popular song from Dubrovnik "Na palme njisu grane" in the ekavian dialect prevalent around Belgrade.

When it comes to language knowledge, most of the second generation *tamburaši* can carry on a simple conversation in Serbian or Croatian, which they learned as children from their immigrant parents. Most of the next generation, many of mixed background, know only a few words and phrases in Serbian or Croatian. Despite this lack of language facility, almost all tamburitza song repertoire continues to be sung in Serbian or Croatian, learned by rote, and often mouthed without understanding. There has been no significant move toward adoption of songs with English lyrics.

Language can be a point of contention between younger *tamburaši* and the older or recently immigrated audience members. When an old-timer comments that the singers are mispronouncing the lyrics, young *tamburaši* tend to react defensively. A few of them, however, have made an effort to better learn Croatian or Serbian, especially in recent years when they have made transatlantic trips and interacted with the European *tamburaši*.

A network of acquaintance and friendship exists among combo musicians across the North American continent. Moreover, the network has increasingly spread to Croatia thanks in large part to the few *tamburaši* from Europe who became Duquesne Tamburitzans, like Vjeko Dimter and Dario Barišić, and to Jerry Grcevich, who spends a good deal of time in Croatia, playing with the musicians there. *Tamburaši* follow each other's music, attend performances by other groups, and travel to events like the TAA Extravaganza, the CFU's TamFest, and the Junior Tamburitzans' annual conclave. They often tip each other in the traditional manner.

Tamburitza combos show no sign of disappearing from the American musical scene. Young musicians are brought into established groups when a vacancy occurs, and talented young musicians continue to form new ensembles. Sometimes tamburitza music seems to be an inherited addiction; the children of many important combo musicians have carried on the tradition. In Zagreb, one of Milwaukee's combos, Father Steve Jurkovich, his son Michael, daughter Patsy, son-in-law Paul Lucas, and nephew Ivo Kućan made up the ensemble. In Chicago, the Sinovi combo began with sons of Kirin and Gornik family *tamburaši* plus a few unrelated friends.

Sometimes an older *tamburaš* will help a young combo to get started. Nick Skertich, formerly of the Skertich Brothers and Veseljaci, assisted and played with the young members of the northwest Indiana combo Plavi Vjetar until they were prepared to continue without him. Old combos break up, elder *tamburaši* pass away, but always new groups form and the American tamburitza combo tradition seems to have a bright future.

SMALL ENSEMBLES IN EUROPE

In Croatia small tamburitza ensembles also are plentiful. Nearly every village, town, and city in inland Croatia (and in parts of Vojvodina) has one or more musical groups featuring tamburitza. The majority of such assemblages are rather informal. Most of the time they maintain only a potential existence. When an occasion arises that calls for this type of music, the players get together, rehearse a time or two, and play for the festivity, possibly a relative's wedding, a traditional holiday, or a folklore festival. Afterward they go back to their regular occupations, perhaps not playing again for many months until the next occasion arises. Such musicians may have learned to play tamburitza solely by ear, in a school orchestra, or as a member of a KUD (cultural and artistic society). Often there has been a combination of formal and informal learning. A musician might learn the basics in school and then improve by jamming with other musicians.

Ensembles of this type may be paid a fee or only receive drinks and food for playing. Because the KUD that performs at a folklore festival is defined as an amateur society, everyone usually performs for free. Since the money to be divided is not a concern, as long as a player can contribute musically an attitude of "the more the merrier" prevails. The ensembles may become large—ten or twelve players are not uncommon.

There are also situations when a KUD hires a professional band to accompany them for an important performance. Since the professional bands can receive high fees for playing weddings and similar private festivities, they are sometimes reluctant to accompany a KUD that cannot usually afford to pay as well.

The more business-like model is typical for American *tamburaši*. Although impromptu combos of junior tamburitzans or adult players may form to play for dances, have jam sessions, and the like, a working combo that performs professionally normally has its official name, business cards, recordings to sell, and some have created websites. In some cities, in order to play in taverns or restaurants, it was necessary for them to become members of the local musicians' union. A different musician might substitute for an absent player at a job or an extra part might be played by someone "sitting in," but the regular combo members always understand that musician's temporary status in the combo.

There are, of course, formally organized bands that play in Croatia as well. In the 1970s and 1980s, most of the groups that played professionally in public venues and for weddings and private dances were rural pop music or *narodnjak* bands. However, there were tambura groups like Bisernica (the ensemble that played regularly at the Zagreb brewery's restaurant), Zagrebački Muzikaši, and Ex Pannonija: *tamburaši* originally from Slavonia who formed a band in Zagreb. Farther east there was Tuce Nikolić's Slavonski Bećari; Čingilingi čarda, a group that played in Osijek and Beograd; Tamburica 5 from Tuzla; Đelem Đelem, composed of Vojvodina Romani players; and Cigani Ivanovići, specializing in Russian and Romani material, and many more.

In the 1970s and 1980s, small Romani bands remained important in Vojvodina and also in parts of Slavonia and Podravina, in areas close to the Hungarian border. While Romani continue to face prejudices from the mainstream population, their music is nonetheless greatly appreciated. Because of their social position, Romani performances traditionally were imbued with the notion that entertainers were socially inferior to their mainstream audiences. The situation was similar for

Jewish klezmer musicians in Eastern Europe and for African American musicians in the United States.

Since many Romani specialized as professional musicians, they were also obliged to cater to their audience's tastes. In order to receive tips, they may have had to ignore ethnic slurs against them. Many songs in their repertoires have lyrics that perpetuate stereotypes about Romani, frequently using the term "Cigani," which many Romani feel is pejorative. The so-called Gypsy style tends to emphasize minor keys, frequently uses the czardas rhythm, accelerating tempos and showy virtuoso instrumental pyrotechnics.

The negative social attitude about Romani is part of a general prejudice against professional musicians, excepting classical performers. A *tambura*š from Slavonia, Gavro Bajic, told me that the statement "svirač ne može biti dobar domačin" (a musician cannot be a good head of the house) was practically a proverb in his village Voćin. Chicago tamburitza maker Michael Hlad (a son of the noted artisan Ivan Hlad) related

Milan Marković, leader of a Romani tamburitza group from Novi Sad, Serbia, performing in Pittsburgh, 2004. (Photo by author)

the following story to demonstrate that attitude. As a boy in his native Veliko Trgovišće (a town in Zagorje, Croatia), Mike was secretly working on a little tambura, learning to make the instrument. His grandfather discovered him working on it and asked the child where he hid it when not at work. Unsuspecting, Mike told him. The next day he found that the old man had deceived him; he had taken the small instrument from the hiding place and burned it in the stove. "Why?" I asked. "He didn't want me to be a bum. They say guys who play music never amount to anything" (M. Hlad 1977).

In Europe there are numerous regional stylistic distinctions among small tambura groups, but they may be divided into two general zones, eastern and western. The eastern zone includes Banat, Bačka Srem, and Slavonia, while the western embraces Podravina, Međimurje, Banija, Zagorje, Prigorje, and Gorski Kotar. Outside musical influences from Rumania, Serbia, and Hungary predominate in the eastern zone. In the west they come from the Alpine Slovenian/Austrian area but also from Hungary.

The music of the most common dance forms in the two areas can illustrate the musical differences between the zones. In the East, the kolo is predominant. For a kolo, a lead *prim* or violin plays intricate improvisation on a relatively simple unarticulated melody to the rhythmic backing in 2/4 time of a *bugarija* and *berde*. Music for the kolo is a short repetitive figure, which may stay in the same key or modulate to other keys following the circle of fifths (C–G–D–A–E, and so forth). The repetitive, circular sense of the music is enhanced by the melodic segments that often end on a dominant chord, leading the music back to the tonic at the beginning of the next phrase.

In contrast, in the West, *drmeš* is the predominant dance form. Like the kolo, it is in 2/4 time, but the melody lines are more articulated, played with less improvisation or embellishment, and the chordal patterns are symmetrical, moving from tonic to dominant and back to tonic.

These distinctions may illustrate the prevailing trends in the two zones, but there is also much overlap. Musicians in each of the zones often play pieces that originated in the other zone, and some pieces originating in the eastern zone have more western features and vice versa.

In the eastern zone there are more small groups using only *tambure*. In the western area, an accordion playing in an Alpine-influenced style is quite frequent. While violins are used in both zones, the western area has quite a few ensembles (*muzikaši*) in which the melodic lead is played by two violins, commonly called *gusle* in local dialect. Rhythm is provided by a small bowed string bass, called *bajs*. Especially in Podravina, a hammered dulcimer is often included in the ensembles.

In Europe as in America, by the 1970s some small tamburitza ensembles evolved into something approaching a rock band, including electric guitars, drums, amplified accordions, or keyboard synthesizers in the instrumental lineup. But even then, when my original research was conducted, the differences between the music of American and European tamburitza combos were quite distinct. In the next chapter, we will see that communications and travel advances have combined to diminish these distinctions.

CHAPTER 8

My Little (Global) Village

At the beginning of September 2003, five young musicians from the Philadelphia, Pittsburgh, and Cleveland areas, members of a recently formed tamburitza combo with the potent-sounding name Otrov (poison), jetted to Croatia to participate in Zlatne Žice Slavonije 2003, a festival of tamburitza music in Slavonska Požega. Although at that time Otrov had been in existence for only a few months, the musicians had known each other and most members had played together in various other aggregations during the past several years.

The message board on the Tamburaland website (www.tambura land.com, no longer accessible) filled up with good wishes to the band, which consisted of five American-born *tamburaši* in their twenties plus their bandmate and musical mentor Vjeko Dimter, then thirty-four, a Slavonac from Osijek, who had lived in Pennsylvania since 1989.

The next batch of messages was from tambura musicians and enthusiasts seeking and receiving advice on how to see or hear Otrov's performance in Požega, either online or via satellite TV. There were appreciative comments about their playing of "Selo moje malo" (My little village), an original tune composed by the group's *bugarija* player Vjeko Dimter. Otrov plays a lot of original material, much of which is composed by Dimter, who sometimes coauthors songs with Otrov's *primaš* Peter Kosovec, a fourth-generation American Croatian. On the message board there is a link to Otrov's picture as it appeared in the Scena section of the Zagreb newspaper *Večernji list*, a sponsor of the event.

On the day after the Požega festival, at a rehearsal of Graničari, an adult amateur tamburitza orchestra and choir in the Milwaukee area, the director Patsy Jurkovich-Lucas played three tunes from the *Zlatne Žice Slavonija* 2003 sampler CD that she downloaded to her home computer that morning. Members of Graničari especially liked the song "Tajna" (Secret) by a combo called Estam, a group they had never heard of before. By the next week, using music notation software on her computer, Patsy had written and printed out her arrangement of "Tajna," which the group immediately began to rehearse. Graničari included the song in their program when they traveled to Pittsburgh in late October 2003 to perform at TamFest 2003, a gathering of North American adult amateur tamburitza orchestras sponsored by the Croatian Fraternal Union.

The Otrov tambura band, 2005. (Courtesy of Otrov)

A few days after the Požega festival, Vjeko Dimter, the webmaster of Tamburaland.com, stated that he would post pictures of the festival. Soon dozens of photos taken by Otrov members appeared on the website documenting not only their performance and travels but also their jam sessions and bacchanalian visits with friends and relatives in Croatia. Humorous, sarcastic, and appreciative comments about the pictures flooded the Tamburaland message board.

The events just described are typical but notable happenings on the contemporary tamburitza scene in the United States and Canada. Such doings, of course, would have been impossible in 1983 when I finished the original version of this work. Otrov's trip to Požega in September 2003 and its musical repercussions constitute a complex act of cultural communication taking place in a contemporary context where technological advances have accelerated the transmission of traditional knowledge and creative expression. Tamburitza once was limited to oral transmission, but it has since entered whatever medium of communication available in its cultural environment. Little could we have dreamed twenty years ago that the available media might expand so rapidly and that an instantaneous worldwide communications network like the Internet might arise.

The tamburitza tradition, like everything else, has changed, especially over the past twenty or so years. In addition to the effects of communications and travel technology, there have been effects stemming from the big political changes in Croatia and Vojvodina, the downfall of Communist political rule in Europe, the establishment of Croatia as an independent state, the breakup of former Yugoslavia, and the Homeland War. And these changes may be linked. Some commentators have seen a causal connection between the international communications revolution and the downfall of authoritarian regimes (Katz 2000, 4).

There is one thing about the tamburitza tradition in the United States that has not changed: it remains virtually unknown to most Americans who are not of Croatian or Serbian descent. The Pittsburgh area is, on the other hand, something of an exception. There, the Duquesne University Tamburitzans have a higher public profile, but most Pittsburghers know Tamburitzans only as the name of one specific group,

Duquesne University's performing ensemble, not realizing it is also the name of a family of instruments and a music tradition.

Despite occasional performances in auspicious settings such as the Smithsonian Folklife Festival and the National Folk Festival, tamburitza music remains little known to many if not most Americans. While introducing the outstanding Pittsburgh *primaš* Jerry Grcevich performing for the prestigious Folk Masters concert series with Chicago's Slanina orchestra, the folklorist Nick Spitzer called tamburitza "a great, unknown American traditional music" (Spitzer 1992).

Virtually no broadly conceived studies of American tamburitza have been published since Walter Kolar, the former director of the Duquesne ensemble, wrote *A History of the Tambura* (Kolar 1975). A welcome exception is the article "Hrvati i tambura u Sjedinjenim Državama" by Stjepan Sremac (Sremac 2002). In addition, it would have been surprising for a group that was formed only a few months before to be performing at an important festival. It also would be surprising twenty years ago to have a combo with members from three different fairly distant cities. These days the personnel of tamburitza combos is much more fluid. A cadre of thirty or forty of the best musicians, living in various cities in North America, all know one another and are capable of getting together and making excellent music together. This situation is parallel to what happened in certain other ethnic musical traditions in America. Commenting on his Irish American group The Green Fields of America, the folklorist/performer Mick Moloney said, "There's kind of a network of about maybe twenty musicians around, and then people come over from Ireland, like Tommy Sands, to join us now and again. At a moment's notice, a group can evolve" (qtd. in Winick 1993).

An example of how this can happen in the tambura world occurred at the Midwest Folklife Festival in Waterloo, Iowa, in June 2001. Almost a year in advance, the festival's organizers had booked Vatra, a Croatian tamburitza combo from Milwaukee. In the meantime, though, the combo had started to fall apart. A marriage, job changes, and relocations had altered the lives of the young men who made up the group, and they stopped playing actively a few months earlier. Wanting to honor the contract to play this important job, the Vatra Milwaukeeans called upon three members of the talented Kosovec family from

Detroit to join them: the multi-instrumentalist Peter, his cousin David (*berde*), and Peter's sister Sonya, a vocalist. They flew into Waterloo a few hours before the performance, rehearsed together for less than two hours in their hotel rooms, and played an outstanding program on the festival's main stage. Their music was polished, well received by the audience, and especially appreciated by a large number of Bosnians, mostly from Velika Kladuša, who now live in Waterloo.

At the beginning of the 1980s most tamburitza combos in the United States and Canada were comprised of musicians who lived in the same city. The membership in these bands changed slowly, as did the core repertoire expected by their fans. Such bands generally had a regular engagement at a certain tavern or hall. For example, in South Chicago you could hear the Star Serenaders every week at the Golden Shell restaurant. A short drive away there was the Rafters, a tavern that always featured local tamburitza combos like the Kapugi Brothers, Dunav, or the Popovich Brothers. In Milwaukee, Jack Yelich played regularly at the Saratoga, a bar on South Sixteenth Street. Similar tamburitza bars with a regular house band or a rotation of a few bands existed in many North American Croatian and Serbian communities.

In recent years, fewer taverns and restaurants offer any sort of live music. Moreover, fewer still would want to offer an esoteric form of ethnic folk music because most seek to attract a broader clientele. Furthermore, restaurant owners face another disincentive to hiring live musicians: the substantial payment sought by representatives of the ASCAP and BMI music publishing organizations. These organizations have become increasingly aggressive in seeking payments for the live performance of material copyrighted through them (Wierichs 2003).

Now there are virtually no tambura bars in the Midwest. Bronko's Restaurant in Crown Point, Indiana, operated by Montenegrin American Nick Tarailo, himself a musician, perhaps is the only such venue that regularly books tambura combos. A few bars, like the Milwaukee Ale House, the Nomad (also in Milwaukee), and the Gypsy Café in Pittsburgh feature an eclectic array of "World Music" performers and occasionally book tamburitza combos.

Because tamburitza enthusiasts can seldom head for a neighborhood tavern or restaurant to hear the music in their local community, there is a greater reliance upon a network community, the Croatian ethnic events, picnics, dinners, dances, and festivals, especially those sponsored by lodges of the Croatian Fraternal Union. These events are planned long in advance as tamburitza music is considered an important component and it always featured in their advertisements. For the larger events, like the CFU Ski Holiday or the National Golf Tournament, band members from different cities may converge, driving or flying in from a considerable distance. The performers' fee, CD sales, and the generous tips skewered on their tuning pegs by appreciative listeners make it financially worthwhile.

There are now more large national events with a tamburitza music theme, and people are willing and able to travel to them. Promoting amateur tamburitza activity is a core raison d'être of the Croatian Fraternal Union. Their annual Junior Cultural Federation Festival continues to be the most important gathering of North American youth tamburitza orchestras; approximately thirty such ensembles participate every year. Since the mid-1980s the CFU also has sponsored TamFest, a gathering of a growing number of adult amateur tamburitza orchestras. In 2003 the adults caught up in terms of the number of groups. Thirty-one adult groups participated.

The Tamburitza Extravaganza continues to be a gathering of professional combos sponsored by the Tamburitza Association of America, and since 2003 there is a new national event, the Tamburaland Festival, held in the Pittsburgh area and organized by the younger musicians involved with the Tamburaland.com website.

With more mobile musicians and audiences, tamburitza music is being created more and more in a national context. As a result, North American regional stylistic distinctions are diminishing rapidly. Cell phones and smart phones are now ubiquitous. This has made it common for musician friends in distant cities to casually hear each other's music. At a recent Graničari rehearsal in Milwaukee, a Pittsburgh friend of the *prim* player Nancy Požgaj called up and listened to a number the Graničari members were practicing. The leader of Chicago's Sloboda Junior Tamburitzans, Joe Kirin, described his phone call from Cincinnati to Philadelphia when he had the honor of being the guest conductor of the "mass performance" of all the youth orchestras at the 2003

Junior Cultural Federation Festival: "Just as the performance was about to begin, I got on the cell phone to call Vjeko [Dimter] so he could hear the performance. A couple of directors and maybe others saw me and were [thinking] like, 'Oh my God, he's talking on the cell phone during the performance.' So I became the first director to use a cell phone during a mass performance and a new age has begun" (Kirin 2003).

Twenty years ago it was still easy to pick out regional styles in the tamburitza combos of North America. There was indeed a distinct sound from groups in Chicago, Pittsburgh, or Youngstown. Nowadays, the younger musicians are more likely to play in a unified style more influenced by Croatian bands like Zlatni Dukati (now called Najbolji Hrvatski Tamburaši), Gazde, Patria, or Berde Band, whose recordings have become readily available, than to play in the style of the older *tamburaši* in their local communities. As a result, the differences that used to be obvious between an American and a Croatian tamburitza group also are becoming less apparent. To sound like the European bands and therefore more "authentic" has long been a goal of most American *tamburaši*. The American stylistic "accent" developed as a consequence of their degree of isolation from the wellsprings of the music—in Croatia and Vojvodina.

There is also less isolation and there are increasing cross-Atlantic influences in the tamburitza tradition. Moreover, the direction of musical influences is not exclusively from Europe to America. Pittsburgh's Jerry Grcevich has emerged since the 1990s as one of the world's finest tamburitza musicians. Jerry grew up playing with his father Joseph and uncle Marko in their Sloboda tamburitza combo. In 1976 the CFU Junior Federation Festival was held in Zagreb for the first time. Jerry, still a teenager but already an excellent musician, participated. He traveled also to Novi Sad, where he met and established a lasting connection with Zvonko Bogdan and Janika Balaž.

Around 1980, Jerry produced two influential LP albums on which he played all five types of tamburitza instrument, recorded sound-on-sound. His music was imbued with a profound influence from the Romani style of Janika Balaž and the Bunjevac style of Zvonko Bogdan. There was an unprecedented emphasis on instrumental virtuosity in all sections of the score. Younger American *tamburaši* were stunned.

Writing for Tamburaland in 2002, Chicago's noted *brač* player Joe Kirin, then director of the Sloboda Junior Tamburitzans, a former member of Sinovi and Slanina, and currently the leader of Tamburitza Rroma, commented, "I . . . became hooked on Jerry and his playing. When his second album came out, I listened to it correctly and was again amazed. I tried to learn much of the material and had difficulty with it. His music caused a major shift in the style and technique of the music I was performing" (Kirin 2002).

Jerry proved to be a conduit for the influence of the Romani players, especially the Janika Balaž Orchestra. Like Jerry and Janika, many American *tamburaši* began to retune their instruments a whole step higher and to use larger, rectangular bone picks. The preference of Janika's group for the high-quality instruments made by the Sombor luthier Lajos Bocan spread to American players. The emphasis on technical virtuosity required finely crafted instruments. Today, in addition to the Bocan instruments, skilled players obtain *tambure* from Lado Krklec in New York City or Marinko Katulić, a luthier who lives south of Zagreb in Turopolje.

Jerry Grcevich.
(Courtesy of
Jerry Grcevich)

Zvonko Bogdan and another important singer, Miro Škoro, had extended sojourns in the United States during the 1980s. Both wound up in musical collaboration with Jerry making recordings with him. In a 1998 interview, Bogdan placed Jerry alongside Pero Tumbaš, Macika Petrović, Maksa Popov, and Janika Balaž in the ranks of the five greatest *primaši* of all time (Spiranović 1998). Shortly before the outbreak of the Homeland War, Miro Škoro and Jerry coauthored and recorded "Ne dirajte mi ravnicu," a song that became immensely popular in war-torn Croatia. The song's lyrics proclaimed "ja ću se vratiti" (I will return)—a sentiment that gave voice to the yearnings for home of refugees and displaced persons.

Because of his high musical standards and his practice of playing all the parts on his recordings, it was rumored that Jerry was too much of a musical perfectionist ever to have a live band. But Jerry defied those predictions, forming the Jerry Grcevich Tambura Orchestra in 1993.

During the past few years, Jerry has spent several months living and making music in Croatia, recording with some of the finest Croatian *tamburaši*. His example has led the way for other American groups to travel to Croatia, seeking opportunities to play on an equal footing with their Croatian peers. For example, in 2002 and again in 2003 the Chicago group Boduli, which perform bluesy, rock-influenced numbers along with more traditional tambura repertoire, traveled to the Brodfest tamburitza music festival in Slavonski Brod.

Joe Kirin's comments provide the ultimate confirmation of Jerry Grcevich's stature in the world of tamburitza music: "Jerry is the best tambura player that I know, period. There has been Janika (Balaž), Hrvoje (Majić), Tuce (Antun Nikolić), and many others that we could argue who is better. None of them could play every position/tambura like Jerry" (Kirin 2002).

As they grow in their music, *tamburaši* seek out and learn new repertoire. The professional combos have adopted the "hit tune" model to attract attention. Even many amateurs are not content just to play and replay the old standards. In the past the American *tamburaši* always had to scrounge for new songs. "To get new repertoire, we used to have to wait for somebody to come back from a vacation in Europe with a suitcase full of 45s from the Jugoton store," commented Michael

Jurkovich, a noted *bugarija* player from Milwaukee (Jurkovich 2003). They needed to hear those records because very little composing of new repertoire was happening in America. By the 1960s, most of the *tamburaši* were American-born; they had limited Croatian or Serbian language skills. Very few American *tamburaši* composed songs in those languages. But the *tamburaši* did not follow the path taken by Polish American polka bands, adding many English-language songs to their repertoire. Except for an occasional American pop tune to sing at weddings, American tamburitza combos continue to shun singing in English.

Before the independence of Croatia, relatively few tamburitza recordings were produced in Yugoslavia so American *tamburaši* often learned the songs of the *narodni orkestri*, which emphasized the accordion played in an Eastern style. Many Serbian and Bosnian *narodnjak* songs, like Meho Puzić's "O majko, majko," Tozovac's "Jeremija," and Predrag Gojković's "Kafu mi draga ispeci," became common in the repertoire of American *tamburaši*, regardless of whether the instrumentalists were of Croatian or Serbian heritage.

After the outbreak of the Homeland War, inter-ethnic tensions between Croatian Americans and Serbian Americans increased, and some very vocal elements of audiences, both Serbian and Croatian, denounced the ethnically mixed repertoire. The Homeland War accelerated the process that was already going on in Serbian American communities to de-emphasize the tamburitza in favor of the accordion- or synthesizer-dominated *narodni orkestri*.

In contrast, Croatian American tamburitza was reinvigorated. The new political conditions in Croatia favored more tamburitza recordings. The appearance in 1989 of Zlatni Dukati's *Hrvatska Pjesmarica* album of previously suppressed patriotic songs was influential. Old, nearly forgotten songs like "Glasno jasno" and newer patriotic compositions like "Slavonac sam" worked their ways back into the repertoire. The story of how this earthshaking album came to be recorded reveals a fascinating connection between the Croatian and American tambura worlds.

The CFU continued the practice begun in 1979 with the Kićo Slabinac tour of sponsoring tours of the United States and Canada by groups from the homeland. In the summer of 1988 the featured band on the CFU tour was Zlatni Dukati, a group originally formed in 1983 in Štitar, the Slavonian hometown of several of its members. On the website of the group, renamed in 1996 the cocky moniker Najbolji hrvatski tamburaši (the best Croatian tamburitzans), we read: "On the CFU tour in America the idea was born to record an album of patriotic songs *Hrvatska Pjesmarica*, which would contribute a lot to the popularization of the band and tamburitza music in general, and at the same time would be a big contribution by our group to the liberating of the national spirit" (http://www.najboljihrvatskitamburasi.com/). The younger American *tamburaši* appreciate the old well-known songs from Kićo Slabinac and Vera Svoboda, but they become more excited by newer tunes from younger bands like Ex Panonnia, Berde Band, and Patria.

New repertoire from Europe has become much easier to access, ultimately leading to today's Internet postings and downloading of MP3s, to YouTube videos and Facebook connections. But having an artist like Vjeko Dimter, a talented and prolific composer of new tambura material, living and performing in the United States really is something new. Vjeko was born in Osijek in 1969. His father, Edgar Dimter, was a trumpet player in local dance bands. Vjeko began to play tambura and guitar at the age of ten and later became a member of the KUD Milica Križan amateur tamburitza ensemble (Dimter 2003).

In 1989 Vjeko went with Milica Križan on a performance tour of the United States. He had the opportunity to audition for the Duquesne University Tamburitzans and was awarded a scholarship. From 1989 to 1993 Vjeko studied psychology and jazz guitar, and performed all over the United States with the Duquesne Tamburitzans. During his college years he began to compose both tamburitza and popular music. He played in American pop and tamburitza combos, including the Jerry Grcevich Tambura Orchestra.

In 1995 and 1996 Vjeko relocated to Zagreb, where he collaborated with the well-known tamburitza groups Šarmeri and Gazde, composing some of their most successful hits—for example, Šarmeri's "Znam da me ne voliš" and Gazde's "U snu i ljubavi." Since late in 1996 Vjeko has lived in Philadelphia, working a day job as a computer specialist for a financial firm while also successfully pursuing his artistic efforts.

He put his computer skills to artistic use, launching the Tamburaland website late in 2001. Tamburaland connected tamburitza musicians and enthusiasts from around the world. The year 2002 brought many successes. Collaborating with Croatian pop star Oliver Dragojević, Vjeko composed "Sve bi dao za nju," which won the Croatian recording industry's Porin award for song of the year 2002 (the award is Croatia's equivalent to the American GRAMMY) (Dimter 2003). Also in 2002 Vjeko produced *Kuda idu godine*, a CD featuring mostly his own compositions that astonished the American tamburitza scene. On the CD he collaborated with Peter Kosovec, an outstanding young American tambura player who was then just twenty-one. Peter demonstrated the full blossoming of his talents on this recording.

Along with players like Ryan Werner of Milwaukee and Robi Sestili of Pittsburgh, Peter Kosovec is one of an amazing crop of young American *primaši* that have emerged in the past few years. The Kosovec family of Detroit has had a longtime influence upon the American tamburitza scene. Peter's grandfather Ludwig was a leader of the Detroit Tamburitza Orchestra. His father, Kenneth, has been a member of Lira and Momci with his brother Dennis. Ken was also the instructor for the youth group Detroit Star Tamburitzans. His mother, Bonnie, is an excellent vocalist. Peter got an early start in music. He recalls the moment at age five when his father put an instrument in his hand: "I remember the exact time he gave me the tambura in my living room. It's the same one I use today" (P. Kosovec 2003; Mikolajek 2001). His talent was obvious after just a few years in the Detroit junior group. He recorded his first CD in his basement studio at the age of thirteen, sharing vocal tasks with his mother and his sister Sonya. He and Sonya as well as his cousin David became members of the Duquesne University Tamburitzans.

Because of his virtuosity and his self-produced sound-on-sound recordings, Peter was thought of as the next generation's Jerry Grcevich, but there also are significant differences. Jerry developed his amazing talents in a greater degree of isolation. Before the 1990s, he seemed to be something of a reclusive genius. Through the 1980s, tamburitza enthusiasts eagerly anticipated the emergence of Jerry's inspiring self-produced recordings created in his home studio. As a Duquesne

Tamburitzan, Peter's musical skills were showcased in live shows far and wide. After graduation he remained in Pittsburgh and was one of the founders of the Otrov combo, bringing us full circle.

Since 2005, YouTube and other video-sharing sites have emerged as a major form of communication. Videos are recorded ever more commonly at any occasion, and you don't need to have sophisticated equipment to make a video. Not only are most compact digital cameras capable of recording videos, but smart phones have high-quality video recording capabilities. You can make a video of whatever you see and send it to your friends or post it on YouTube, your blog spot, or Facebook. The number of videos of tamburitza performances, recorded both in the United States and in Europe, is growing daily.

Today the American tamburitza tradition is healthy and shows no signs of decline. Young people continue to learn to play the tambura in more than thirty youth groups, mostly associated with the CFU Junior Cultural Federation, and their professional combos are making their mark. At the 2003 Tamburitza Extravaganza in Chicago, the teen members of the youngest participating professional combo, Mladi Fakini from Milwaukee, were greeted with much enthusiasm.

Tambura remains closely associated with the institutions of the Croatian ethnic community in America, even when, through intermarriage, many of those learning to play today have fewer Croatian ancestors. The younger generation takes for granted the availability of the Internet, multifunction cell phones, videos on YouTube, and easier travel, all of which are making the tamburitza combo tradition a more unified, global musical scene.

CHAPTER 9

Tamburitza Orchestras

s an "uplifted" form of peasant culture, the large tamburitza
orchestras are the most direct descendants of the musical ideas
of Ljudevit Gaj and the Illyrian movement. When I did my
field research in the 1970s, tamburitza orchestral ensembles were most
numerous in Croatia while Subotica in Vojvodina and Ruma in northern Serbia had important orchestras. The sphere of large tamburitza
orchestras includes professional orchestras, school orchestras, and adult
as well as youth amateur tamburitza societies.

Professional tamburitza orchestras have been a component of the
musical staff of government-sponsored radio and television stations.
In Vojvodina and Bosnia, respectively, Radio-Televizija (RTV) Novi
Sad and RTV Sarajevo maintained such orchestras. The strongest such
ensemble was established in Croatia in 1941 at RTV Zagreb, now called
Hrvatska Radio-Televizija (HRT). Many of the tambura musicians also
played other instruments in popular or classical ensembles. They rehearsed and performed pieces for broadcast as the featured attraction,
as on Radio Zagreb's longtime Friday morning broadcast *Sitne žice
tamburica*, or to accompany vocalists, generally professional popular
or operatic singers. Such singers required the accompaniment of an
orchestra for radio broadcasts, on recordings or at live performances,
which have been held since the 1960s in various cities and towns around
the country. Today, most festival performers are the best-known urban

popular recording artists. At the festivals they debut performances of compositions by songwriters who endeavor to compose new popular songs using elements of the host location's regional folk music. Those festivals in regions where the tamburitza is common regularly call upon a tamburitza orchestra to accompany the singers. For example, the HRT tamburitza orchestra has performed at festivals in Krapina, Slavonska Požega, Slavonski Brod, and Zagreb (Njikos 1978).

In Novi Sad and Sarajevo the majority of the musicians in the radio orchestras were of Romani ethnicity. Many of them began to play as aural musicians who became musically literate through working in the orchestra. As mentioned earlier, in addition to their full-time orchestra jobs, many of the Romani musicians play in smaller ensembles at taverns or restaurants (ibid.).

In Zagreb, in addition to the HRT orchestra, the national folk dance ensemble Lado employs an orchestra of about fifteen musicians to accompany the dancing-singing troupe. Although the Lado musicians play several types of Croatian traditional instruments, *tambure* are most frequent in their performances. Božo Potočnik, born in Zagreb in 1932, served as the ensemble's director for more than thirty years beginning in 1955. Božo Potočnik is an important composer of the core repertoire of Lado (suites of folk songs and dance tunes in a style that remains close to the village original). His music has been popularized through the performances and recordings of Lado. Amateur groups both in Europe and America have long been performing Lado-originated music and dance routines. The spread of Lado material has been aided by former Lado dancers and musicians who teach school orchestras or local amateur cultural and artistic societies (KUDs).

Though numerically few, the professional orchestral *tamburaši* have played an influential role. Many of the directors of the prominent orchestras also tend to be composers and arrangers of the music. Their compositions have been published and the sheet music distributed by the Prosvjetni Sabor Hrvatske (Department of Education of Croatia). Orchestras throughout former Yugoslavia and, to some extent, junior orchestras in North America, use these orchestral arrangements. A few of the most important composer/arrangers are Julije Njikoš, Sava Vukosavljev, Željko Bradić, Siniša Leopold, and Božo Potočnik.

Julije Njikoš (Osijek, 1924—Zagreb, 2010) began to play as a young member of the graphics workers' amateur tamburitza orchestra Tipograf (typographer). He became the director of the tamburitza orchestra in KUD Kraš and, in 1951, the director of the Radio Osijek tamburitza orchestra. He was an initiator and the first conductor of the Pajo Kolarić tamburitza orchestra, a still-active amateur group. In 1961 he was a founder and a driving force behind the ongoing Međunarodni festival hrvatske tamburaške glazbe (International Festival of Tamburitza Music) held annually in Osijek.

In the mid-1960s Njikoš and his wife, Vera Svoboda, a renowned singer, began a decades-long career of producing recordings of Slavonian and other Croatian folk songs on Jugoton Records (later Croatia Records). Some of the songs were arranged by Njikoš himself, and he directed the accompanying orchestra.

Njikoš proved to be one of the most prolific composers for tamburitza orchestra. He gained a deep knowledge of the music of Slavonian villagers, and as a result his compositions draw upon and remain close to the spirit of folk music. The titles of his compositions such as *Slavonska rapsodija* or *Šokačka predigra* proclaim their grounding in Slavonian traditional music. Indeed, his music cites passages from folk song and dance melodies. Because of their close ties to folk music, his works are musically accessible to wide audiences, and some of his pieces— *Pjesma bez riječi* (Song without words), *Izgubljena nada* (Lost hope), and *Romanca u G-duru* (Romance in G-major)—have become among the most popular and frequently performed of all orchestral compositions for tamburitza (ibid.).

While some leading twentieth-century composers for tamburitza, like Ernö Király or Tihomil Vidošić, utilized atonality and dissonance, this style seldom meets with common appreciation from a wide audience, although respected by sophisticated connoisseurs of classical music. Therefore these compositions are performed less frequently and then only by an orchestra with a highly sophisticated director. Njikoš, through his interesting juxtapositions of folk melodic motifs, was able to satisfy both the musically trained and untrained audiences.

Njikoš's work was best known in former Yugoslavia, but by the late 1970s, a few American orchestras began to discover his compositions.

On their 1979 American tour organized by the CFU, the Pajo Kolarić Orchestra from Osijek opened their show with Slavonska rapsodija, and soon thereafter a number of American tamburitza instructors were clamoring for the score. Thus the piece has entered the repertoire of several American junior tamburitza orchestras. In June 1982 Njikoš himself directed the Detroit Tamburitza Orchestra, the most proficient orchestral tamburitza group in North America, to accompany vocal performances by his wife, Vera Svoboda.

Njikoš remained extremely active his entire life, publishing an overview of the existing musical literature for tamburitza orchestra in 2007, only three years before he passed away in 2010 (Ferić 2011, 366–67).

Sava Vukosavljev (1914–96) made a great contribution to orchestral tamburitza music during his many years as director of the Tamburaški orkestar of Radio-Novi Sad. Born in Zagreb in 1914, he spent most of his life living in Belgrade and Novi Sad. His compositions such as *Pred spomenikom Paje Kolarića*, *Concertino za brač*, and *Vojvođanski popuri* blend modern, classical, and traditional music concepts. They remain popular with tamburitza orchestras in Croatia and Vojvodina. Vukosavljev also performed an invaluable service by helping to broaden the musical knowledge of his orchestra's *primaš*, the immensely influential Janika Balaž.

Željko Bradić, born in 1934 in Petrinje, has been a central figure in tamburitza education for more than fifty years. He comes from a musical family, and the compositions of his father, Zvonko Bradić, still are performed by Croatian tamburitza orchestras. Željko graduated from the Higher Pedagogical School in Zagreb in 1957 and became a music teacher in Samobor, achieving notable results with the children's tamburitza orchestra of the Janko Mišić elementary school. He was a founder of the Ferdo Livadić youth tamburitza orchestra in Samobor, one of the most award-winning ensembles of all time. Beginning in 1956, Željko instructed music teachers through the Croatian Pedagogical Academy in Zagreb and in summer seminars on the Adriatic coast to prepare them to direct large and small tamburitza orchestras. He is the author of a number of tamburitza instruction books, and he directed the tamburitza groups of the Zagreb-area amateur KUDs. In addition, Željko has written many orchestral arrangements of folk and popular songs, especially the folk songs of the Samobor vicinity (Ferić 2011, 379).

Since the mid-1980s, Siniša Leopold has emerged as arguably the leading figure in orchestral tamburitza music in Croatia. Born in Grubišno Polje in 1957, his family moved to Samobor when he was a child. He began to play tambura in the Janko Mišić elementary school orchestra with Željko Bradić as his instructor. As a youth he was active in the Ferdo Livadić orchestra. Leopold graduated from the Music Academy in Zagreb and in 1985 became a lecturer in the tamburitza section of that institution. The same year he became the chief conductor of the tamburitza orchestra of Croatian Radio-Television (HRT). Leopold increased the visibility of tamburitza on Croatian television by producing and directing numerous televised concerts. His New Year's Eve concerts titled *Valceri, polke i druge špelancije* (Waltzes, polkas, and other frolics) are a holiday TV ritual. Leopold continued and strengthened the tradition of excellence that the Croatian Radio-Television orchestra has maintained since its founding in the 1940s. In addition to playing the works of the earlier composers for tambura, Leopold has added to the repertoire his own compositions: *Lipo ti je kad se kuruz sije* (Corn planting time is pleasant) and *Tamburaško sijelo* (Tamburitza work bee). In 1992 he coauthored a tambura instruction book with Željko Bradić, and in 1995 he published *Tambura u Hrvata* (The tambura among the Croatians), an informative book on tambura music and history (ibid., 373–74).

While Leopold is dedicated to advancing the capabilities of tamburitza in serious orchestral music, he also has an appreciation for a wide variety of musical idioms: folkloric music, musical theater, contemporary classical-popular music fusion, and *etnoglazba*, the Croatian term for a type of world music that blends folk music with modern popular rhythms and new instrumental technology. Leopold has rearranged classics like "Storm," the final movement of Vivaldi's "Summer" concerto from *Le quattro stagioni*, and Beethoven's "Moonlight Sonata" (Sonata 14, op. 7, no. 2) using modern dance rhythms and synthesizers for the flamboyant Zagreb cellist Ana Rucner. He composed the music for the first tamburitza musical, *Janica i Jan*, about the Croatian Olympic skiing sensations Janica Kostelić and her brother Ivan Kostelić.

He has conceived three musical television series that have played on HRT for several years, *Svirci moji* (My musicians), *Za srce i dušu* (For heart and soul), and *U ozračju tambure* (In the atmosphere of the tambura), which showcase performances by performers of folk, classical, and vernacular music. He has composed music for television and film, winning the Golden Arena award (the Croatian equivalent of the Oscar) in 2004 for the soundtrack of *Duga mračna noć* (Long dark night), starring Goran Višnjić (the Croatian actor best known as a longtime regular on the U.S. television series *ER*). Recently he composed the music for the 2011 film *Kotlovina* (Grilled pork chops).

Although open to modern innovations, Leopold is dedicated to preserving older forms of Croatian traditional music. He serves as a music instructor for the School of Croatian Folklore and devotes considerable effort to advancing tambura in Croatian emigrant communities. Leopold often travels to North America, South America, and Australia to conduct folklore seminars in Croatian emigrant communities (Leopold 2011).

In September 2004, the HRT tamburitza orchestra, directed by Leopold and joined by the singers Barbara Orthman and Đani Stipaničev, was featured on a CFU-sponsored tour of Croatian communities in several American cities. They made a tremendous impression. Blogging on the Tamburaland.com website, Ken Kosovec, the director of the Detroit Tamburitza Orchestra, in 2011 raved about their performance and spoke of the near-mishap that demonstrated their aplomb.

I had the pleasure to witness the first performance ever in America of this ensemble on Friday Sept. 17, 2004, in Kansas City. Unfortunately, due to hurricane Ivan, their connection in Georgia delayed their arrival almost eighteen hours! . . . There was however a major problem. One of their luggage pieces that did not arrive contained all of their [sheet] music. At the airport they were assured it would be arriving on the next flight and delivered immediately to them. Well, the concert started at 7:30 p.m. with no music! As true professionals under the capable direction of Siniša Leopold, they began the program anyway with some changes from their original program. Fifteen minutes into the program the music arrived and they briefly paused and then continued their original program. (http://www.tamburaland.com, no longer accessible)

Their subsequent performances in St. Louis, St. Paul, Chicago, Cleveland, and Pittsburgh thrilled the largely Croatian American audiences and inspired American *tamburaši*.

Although the professionals are influential, the overwhelming majority of tamburitza orchestra members are amateurs. This tamburitza musical amateurism remains strong. In Europe, tamburitza orchestras are most common in Croatia and in the Vojvodina province of Serbia, with a few additional orchestras in northern parts of Serbia. There are also amateur orchestras in Slovenia and in Bosnia-Herzegovina.

Tamburitza in Croatian Schools and Amateur Societies

Since 1952 tamburitza instruction has been a regular feature of music education in Croatian schools, contributing to the abundance of tamburitza orchestras in Croatia. At the Pedagogical Academy and at summer seminars on the Adriatic coast organized by the Prosvjetni sabor Hrvatske (Department of Education of Croatia), music teachers have an opportunity to learn or improve the skills to form and lead tamburitza orchestras. Smaller schools in rural areas, which may not be able to afford classical or band instruments for their music education program, often view tamburitza as a less expensive but culturally valuable and appropriate form of music education for their communities.

Tamburitza instruction and orchestral activity based in the schools has become a part of community life in most regions of Croatia. School tamburitza orchestras typically perform at various events in their locality, or even at larger national music festivals. They may play instrumental music only, or they might combine with choirs or solo singers to perform vocal pieces. Frequently amateur orchestras are called upon to participate in festive occasions or official holiday observances. On outdoor stages in parks and on public squares, tamburitza orchestras made up of school children often perform between the speeches of local politicians on national holidays, at anniversary observances of local cultural institutions, or even at a ribbon-cutting ceremony for a new school building or newly paved stretch of highway. From the stages of school auditoriums or in small-town movie theaters, tamburitza-strumming music pupils treat their hometown crowd, including their proud parents of course, to choral and instrumental performances.

Few of these orchestras are prepared to perform lengthy programs of complex orchestral numbers, and since there is a constant turnover among the young members, it is difficult for a school orchestra to build up a large repertoire of concert pieces. Some school orchestras have now opted to reorganize as a section of KUDs. In Samobor, for example, the excellent Ferdo Livadić orchestra developed from a high school tamburitza ensemble.

Only a minority of KUDs include a tamburitza orchestra among their cultural activities. More of them emphasize other offerings: folklore dance troupes, drama societies, chamber music ensembles, and poetry clubs. In inland sections of Croatia and in Vojvodina, though, tamburitza orchestras may be the most numerous type of KUD. The Đuro Salaj KUD from Slavonski Brod featured, among other activities, an outstanding accordion orchestra as well as one of the finest amateur tamburitza orchestras directed by the passionate tamburitza promoter and musician Mihael Ferić.

The educational efforts of schools and KUDs in tamburitza playing have helped create and retain a strong base of popularity for the instrument. *Tambure* remain quite popular despite the onslaught of newer amplified electric instruments. In a survey of Slavonian school children conducted in the 1950s, more than two-thirds indicated a preference for the tamburitza over other instruments (*Tamburaška glazba* 1957, 30). Many of these children would have likely retained that musical preference when they became mature adults in the 1970s and 1980s, and the persistence of tamburitza into the twenty-first century indicates that yet another generation has remained devoted to the instrument.

Since the 1960s, young people began to prefer electric guitars and drum sets, but still, *tambure* have retained a niche, in part for practical reasons. In 1978 I had a conversation with some young rock musicians from Sveta Jana in western Croatia. They told me their combo still used their "hollow" (*šuplji*) *tambure*, which require no electricity, when they played for outdoor *pohodi*, those traditional events such as wedding processions and other door-to-door holiday rounds.

In addition to their place in the formal curriculum of public schools, tamburitzas are frequent in the activities of extracurricular cultural and artistic societies in many localities. Prominent among KUD members are young unmarried people, but KUDs may include some middle-aged and elderly in their ranks.

The formation of KUDs accelerated in the 1970s in former Yugoslavia, owing in part to the adoption of the new national constitution in 1974 that granted a greater degree of power to the Yugoslav republics and to local self-governing communities. The power to disperse funds for local cultural activity, such as the purchase of instruments or dance costumes for a KUD, frequently became the purview of a town or neighborhood council (*mjesna zajednica*). These days in independent Croatia, local governments still are able to distribute finances for such purposes provided by the fund for cultural and artistic amateurism of the Ministry of Culture. Another stimulus to the formation of KUDs involving tamburitzas was the revival of the concept of authentic folklore and the accompanying establishment of festivals in such locations as Zagreb, Vinkovci, and Đakovo, providing an opportunity for amateur groups to perform.

The sheet-music collections of orchestral tamburitza ensembles typically include older scores that the group may have inherited from an earlier generation or a predecessor organization, sometimes even hand-scored by an erstwhile director. Other scores may be the personal property of their director who may instruct and conduct more than one orchestra. Still others are more recent acquisitions of scores published by the Hrvatski sabor kulture or other music publishers. The compositions vary in complexity and musical sophistication. Some are simple orchestrations of folk or *starogradska* songs or perhaps the composer connected a few such melodies from a particular region or era into a suite. There may also be tambura adaptations of overtures from Croatian, Italian, or Viennese operas, along with the more aesthetically challenging modern compositions by Király and Vidošić. In

addition to their concert repertoire, many orchestras can also play a
lighter program, songs and dance tunes of their region's folk music and
starogradske pjesme.

I had a chance to observe several amateur tamburitza orchestras for
youth at the Festival of Youth and Children's Orchestras of Croatia.
The twenty-first annual festival, which took place in May 1978, included
thirty-seven musical ensembles of all types. Fifteen were tamburitza
orchestras, twelve were accordion orchestras, five bowed string ensembles, three brass bands, a mandolin orchestra, and an orchestra comprised of accordions, melodicas, and harmonicas.

The 1978 festival was held in Gospić, the main market town in the
mountainous rural province of Lika. One of the participating music
teachers remarked that the location was clearly a political and not an
artistic decision. The festival had previously been held for several years
in superior facilities in Varaždin in northeastern Croatia. Varaždin is a
small baroque city with a long tradition of high culture, a music school,
and an opera house. In contrast, Gospić, despite some recent improvements, was still a provincial backwater with barely adequate facilities to
host this event.

The concerts were held in the auditorium of the local movie theater
with its rather small stage. Some of the teachers groused about the
acoustics of the hall and complained that there was scarcely any back-
stage space or other green-room space in the building. As a result, the
orchestras had to tune their instruments in an office building across
the street, pass outside into the cool springtime mountain air, and then
go back into the heated auditorium, the temperature changes causing
the just-tuned *tambure* to go out of tune again.

However, the enthusiasm of the children, happy to be on an outing
with their schoolmates, was unscathed and undampened. Gospić did
not have adequate space to lodge the members of all the orchestras,
so accommodations were arranged in an assortment of dormitories
and barracks, often many miles away. The young people did not seem
to mind being bused to and fro. They seemed excited at the prospect
of playing, being recorded for television (TV Zagreb videotaped the
event), and mostly just being away from home, seeing other young
people from different towns.

The festival opened on a breezy Friday afternoon on the central square of Gospić. There were three brass bands, which played the Yugoslav and Croatian anthems, and speeches by politicians and education officials. Zoran Palčok of the Prosvjetni sabor Hrvatske (Croatian education department), a sincere enthusiast, fervently declared, "Young people who dedicate their free time to music are dedicating their youth to a wonderful international art which ties the whole world together."

Indeed, an enthusiastic and selfless love of music seemed to permeate the whole festival. The teachers were excited at the chance to display their students' achievements, engage in discussions with their colleagues, and share musical ideas. For example, I had breakfast with Milan Jadrošić of the Varaždin Music Academy, Željko Bradić, and Julije Njikoš. After eating, Njikoš spread out his latest composition on the table and sang the melody line out loud. "Now isn't that beautiful?," he beamed.

Nearly every important figure in the world of Croatian orchestral tamburitza was present, as a teacher, conductor, or judge. The orchestras included groups, which represented a high level of musicianship despite their amateur status. Groups like Ferdo Livadić, Đuro Salaj, and the orchestra of the Varaždin Music Academy were surpassed in skill only by the professional RTV orchestras.

Following the welcome, there was an outdoor program by the three brass bands, followed by four concerts held in the auditorium on Friday evening, Saturday morning, afternoon, and evening, in which the thirty-four remaining groups performed. Inside the theater, in the middle of the movie screen, there hung the symbol of the festival: a large wooden disk painted with the silhouette of a vaguely female figure in a balletic pose, the muse of music perhaps, the finger of her extended arm touching the top of a towering harp, the whole scene surrounded by a laurel wreath.

Otherwise there was little attention to the appearance of the stage. It was cluttered with stackable plastic chairs and foldable wire music stands. Most of the orchestras performed in basic white shirts or blouses and dark pants or skirts. A few of the tamburitza orchestras played in folk costumes of their home region. The Matije Gubec orchestra from

Zagreb performed in *prigorsko nošnje*, the costume of the hill country on the city's north side. It was ironic that despite their folk costumes, the performance was not folkloric but classical. They played somewhat dissonant or atonal compositions by contemporary Yugoslav composers like Boris Krnić and Nikša Njirić. Other performing groups that wore folk costumes included the tamburitza orchestra of the Oriovac Elementary School and the ensemble Knežija that hailed from the neighborhood of that name in Zagreb.

The music performed at the four concerts fell into two general categories: pieces that took their inspiration quite literally from folk music, especially Slavonian, or classical music, in a modern style mostly influenced by composers like Igor Stravinsky. Some of the classical works by Croatian composers like Slavko Zlatić and Božidar Širola incorporated the scales or *melos* of Istria or other Croatian regions.

Even though the melodious folk-style pieces seemed to engender the most enthusiasm from the audience, the judges distributing gold, silver, and bronze awards favored the more avant-garde repertoire. The tamburitza orchestra that won the gold award, Đuro Salaj from Slavonski Brod, conducted by Mihael Ferić, played the atonal composition *Study Number One*, by Ernö Király, a composer of Hungarian ethnicity from Novi Sad. In this piece, reminiscent of John Cage's compositions, the composer sought to break the boundaries of conventional musical practice with such experimental techniques as tapping on the tamburitzas and noisily scraping a pick vertically up and down the *berde's* strings.

Four of the fifteen participating tamburitza orchestras used a folkloric format. These groups frequently provided accompaniment to dance groups and a few of them seemed a little uncomfortable in the center of attention. The groups taught by Antun Barić, a longtime musician in Lado's ensemble, were confident and poised. Unlike the concert orchestras who performed seated, reading from sheet music, and led by a conductor, the folkloric groups played standing, without written notes; the group from the Slavonian village of Bošnjaci did not even perform on stage but stood in front of the first row of seats. The leaders of the folkloric groups "conducted" facing the group while playing an instrument, usually a *prim* but in one case a *berde*, nodding and gesturing with the instrument to direct the ensemble.

Although admission to the concerts was free, there was no over-whelming turnout of the local populace of Gospić. It might have been the lack of local ensembles on the program. There was only one ensemble from Lika, a brass band that played on Friday afternoon. The rest of the participating groups were from central Croatia, Slavonia, or Dalmatia. The few locals who attended listened and applauded politely, but many seemed unimpressed by the dissonant compositions. The folk-oriented pieces and the folkloric tambura groups received notably more applause. For the most part, the audience was made up of the music teachers and members of the participating orchestras, sizing up the competition or listening for inspiration.

Unlike the performances of American junior tamburitza orchestras, which are sponsored by community-based organizations that arrange social meals and dances in connection with their concerts, there were not organized opportunities for the youth from the various groups to socialize. A few of the male *tamburaši* had an impromptu jam session on the street, with a few girls dancing a kolo to their music. To tease the girls, the boys sang a *bećarac* song with suggestive lyrics.

Impromptu combo of Croatian teenagers jamming in Gospic, 1978. (Photo by author)

On the whole, the festival was a serious educational and cultural event, not a social one. Although the event was filmed for television, it was not necessary for the music educators in charge of the festival to compromise their sophisticated aesthetic choices in order to please a broader audience. Some of the ensembles did play more popular music, but this was not rewarded by the judges.

An outstanding accomplishment culminating from the decades of tamburitza activity in the professional, amateur, and educational spheres are the performances since 2006 of Hrvatski tamburaski orkestar (Croatian tamburitza orchestra) otherwise known as the One Hundred Tamburitzans. On their ninety-fifth anniversary, the Croatian cultural society Šokadija-Zagreb, an organization of Zagreb residents whose family roots extend back to Slavonia, assembled a colossal tamburitza orchestra. Outstanding musicians hailed from twenty cities in Croatia and also included a few players from Subotica in Vojvodina, from Tuzla in Bosnia-Herzegovina, from Croatian communities in Austria, Belgium, and Hungary, and two American *tamburaši*, Jerry Grcevich from Pittsburgh and Steve Ovanin from Chicago. After four concerts in Zagreb and one in Šibenik, they toured internationally in 2009 to play in such venerated concert houses as the Wienerkonzerthaus in Vienna and the Muvészetek Palotája in Budapest.

AMERICAN TAMBURITZA ORCHESTRAS

In Croatia there is to this day considerable support for tamburitza coming from important official institutions. In North America the situation is quite different. Tamburitza orchestras operate in America with little or no official support. Amateur tamburitza playing takes place in junior and adult tamburitza orchestras, which can be found in most of the larger Croatian and also a few of the Serbian ethnic communities in the United States and Canada. The only larger Croatian American communities without tambura groups are the predominantly Dalmatian and Istrian communities such as those in San Pedro, California, and Queens, New York. The coastal people seldom identify strongly with the tamburitza, favoring instead their regional Adriatic musical traditions.

The American orchestras are grassroots community organizations, sometimes informal, sometimes legally incorporated and governed by a small board of directors. Some are sponsored by a church or an ethnic fraternal lodge. The earliest of the currently active youth orchestras were founded in the 1950s and 1960s. Additional groups have continued to be formed and some have disbanded over the decades. With slight fluctuations in number, there are currently about thirty to forty active youth groups in North America. Most of the Croatian junior tamburitzans are affiliated with the Croatian Fraternal Union's Junior Cultural Federation, an umbrella group that provides various kinds of support and networking, and since 1967 it has organized an annual youth tamburitza festival. The CFU considers the tamburitza activities a core purpose of the fraternal organization. On their website, the long-time CFU president Bernard Luketich declared, "Both the CFU Junior Cultural Federation Festival and the Adult TamFest remain the premier events of the Croatian Fraternal Union."

At the beginning of the school year, the CFU weekly newspaper *Zajedničar* carries notices from numerous junior tamburitza groups seeking new members. For example, the September 2, 2009, issue had six such notices in the form of brief articles. In addition to the practical information about the times and locations of practices, some explained the groups' mission. Paul Lucas, a key supporter of the Milwaukee CFU Tamburitzans, a former junior tamburitzan, a member of the Graničari adult orchestra, and husband of Patsy Lucas, a tambura music director, wrote, "Our core mission is to do our part to showcase, promote and preserve our Croatian heritage. . . . Participation in such organizations has proven to be a rich and rewarding experience for these young people, one that often leads to lasting participation in other Croatian organizations as adults" (Lucas 2009, 8).

Among many Croatian Americans the tamburitza orchestra is considered the primary way to involve youth in the culture of their ethnic community and thus extend the community's cohesiveness across generations. In a feature article in the *Pittsburgh Tribune-Review,* Mary Franko-Dorfner, the choreographer for McKeesport, Pennsylvania's Sacred Heart Tamburitzans, joked, "It feels like I've never *not* been a tamburitzan." Beth Cindric, then a twenty-year-old member of the

The Silver Strings Junior Tamburitzans rehearsal, Milwaukee, 1980.
(Photo by Timothy Sharko)

group, asserted, "Without a doubt, my children will be tamburitzans."
Ivan Begg, the president of the Sacred Heart group, noted that some
of the tamburitzans are third- and even fourth-generation performers
(*Pittsburgh Tribune-Review*, April 3, 2005).

The current youth groups are the latest manifestation of a tradition that goes back at least to the beginning of the twentieth century.
The efforts of Charles Elias Sr., musician, instructor, and author of
the 1924 instruction book *Škola za tamburaše*, were discussed in chapter 5. Elias, who immigrated to Milwaukee in 1903, gained an ally in
his teaching efforts in 1906 when George Beleg, a former seminary student from Elias's Croatian hometown of Suhopolje, immigrated to the
United States. Beleg, born in 1876, had already been an active *tamburaš*
in Croatia. He settled in the Turtle Creek Valley area east of Pittsburgh,
where from 1910 to 1949 he served as the instructor for numerous
tambura groups. When Beleg was posthumously inducted into the
Tamburitza Association of America (TAA) Hall of Fame in 1984, the
anonymous author of his tribute indicated that he taught as many as

twelve orchestras at a time, over the years teaching a total of thirty-four groups in several Pennsylvania mill towns like Clairton, Rankin, Braddock, Wilmerding, Trafford, McKeesport, Duquesne, Homestead, and Monessen.

The next generation of tamburitza instructors in America included Paul Perman and Ivan Rožgaj, who were, like Beleg, TAA Hall of Fame members. Perman was born in 1896 in the village of Jusići near Opatija, Croatia. He began to play in a tambura ensemble in his home region in 1907. He immigrated to Pennsylvania in 1912 and formed a six-piece tambura combo in the small coal-mining town of Acosta in 1913. During the next decade he instructed seven different groups. In 1925 Perman moved to Sharon, Pennsylvania, near the Ohio border, and joined the Croatian String Quintet. The group became early radio pioneers, broadcasting regularly from 1926 to 1932. With the appearance of Srijemski-system tamburitzas in the later 1920s, Perman became an avid advocate for adopting these more versatile instruments and ultimately became an instrument maker and instructor. He was apparently an old-school European-style music teacher. His TAA Hall of Fame tribute writer stated, "Perman was a firm believer in the student knowing all the theory and fundamentals of music before putting an instrument in his hands." Moreover, he was "a stern taskmaster" who didn't care whether the pupils liked him or not as long as they made progress. In 1960 he returned to his native village, where he passed away in 1967.

Ivan Rožgaj was born in 1898 in Ribnik, Croatia, in the Gorski Kotar region. He immigrated in 1913 to Kansas City, where he studied violin at the Western Conservatory of Music. In 1922 Rožgaj relocated to Whiting, Indiana, an industrial town abutting South Chicago. There he began his extensive tamburitza teaching career, initially with a group in Whiting and another in nearby East Chicago. He instructed the orchestra at the Croatian Children's Home, an orphanage in Des Plaines, Illinois, and toured as a performer for nearly six years in a combo with the famed Vasil Crljenica. After 1928 he devoted himself to teaching efforts, ultimately teaching twelve tamburitza groups in the Illinois-Indiana area.

Later, Rožgaj became the music instructor at Memorial High School in Campbell, Ohio, a position he held for many years (Campbell has a strong tamburitza tradition and is located very near where Paul Perman lived in Sharon). There was such demand for his tamburitza teaching abilities that Rožgaj had the opportunity to instruct an additional sixteen tamburitza orchestras in the Youngstown, Ohio, area and in Western Pennsylvania.

These early instructors—Elias, Beleg, Perman, and Rožgaj—labored in the mines and mills like most men in their communities yet managed to scrabble together a music business within the ethnic community to support themselves as teachers, performers, and instrument makers. They played no small part in making the Milwaukee/Chicago/ Northern Indiana and the western Pennsylvania/eastern Ohio areas the two biggest hotbeds of tamburitza in the United States. Their most talented students became combo musicians, Duquesne University Tamburitzans, and the next generation of tamburitza instructors.

The region around St. Louis, Missouri, also emerged as an important hub of tamburitza activity thanks in large part to the dedicated music instructors of the Lusicic family. Ivan Lusicic, born in the village of Grižane in Primorje in 1897, was a *tamburaš* in Croatia before immigrating to St. Louis in 1924; there he joined an active community of Primorci in that city. By occupation Ivan was a stone carver and made burial monuments, but he and his wife, Anna, devoted their free time to teaching local Croatian choirs and tamburitza groups such as the Walnut Park Juniors in north St. Louis, and the Primorci in the Bribirsko selo (Bribir village) neighborhood of south St. Louis. There was a decline in musical activity at the beginning of the 1930s because of the onset of the Great Depression, but in 1935 Ivan and Anna established a new group, Hrvatski Pomladak (Croatian Youth), in which their own children Eleanor (b. 1927) and Ivan Jr. (b. 1928) were among the members. When in 1938 Ivan Sr. initiated the *Croatian Radio Hour* in St. Louis, Hrvatski Pomladak regularly performed on radio broadcasts. The group disbanded in 1942 because many of the older boys had been drafted.

Eleanor Lusicic Eaves emerged as an exceptionally talented musician and artist. At the age of six she began to play Farkaš *bisernica* in the Primorci group taught by her father, and in 1935 she moved on to Hrvatski Pomladak. After 1942 she became active in the Hrvatska Vila Croatian choir, a new organization also directed by her father. There she sang in the choir, became their pianist, and eventually took over as music director after Ivan Sr.'s death in 1964. She had been offered a scholarship to become a Duquesne University Tamburitzan but opted to remain in St. Louis, where she attended a business college, helped as a designer and bookkeeper in the family's monument business, and studied violin, piano, and voice at a music conservatory.

In 1961 the junior tamburitza group was revived, after a hiatus of nearly two decades. Initially meeting in the home of Ivan and Anna Lusicic, the group was named the Croatian Junior Tamburitzans of St. Louis. It is interesting that the Croatian Juniors initially selected Janković-system *tambure* for the group; to my knowledge this was the only American group ever to do so. Hrvatski Pomladak had used Farkaš instruments, which by 1961 were considered archaic. The Janković system had been originated by Slavko Janković, a noted musician, athlete, judge, and musicologist born in 1897 in Novi Mikanovci near Vinkovci in Srijem (Ferić 2011, 359). His system's *tambure* were tuned in fifths, like violins, to take full advantage of all four fingers on the player's left hand. The system was adopted by many schools in Croatia and remains in use, although there has been a resurgence of use of the Srijemski system in Croatia. Eleanor Eaves wrote in English an instruction manual for Janković system *tambure*. Within a few years virtually all other American *tamburaši* were using the Srijemski system; the group switched to Srijemski and Eleanor wrote another instruction manual to ease the transition. Fifty years later Eleanor, in her eighties, continues to lead the group with assistance from her nephew Dan and his wife Linda Lusicic (TAA).

Angie Zadravec of Youngstown had an enduring career as a tamburitza instructor. Born in Youngstown in 1921, she was in the all-female, five-piece ensemble Danice with four of her sisters during the 1930s. The group disbanded due to marriages, work, and parental responsibilities, and Angie worked as a welder during World War II. When the director of the local junior group Fala Tamburitzans, in which her two daughters participated, retired in 1966, Angie stepped in, reorganized the group as Vesela Srca (Happy Hearts) Tamburitzans, and added a dance choreographer. She became music director of the group, which at one point had seventy students. Angie remained in the music director position for thirty-nine years until 2005. In the 1980s she organized the adult tamburitza orchestra Od Srca (From the Heart) and until the age of eighty-nine was still directing the group.

The TAA Hall of Fame also includes the three remarkable Puskarich sisters, Caroline Bahr, Rose Husnick, and Marilyn Repasky, all born during the 1930s on a farm in Plum Boro, Pennsylvania. All three had excellent singing voices and all became Duquesne Tamburitzans. After graduation, Rose married another Tamburitzan, Fred Husnick, in 1957 and the next year they established Veseli Tamburitzans, a combo that is still active. Rose also instructed junior and adult orchestras in Sharon and Farrell, Pennsylvania. Caroline moved to California in 1960, eventually settling in Mountain View, where in 1965 she organized Veseli Seljaci (The Merry Villagers), an adult orchestra. Reversing the usual pattern of forming an adult orchestra only after a youth group has been active for several years, Caroline organized a youth group, the Santa Clara Valley Junior Tamburitzans. Marilyn became the instructor of the Golden Triangle Tamburitzans in Pittsburgh, performs as a vocalist with her sister Rose in Veseli, and for more than twenty years has been a kolo dancing instructor for adults.

From the influential tambura careers of these women, it is apparent that women, especially those born after 1920, have played key roles in the junior and adult amateur tamburitza sphere. As early as 1930, Nada Rashovich became the leader of Balkan Serenaders, a ten-piece youth orchestra affiliated with the Holy Resurrection Serbian Orthodox Church in Chicago, a group that included *tambure* (Opacich 2005, 90–91). We read earlier that the tamburitza combo domain is male dominated, but the equal or greater number of females who have received tamburitza instruction in the junior groups and in the Duquesne Tamburitzans have nonetheless found significant roles in instructing youth groups and subsequently as members or leaders of adult amateur tamburitza orchestras.

The list of youth orchestras on the CFU website showed in January 2011 that 40 percent of the listed music directors were women. More than 75 percent of the choreographers and dance instructors are women, and when all of the listed leadership positions are considered, women constitute 63 percent of these (http://www.croatianfraternal

union.org/, accessed 2011). Unlike the male teachers of the early twentieth century, those who have moved into these positions since the 1950s do not expect to be able to earn their livelihood teaching tambura or kolo dancing. The key leaders do receive honoraria, but the groups are not run by professional staff. They couldn't function without a high degree of voluntarism from parents and boosters, much of it carried out by women.

Lara Sees, the assistant director of Pittsburgh's North Hills Junior Tamburitzans, stated, "We have grandmothers, aunts, people's neighbors who come and sew for the kids, sell tickets, man booths" (*Pittsburgh Tribune-Review*, April 3, 2005). Most of the fund-raising events for the groups involve food sales—*sarma* (cabbage rolls), pierogi (Polish dumplings), Christmas cookies, lamb, chicken, or sausage dinners. The men gravitate to raising funds by selling advertisements in the program books for groups' annual concerts or organizing raffles. With the traditional concern for family welfare and cohesiveness, and for children's upbringing, women are indispensable in the continuing success of amateur tamburitza groups.

The active support of the CFU also has been crucial to the continuing success of the youth orchestras. The opportunity to participate in the CFU's annual Junior Cultural Federation Festival, held since 1967 on the weekend closest to the Fourth of July holiday, is a major incentive for the youth orchestras. The festival draws about thirty junior tamburitza orchestras, usually in one of the tambura-rich American or Canadian cities, like St. Louis, Chicago, Pittsburgh, Detroit, or Toronto. Since 1976 the event has been held every fifth year in Zagreb, with a hiatus occurring during the Homeland War (1991–95). Before or after the festival, the groups usually tour Croatia for a week or more.

Preparing for their annual concerts, the festival performance, and raising the needed travel funds are major challenges, which the groups usually manage to meet successfully. The festival includes two concerts during which each group presents a short performance, but the concerts are not the only attraction. There is a great deal of socializing, and there are parties and jam sessions late into the night. At the festival, the children also are learning the community's accepted style of festive behavior.

A highlight of the event is the combined performance. Typically more than seven hundred junior tamburitzans are assembled on a stage to be directed by the guest conductor, an annual honoree, usually a longtime music director of one of the groups. To be selected is considered a major honor in the Croatian American community. (The CFU lists all of the past honorees on their website.)

Lacking support from an ethnic fraternal organization, the number of Serbian American junior tamburitza groups has diminished since World War II. Among Croatians there is near universal recognition of the tamburitza as a national symbol and that junior tamburitza groups are the prime way to involve the youth in their cultural heritage. Not so among the Serbs.

There remain only a few junior tamburitza orchestras associated with Serbian communities, typically through a Serbian Orthodox church such as St. Sava Church in Milwaukee and St. Nicholas in Wilmerding, Pennsylvania. In the bimonthly magazine *Serb World* Milan Opacich lamented, "For me the greatest enigma is 'Why are there few, if any, new Serbian tamburitza groups being formed in our colonies?'" (Opacich 2005, 92). Noting that most of the earlier Serbian immigrants came from Vojvodina or various regions of Croatia where the tamburitza is widespread, he wrote: "Many of our later immigrants came from regions where tamburitza was not as popular—like Serbia, Montenegro, and Herzegovina. For some of them the discovery of tamburitza among the Serbs in America was a new experience. Many times I have been chagrined when told, 'To nije naša muzika!' [That is not our music!]" (ibid., 98).

Many of the more recent Serbian immigrants are indifferent to the tamburitza and a few are overtly hostile, declaring that the tamburitza is only Croatian and advocating for Serbian *narodna muzika*. This division in the community makes it an uphill struggle for the Serbian American tamburitza enthusiasts. Opacich stated, "We adults, along with the remaining Serbian *tamburaši*, somehow have failed. I see few youngsters learning tamburitza and . . . if there is not a resurgence . . . it will soon disappear" (ibid.).

Adult amateur tamburitza orchestras have existed in North America since early in the twentieth century, in those days often connected to singing societies. An event that stimulated the formation of larger adult orchestras was the "Yugoslav Day" program at the Chicago World's Fair on July 2, 1933. For the occasion, a tamburitza orchestra with more than forty members, mostly members of Chicago-area combos such as Javor, the Kapugi Brothers, Jadran, the Popovich Brothers, and others, played under the direction of Adam Popovich. This aggregation had a continued existence until later in the 1930s as the Chicago Tamburitza Club (ibid., 197–98). The Cleveland United Tamburitza Orchestra and the Detroit Tamburitza Symphony were similar large aggregations active in that era, all relatively short-lived.

In 1957 the Detroit Tamburitza Orchestra (DTO) was formed, the most successful and enduring large adult orchestra in North America, and the orchestra that has attained the highest quality in terms of classical music attributes. Originally named the Detroit Senior Tamburitzans, the first director was Andrew Benda, a Detroit combo musician and a youth orchestra leader. At their first concert in 1958, they had to rely on playing from a few old surviving scores inherited from the 1930s Detroit Tamburitza Symphony. Later in 1958, Benda traveled to Yugoslavia to acquire new scores. He also met and established relationships with tamburitza composers and the directors of the Yugoslav tamburitza orchestras.

In 1966 Andrew Benda became ill and died. Fortunately, Detroit had Steve Pavlekovich, a qualified replacement. Steve was a veteran combo musician and, inspired by the recording innovations of Les Paul, he was the first tamburitza musician to produce sound-on-sound recordings, playing all the tamburitza instruments and parts himself. The opportunity to direct this skilled orchestra inspired Steve to compose several orchestral arrangements of folk song suites, many of which remain in the orchestra's library. In 1967 Steve was honored as the first Guest Conductor of the combined group at the CFU junior festival.

When Pavlekovich retired from leading the group in 1974, James Guracech became the new director. "Kum Jim" (Godfather Jim), as he was known, had been a tambura student of Andrew Benda's in the late 1930s; he also trained as a classical violinist at the Detroit Conservatory of Music. Jim enlisted in the U.S. Army in 1951, serving for three years in occupied Germany as a violinist in the U.S. Army's European

Theater Symphony Orchestra, which played goodwill concerts for German audiences. After returning to Detroit in 1954, he joined the Balkan Cavaliers, a local tambura combo. Jim's solid classical music training and experience, along with his tamburitza grounding, made him an ideal director to advance the Detroit Tamburitza Orchestra in its "serious music" direction. John Belavich, a member of the group, stated that Jim "incorporated a more disciplined, serious method of musical interpretation than our orchestra had ever experienced before. His strictness in enforcing us to 'play as written' has enabled the Detroit Tamburitza Orchestra to reproduce each musical composition exactly as the composer meant it to be."

James Guracech retired in 1994 and turned the baton to Ken Kosovec, a member of the talented musical Kosovec family. Ken had been an orchestra member, and the son of Ludwig Kosovec, a DTO founder. Ken has been both a former junior orchestra director and an accomplished combo musician. He and his brother Dennis played in two of Detroit's great combos, Lira and Momci. His son and daughter, Peter and Sonya, and nephew David are among the elite *tamburaši* of the younger generation. Under Ken's skillful leadership, the DTO continues to enjoy the status of one of the most accomplished tamburitza orchestras playing in the classical music manner.

In North America, there are, however, few adult orchestras and virtually no youth orchestras that attempt the classical music model. Nearly all of the repertoire of junior orchestras emphasize a folklore direction. Among the adult groups, aside from the DTO, there is only one other group that consistently performs in the classical music manner, the Prijatelji Orchestra of Chicago, directed by John Gornick. John was a student of Ivan Rožgaj at the Croatian Children's Home, played *bugarija* as a longtime member of Tony Muselin's Continentals combo, and is the father of Joe and Nick Gornick, mainstays of Chicago's Sinovi combo (Gornick 2004).

The number of adult orchestras expanded substantially in the 1980s when the CFU took an interest in promoting their expansion. Noting that graduates of the junior tamburitza groups lacked opportunities to continue their involvement with the music, the CFU announced that in the fall of 1987 they would organize TamFest, an annual festival of adult orchestras similar to the junior festival (Luketich 1998). With stimulus from TamFest, the number of adult orchestras expanded from a dozen or so to more than thirty. In January 2011 there were thirty-nine adult groups listed on the CFU website. From 2003 to 2008, I participated as a *čelo brač* player in Milwaukee's Graničari adult orchestra, one of the groups established in the 1980s. Regionally, the adult groups are most numerous in Pennsylvania where there are eleven orchestras. Canada's Hamilton and Toronto areas nearly match Pennsylvania with ten groups; the remaining orchestras are mainly in various industrial midwestern cities like Chicago, Milwaukee, and St. Louis.

Most of the adult orchestras, which range in size from about fifteen to forty members, perform in the manner of a large combo. The groups may perform standing or sitting, with or without music stands. When they sing, the *prim* and *brač* players usually cease playing, leaving only the *bugarija* and *berde* players to provide rhythm. Some of the groups include a choir of singers who do not play *tambure*. In Graničari, most

Graničari from Milwaukee, at TamFest in St. Louis, 2007. (Courtesy of Graničari)

of these choir singers are older participants, many of them immigrants from Croatia. Singing in the choir provides a way to participate for these members who did not learn to play tambura in their youth. Many of the singers have grown-up children who had been members of the Milwaukee CFU Tamburitzans or of a predecessor group in Milwaukee, the American-Croatian Silver Strings. Indeed, most of the tambura players in Graničari were alumni of these junior tamburitza orchestras.

There is a close relationship between Graničari and the Milwaukee CFU Tamburitzans. The Milwaukee CFU group and Graničari share a common director in Patsy Lucas, and most Graničari members have had past experience in one of the junior groups, either as parents or performers. The adult group supports the junior group's fundraisers. For example, in 2007, when the juniors needed extra funds to bring in the popular Otrov combo from Pittsburgh, the adult orchestra voted to cover half of the expense. The bus trips to the festival or to guest performances at the concerts of sister groups are multigenerational family parties on the move. On the bus, food and drinks are passed around, songs are sung, *tambure* are strummed. A near familial relationship among members is encouraged. Steve Jurkovich, Patsy Lucas's father, enjoys being called Bajo (Grandpa) by everyone on the bus, a familial touch.

In addition to the classical and the large combo types of orchestra, three adult tamburitza groups, Kumovi of Pittsburgh, Selo from Columbus, Ohio, and the Croatian Cultural Ensemble Kordun emphasize dance. Kumovi has many members who are former Duquesne Tamburitzans, and Selo has members who were in the Živili Kolo ensemble of Columbus. The choreographer for Kumovi, Željko Jergan, has a remarkable career as a dance instructor and choreographer, reminiscent of the careers of the immigrant music teachers a century ago.

Željko was born in 1955 in Varaždin, Croatia. He was enthralled by folk dancing since childhood. While studying architecture at Zagreb University in 1974, he made an impulsive decision to audition for Lado, the Croatian National Folk Dance ensemble. His parents didn't learn of his career change until they saw him on television dancing in a Lado performance. During his twelve years performing with Lado, Željko also researched folk dance and instructed folklore groups in the Varaždin and Zagreb areas. In 1986 Željko married his American wife Cindy who had come to Zagreb from Pittsburgh in 1984 to study and dance with Lado. They settled in Pennsylvania, where Željko immediately resumed his dance teaching career. By 2009, he had become artistic director of eight different ensembles: three in Pittsburgh, three in Canada, and two in California. He has been hired to teach choreographies to more than thirty American and Canadian junior tamburitza groups and to college and professional dance groups as well (including the Duquesne University Tamburitzans). Beyond the ethnic community, Željko is frequently called upon to teach at the dance camps of recreational international folk dance organizations, and has taught such groups not only in North America but also in Norway, Japan, and China (Jergan 2004). Croatian and other Balkan folk dance is inextricably entwined with the tamburitza tradition and will be treated in chapter 10. Tamburitza orchestras continue to thrive especially among Croatians in the homeland and in North America. In Europe they enjoy greater official institutional support and professional direction through the schools and in government-funded amateur artistic groups. In North America, they enjoy strong community support at the grassroots level. It can be said, they are the beating hearts of the Croatian communities of North America.

CHAPTER 10

Folk Dance Groups

The tamburitza is intimately associated with South Slavic folk dance. Tamburitza and dance exert a substantial mutual influence upon each other. Having replaced earlier traditional instruments like *gajde* and *dude* (types of bagpipes), *dvojnice* (a double fipple flute), or *lijerica* (a pear-shaped bowed stringed instrument) as the most common form of dance accompaniment in many villages, the tamburitza's association with dance music is more recent, coming with the popularization of the instruments in the late nineteenth and early twentieth centuries.

South Slavic folk dances are numerous and varied. In many regions, villagers know several different dances, and one need travel only a short distance over the ever-changing cultural landscape of the Balkans to encounter variants of dance types.

The communities that support the tamburitza tradition have older and newer forms of dance as a part of their festivities and displays of cultural heritage. There is informal dancing in European villages at celebrations of such holidays as Carnival, St. George's Day, and St. John's Day. Traditional dancing also takes place at weddings, christenings, and other important rituals. Informal dancing is also a part of festivities in the North American South Slavic communities. Staged presentations of traditional dance as a display of cultural heritage are common both in the KUDs of the former Yugoslav countries and in their ethnic communities abroad.

Kolo dancing to the Slavonski Bečari, St. Augustine Church hall,
Milwaukee, 1979. (Photo by Timothy Sharko)

Although today most traditional dancing is done primarily for recreation, exercise, expression of heritage, or as a social activity, in the past it is likely that folk dances had deeper religious or magical purposes—to help ensure success in hunting or fruitful harvests, to fight disease, and to ward off spirits. Nowadays, awareness of earlier magical functions may have disappeared or, if not entirely forgotten, transformed into a joke by the majority who no longer believe in its efficacy. Ivan Ivančan, a folk dance scholar and choreographer, mentioned the *zečko kolo* or *zajc* (the rabbit dance) and *dučec* or *nebesko kolo* (jumping dance) as examples of dances with a trace of ritual function remaining: the rabbit dance to ensure good hunting, the jumping dance to encourage flax or hemp to grow tall.

Ivančan and other dance scholars have classified Balkan dances according to the cultural geographic zones developed by ethnologists, to which, for the most part, the boundaries of the dance zones correspond. Of these regions, the Pannonian, Dinaric, and Adriatic zones, which comprise most of the territory of the former-Yugoslav countries, have the most significant connections to tamburitza (Ivančan 1965).

In the Pannonian region, the most important dance type is the closed kolo, dancing in a closed circle. Generally the kolo here is close: each dancer holds the hands not of the adjacent dancers but the second nearest ones. The dancers' bodies are close together with extended arms clasped either behind the back or in front of the adjacent dancers in a "basket" hold. In this tight circle, the dance motions are economical and intricate. There are no leaps, sweeps, or high kicks, but fast patterns of small steps. An erect posture is important, and while some dances call for the upper body to be relatively immobile, others of the *drmeš* type call for rapid shaking above the waist. In both the Pannonian and Dinaric zones, the direction of rotation of the kolo tends to be clockwise in the western but counterclockwise in the eastern portions of the regions.

In the western Pannonian areas there are strong influences of the Alpine zone, namely couples' dances, the polka, and the waltz, with extensive spinning while dancing, either in couples or in small kolos of four dancers. The Slavs share the Pannonian plain with Hungarians, so Hungarian dances, *csardas*, and *koscinto* are common.

Although dance accompaniment used to be played on bagpipes, wooden flutes, or *samice*, tamburitza ensembles are now more common. Accordions and electronic synthesizers have replaced *tambure* in many places.

In the Dinaric zone, both open and closed kolos are known. Some of the dances of this region are among the most ancient folk dances still actively performed; some, such as the silent kolos of Lika and the Dalmatian hinterlands, are danced without musical accompaniment of any kind.

Dinaric dances tend to include a greater number of slow, strolling, dance motions accompanied by songs. The dancers hold the hands of the adjacent persons in the kolo. Thus there is more space between dancers than in the basket-hold dances. Often one dancer has the role of caller, who directs the kolo when to start, stop, accelerate, or slow down.

The solo *tambure*, *samica*, and *šargija* are frequent as dance accompaniment in the Dinaric zone; tamburitza ensembles are less common, and such ensembles might not include the standard combination of instruments. For example, in the 1978 Smotra folklora, one group from Bosnia had dance music from a group consisting only of three *brač* players.

The predominance of line and circle dances among South Slavs has been attractive to ethnologists because these dances are quite ancient. The communal values expressed by dancing in large circles have been attractive to romantics who idealized peasant life. Even a serious scholar like Antun Radić was swept away into such musings when, writing in the *Journal of Folk Life and Custom* in 1899, he described dancing with Slavonian peasants in their kolo: "At first it was as if I experienced in my mind all that is written in learned books: of the beginnings of rhythmic human motion, of the connection of motion to verse, of the beginnings of poetry and drama; I seemed to imagine the Greek dramatic chorus, later the agora, the forum—until finally all those thoughts left me, and I remained alone with my eyes and ears, and the soul in me seemed to be poured into the souls in the kolo who lived and gloried only in that moment" (Radić 1899, 44). Radić stressed the importance of scholarly research on the dance: "The kolo of the Croats and their closest brothers is an exceptional phenomenon; in this form today in Europe it is unique . . . I cannot imagine more interesting studies than of the kolo" (ibid.).

In light of the strength of Radić's feelings about the kolo, it is not surprising that his followers, the Croatian ethnologists, should have worked intensely to develop the Zagreb *smotre* in the 1930s. The re-establishment of the Smotra folklora in 1966 and the development of other folklore festivals around the world have provided a powerful stimulus to reinvigorate traditional dancing and to organize groups who can perform these dances on stage.

Villagers performing stage presentations of the folk dances are relatively recent developments. In 1925 and again in 1926, an amateur dramatic club from the village of Remete, near Zagreb, presented staged depictions of their Christmas Eve, St. George's Day, and wedding customs. These performances were the earliest noted performances in Croatia of villagers simulating their customs on stage for a general urban audience. Folk dancing by villagers did not take place on stage until the 1935 festival of village choirs (see chap. 4), where choir members from Jasenovac and Sunje in lower Posavina performed their kolos (Bratanić 1941).

Because these performances stimulated a great deal of interest, the panel of experts encouraged all choirs henceforth to perform dances along with their singing programs at subsequent *smotre*. Inspired by these performances, a group of urban amateur folk dance enthusiasts, the Society of Croatian theatrical amateurs, was formed in Zagreb. They performed folk dances at an international festival held in Berlin in connection with the 1936 Olympic Games and were awarded first prize in the competition (ibid.).

Up until the outbreak of World War II, numerous village choirs had developed staged programs of their village's dances and had presented them at *smotre* in Zagreb and at smaller regional *smotre*. The village choirs and dance groups proved to be enduring. They reemerged after the war and in 1945, the Seljačka sloga (see chap. 4) organization resumed its activities organizing festivals.

The postwar socialist regime in Yugoslavia encouraged organized cultural activity in villages. At the same time there was a huge influx of villagers into the cities, bringing village culture into urban areas. Young war veterans, mostly villagers, streamed to cities to work or study. As the new regime established itself, the songs and dances created during the partisan struggle and which were based on peasant models were extensively performed and broadcast. Peasant culture was in vogue in the immediate postwar years.

In Zagreb, amateur folk dance societies formed, named after partisan heroes like Ivan Goran Kovačić and Jože Vlahović. In 1949 the professional folk dance troupe Lado was established. In relation to dance groups, there was also a significant congruent change in emphasis in the cultural-political orientation of their performances. The performance of "pure peasant dances" was replaced by choreographies that presented a more stylized, artistically arranged dance performance, based on but not identical to unstaged village dance.

It was not until the 1960s, when there was an increase in the influence of the ethnologists who had been active in the prewar *smotre*, that a greater emphasis was placed upon presenting dances as they were supposed to have been performed in the villages in nonstaged contexts (Ceribašić 2005, 187–203).

Because of the successful efforts of the activist ethnologists prior to World War II, and the renewed work of Seljačka sloga, both village and urban amateur groups were influenced by the ideas of the ethnologists concerning how to present traditional music and dance. Throughout the former Yugoslavia and especially in Croatia, folklore groups, both urban and rural, have been encouraged to emulate the ethnological ideal of authentic folklore.

Village amateurs are most numerous. Many of the groups active in the 1960s and up until the present trace their origins to the 1930s when they performed at prewar *smotre*. Many of the Seljačka sloga groups still are active and some still bear the same names. But even when the names of the groups have changed—some used the names of local partisan heroes during the socialist Yugoslav regime, and after Croatian independence in 1991, they may have adopted a new name evoking Croatian patriotism—the nucleus of the group often remained the original Seljačka sloga members, their children, and their grandchildren.

The repertoire performed at the prewar *smotre* was regularly noted by the ethnomusicologist/composer Božidar Širola and published in 1940. One can find many of the same songs and dances in the repertoires of groups that have performed later on at Smotra folklora (Širola 1940).

In 1978 I visited a rehearsal of a village group that exhibited this type of continuity. The group was founded in 1923 and located in the village of Mraclin in the Turopolje region, several kilometers south of Zagreb's airport. In its early years the group was called Kopač (the digger), a name evocative of its village setting. During the 1920s and 1930s they performed like an urban choir from written arrangements with a conductor. But after Seljačka sloga eliminated that type of performing group, they did not participate in the Zagreb *smotre* of the 1930s.

By the 1960s they reorganized as an authentic folklore music and dance group named after a Partisan hero, KUD Josip Galeković. They participated in the Smotra folklora in Zagreb in 1966, 1982, and 1990 (Ceribašić 2011). In 1996 the name of the group was changed again to

KUD Dučec, the name of a jumping dance, which is part of the local tradition. In 1978 Franjo Cvetnić, who had played in the group forty years earlier, was still the *primaš* of the KUD's tamburitza ensemble in 1978, and two of his sons were key activists in the group. The membership of the KUD at that time represented a cross-section of Mraclin's society, but the more articulate and better educated villagers were disproportionately well represented. The group remains active today. Now one can view YouTube video clips of their performances, and even though the group's name and the emphasis in its artistic practices varied over the years, Mraclin residents view the present KUD as a continuation of the group originally founded in the 1920s. In June 2008, there was a grand celebration of the eighty-fifth anniversary of KUD Dučec. They were honored to have a performance by Lado featured on the program.

It is important to note the social status of a KUD's various members to understand the group's standing in the local community. Although it is sometimes tempting to urbanites to conceive of peasant society as homogeneous, there are significant social distinctions within that society that continue to sharpen in modern times. For a long time there have been differing levels of education, and even when formal educational differences were small, due to a uniform lack of educational opportunities, there have always been more intellectually curious individual villagers predisposed toward reading, study, and discussion.

The village intelligentsia has often played a crucial role in the establishment and continued functioning of folklore KUDs. This tendency is far from surprising. It would have been readers of the Seljačka sloga magazine who would have first heard and understood the reasons to form village folklore groups. Assembling the group and preparing to present a program along defined ethnological guidelines required organizational, intellectual, and administrative abilities.

Such is the case with the group in Mraclin. In 1978, in addition to agriculturalists, housewives, and woodworkers, the group included educators and engineers. One such was the *primaš* Franjo Cvetnić. He had been a mainstay of the group and was nicknamed "Esperantist" (speaker of Esperanto). Such nicknames are important in villages where but a few family names predominate, and often the nickname totally supplants the official name in everyday usage. Since Cvetnić is quite common in Mraclin, all members of Franjo's direct line are called Cvetnić-Esperantist because several family members were interested in the Esperanto international language movement. Such an interest clearly indicates an intellectual frame of mind. Moreover as Franjo and his son, also named Franjo, explained to me, they saw a relationship between the goals of the Esperanto movement and folklore groups. Both involve communication and sharing, travel, and the development of international goodwill.

While the village intelligentsia serves as major instigators of the folklore KUDs, it is not exclusively their domain. In the 1970s I noticed that the musicians who made and played archaic handmade musical instruments, such as *gajde, diple, dvojnice,* and *tambura dvožica,* tended to be older men from the poorest, least-educated segments of village society—shepherds and poor peasants. Nonetheless they were highly desirable KUD members because the instruments they played were the oldest and, according to the ethnologists' concept, the most "authentic" forms of local dance music. Although their musical talents were appreciated, I heard younger KUD members joke about the rustic behavior and errors of their elder *gajdaš* or *dipljaš* when that unsophisticated musician came with them to the "big city" of Zagreb for Smotra folklora.

When I was doing my field research in the 1970s, it was uncertain that younger musicians would learn to play the archaic instruments. This task was complicated because they usually would have to learn to make the instruments themselves. There were few artisans making these instruments and certainly not in all their regional and local variants. It was often considered part of the traditional role of the musician to make the instrument. Even when the instruments were available, there were few older players who had the desire, temperament, or ability to instruct young aspirants, probably because they themselves had received no instruction. It was a common practice that a young person would learn to play the older instruments in solitude, while tending flocks or doing agricultural tasks far from the village. They would not perform for others until a fair degree of competency was achieved.

Josip Kanaletić, a bagpiper (*mišničar*) from my mother's home town of Nerezine on the island Lošinj, told me an anecdote, which is a good example of this type of musical apprenticeship. Kanaletić told me that after he and his elder brother had worked all day cutting wood far from the village, they set out for home. When they reached a fork in the path, Josip insisted that the longer path actually was the shortest way back to the village. He provoked an argument with his brother, and they parted ways, each on a different path. As Josip walked, he took out the chanter of a bagpipe (*mih*) and began to practice. After several days of this routine, Josip's brother became curious why his younger sibling always took the longer path and secretly followed him. He heard Josip playing, by now quite skillfully, and when they returned to the village the secret was out (Kanaletić 1972).

Learning to play was traditionally done in solitude, and most of the archaic instruments are made to be played solo. In contrast, the social aspects of learning and rehearsing are important to the folklore KUD, which was difficult to connect with the archaic instruments. Therefore there has been a considerable tendency to replace the older forms of dance accompaniment with newer tamburitza ensembles.

I observed in the early 1980s that there were some trends in the opposite direction. Instruction in playing the *sopila*, an archaic double-reed instrument, had been brought into schools in Istria, where it is indigenous. At that time Krešimir Galin taught the playing of old instruments in a summer seminar for folklore group leaders, and this sort of effort has expanded along with the recent revival of *samica* and *šargija* playing. A coalition of Croatian cultural organizations now organize winter seminars held in Crkvenica and summer seminars on the islet of Badija near Korčula, and in Zagreb where instructors such as Đuro Adamović and Vido Bagur have taught dozens of students to play older instruments such as *gajde*, *lijerica*, and *diple*. In addition, a number of artisans have emerged who make these instruments. Intervention by cultural organizations and the instruments' usefulness as accompaniment to folk dance groups seem to have rescued the use of Croatian archaic instruments from extinction.

Folklore KUDs continue to thrive as new groups have been formed both in rural and urban areas. Sometimes their artistic leadership is provided by the most capable KUD members, but outside dance instructors for such groups are much in demand and some manage to teach several groups. They are well paid for their efforts. When the female members of a group are unable to do so, local seamstresses are called upon to repair or produce replicas of village costumes. Thus there are business opportunities associated with KUDs.

The number of occasions for folklore dance groups to perform has proliferated. In 1970s Yugoslavia, I noted that in addition to folklore festivals, a KUD might have been asked to perform at a commemorative ceremony on holidays such as Veterans' Day (Dan borca) or at the dedication of new infrastructure, like public buildings or roads. In the largest Croatian city, Zagreb, in the 1970s stages were erected in several public squares for May Day observances: commemoration of the May 7 liberation of Zagreb from Axis occupation and the arrival of the relay batons (*štafete*) celebrating Tito's birthday (otherwise known as Youth Day) on May 25. Folklore KUDs and other types of amateur artistic groups participated in these events. Since Croatian independence, analogous events to celebrate patriotic occasions continue with the participation of artistic groups including folklore KUDs.

Zagreb's professional folkdance troupe Lado has been very influential not only on Croatian amateurs but also on North American dance groups like the Duquesne University Tamburitzans, junior tamburitza groups, a few of the adult orchestras, and non-ethnic recreational Balkan dance enthusiasts. Founded in 1949, the initial directors of Lado were individuals with a strong background in ethnology—Zvonimir Ljevaković was the first director. He was succeeded in 1974 by Ivan Ivančan, who served until 1983. (Hanibal Dundović served as director from 1983 to 1991 and was succeeded by Ivan Ivančan Jr. in 1992.) The emphasis of these director/choreographers was to present Croatian village dances in a straightforward manner, as close as possible to the village original. The Lado choreographers have eschewed the flirtation dramas and gymnastic stunts that were conventional in choreographies by Igor Moiseyev, the founder of the Russian Moiseyev Dance Company. Moiseyev's choreographic style had become common in the national folk ballet companies of the Soviet-dominated eastern bloc countries. That Lado's founding was late in 1949, more than a year after

Tito's political break with Stalin, may have made it easier to establish a national folk dance company based on a very different aesthetic from the Soviet model. Lado's aesthetic was and has remained closer to the model of the prewar Zagreb ethnologists, seeking to create choreographies that do not call attention to themselves and that change the basic peasant dances as little as possible.

Ivančan articulated his choreographic principles in *Folklor i scena*, a handbook for instructors of folklore groups in which he asserts six major points: "[W]e must satisfy a few basic prerequisites, and these are: (a) familiarity with the authentic material, such as songs and dances, (b) experience of the folk art in the field, (c) carrying over of one's own

Lado album cover, 1970s. (Courtesy of Croatia Records d.d.)

experience to the stage, (d) familiarity with the laws of staging and composition, (e) creation, rehearsal, and maintenance of individual choreographies, and (f) the necessary individual artistic mark of the creator" (Ivančan 1971, 93). Ivančan stressed the need for fieldwork to experience folkdance in its original context in order for a choreographer to create an adequate staged representation, changing it as little as possible only to maintain balance and symmetry on stage.

As a choreographer, Ivančan realized his work cannot be an exact replication of peasant folklore. In a personal conversation, when I asked him about the quibbles of some ethnologists about the so-called authenticity of Lado choreographies, Ivančan stated emphatically, "A picture of a fish cannot be a fish" (Ivančan 1977).

Most Lado choreographies portray a customary event, a holiday, or wedding in a particular village with its associated songs and dances. Care is taken that the costumes, music, instruments, dance steps, and dialect of the lyrics are all ethnographically correct. There are, however, a few Lado choreographies in which the directors attempted to be more experimental. Ljevaković created a dance to portray the wheat harvest in Baranje. Male dancers swinging scythes on stage are followed by stooping women bunching and tying up imaginary shocks of wheat. Ivančan's *Ladarice* choreography is a colorful mosaic of dancers wearing the costumes from various regions of Croatia, a dance spectacle rather than a depiction of a village dance.

The dancers in Lado are mostly young people, some urbanites and others originally from villages. Few if any have had formal dance training, which is unlike the folk dancers in the former-Soviet bloc companies. Indeed, the Lado directors have been chary of including trained dancers lest their movements seem too unlike peasants (Rajković 1978).

Lado has toured all over the world including North America. They have made many recordings, not only on Yugoslav and later on Croatian labels but also on Western European and American labels. The LPs released by Monitor Records in the United States during the 1960s were very influential upon American tamburitza groups. The dance repertoire of most junior tamburitzans, the Croatian repertoire of the Duquesne University Tamburitzans, and the material used by Živili

Kolo of Columbus, Ohio, all are influenced by or are modifications of Lado's dance suites.

The influence has not been exerted only by seeing Lado or hearing recordings of Lado. Over the years many American, Western European, and even Japanese dance teachers have attended dance workshops taught by Ivančan, Stjepan Sremac, Željko Jergan, Srebrenka First, Vlado Salopek, and other Lado-grounded dance specialists. In addition to Željko Jergan, other former Lado dancers who have lived and taught dance in the United States include Milwaukee's Susan Maydak, Nena Šokčić in Los Angeles, and Pittsburgh's Nevenka Vujčic.

In the 1970s the Duquesne University Tamburitzans hired Ivan Ivančan to teach some of his choreographies to their group. Duquesne's material, however, was not limited to Croatia. Their repertoire now includes dances from Rumania, Poland, Bulgaria, Russia, and other eastern European countries. The choreographies that they learned from instructors from those countries are closer to the Moiseyev model. Because the Ivančan choreographies are quite different, Duquesne's concerts have tended to be a heterogeneous mixture of varying influences. Nicholas Jordanoff, the artistic director from the 1970s to the 1990s, tended to place the flashier Moiseyev-style choreographies at high points in the program, such as the closing routine or the last item before intermission. This seemed to place an emphasis on those Bulgarian or Rumanian suites and often caused the Croatian and Serbian American audiences to grumble that the Tamburitzans were not doing enough Croatian material. The lack of a unified aesthetic concept was also evident in Duquesne's performances, which often included recent popular *narodnjak* hits performed by a small combo while the rest of the dancers changed costumes for the next dance suite. Because the American tamburitza combos were likely to play these numbers, they appealed to the American South Slavs, but the directors of Lado or any ethnologically directed group would decry the inclusion of such non-folkloric songs.

As elsewhere in the tamburitza tradition, there is a familiar contrast of the American and European components. While Lado and its choreographic style has emerged out of the ferment of intellectual arguments about the most ethnologically appropriate way of adapting

authentic village dance to the stage, Duquesne's directors were not
trained in ethnology and do not have a deep concern about ethnological issues. Over the years I have had conversations with Duquesne
directors Walter Kolar, Nicholas Jordanoff, and Paul Stafura. All of them
asserted that their concern is to put on a good show, not to present an
ethnographic display. As other American *tamburaši* have been doing
since early in the twentieth century, the Duquesne University Tamburitzans seek to entertain the Slavic and other Eastern European ethnic
communities, and they also hope to validate those cultures to the general American audience.

Duquesne concerts are important annual events in Croatian American communities. Often their concert is sponsored by a local CFU
lodge or a coalition of lodges. As sponsors, they pay the Tamburitzans'
concert fees and the costs for the use of an auditorium as well as the
local marketing costs. Lodge members are enlisted as ticket sellers,
often receiving ten or twenty tickets apiece to sell to their personal
contacts (Leo Sharko 1980). If their travel schedule permits, the Tamburitzans may remain in town to attend a dinner dance, also typically
organized by a CFU lodge at a church or lodge hall. After dinner a
combo plays for informal participatory dancing. Sometimes the combo
players are a few of the Tamburitzans, or sometimes a local tamburitza
ensemble may be hired. The Duquesne directors also urge their college
student performers to mingle with the local crowd (Jordanoff 1987).

These young performers, college students all, have been recruited
mostly from the cream of the junior tamburitza groups. For the past
twenty years, three or four of the thirty Tamburitzans have been from
Eastern Europe. Some of these, like Vjeko Dimter, Dario Barišić, and
Srbislav Cvetković, remained in the United States taking important
roles in American tamburitza activities. All of the Duquesne troupe
members receive scholarships, but they have to earn it by playing sixty,
seventy, or more concerts during the school year in addition to studying for their classes. Every weekend, the spring and winter breaks, and
sometimes even the summer vacation is taken up with touring. Even
when they don't tour abroad, they must report for duty in early July
to learn the new season's program. Until the 1990s they rehearsed the
new program in a camp at the tiny northern Wisconsin town of Lake

Nebagamon. Their first trial performances took place in early August in nearby towns and cities of the Lake Superior region.

The Tamburitzans eventually outgrew the relatively primitive facilities available in Lake Nebagamon. In the late 1980s, in my capacity as folk arts specialist for the Wisconsin Arts Board, I was contacted by the Tamburitzans' leadership and Lake Nebagamon's local officials to help them seek funding to build a suitable practice facility. Unfortunately sufficient funds could not be raised, so the Tamburitzans now rehearse in facilities at their home base at Duquesne University.

Wherever they practice, the hard work of the student performers also has its rewards. Many of the young musicians and dancers become so intensely involved in the music and dance that it becomes a life-long passion. Many become combo musicians, tamburitza instructors, or choreographers for junior orchestras, sometimes even for the same groups from which they graduated themselves years earlier.

There have been a few professional Balkan dance troupes in North America. The Aman Folk Dance Ensemble, started in 1964 by Anthony Shay as a student organization at UCLA, evolved into a professional dance troupe. In Aman's early years their repertoire emphasized Balkan dances although few if any of the dancers were of a Balkan ethnic heritage. Over time the group's repertoire began to include more material from the Americas, the Middle East, and North Africa.

George Tomov, a dancer born in Skoplje, Macedonia, who had experience as a member both of Tanec, the Macedonian state folk dance company, and of Lado, immigrated in 1968 to New York City, where he opened a dance studio on Union Square. Also he taught Balkan dances at camps for international folk dance enthusiasts. In 1974 he founded the George Tomov Dancers, a touring company that was active until 1986. Most of his dancers were his students and, like Aman's dancers, not of Balkan ethnic backgrounds. They performed to recorded music, which was controversial at the time.

Because of its artistic and humanitarian achievements during its thirty-year existence, Živili Kolo has been perhaps the most remarkable American ensemble performing the folk dances of former Yugoslavia. Živili was founded in Columbus, Ohio, in 1974 by three former junior tamburitzans, Drucilla Badurina-Rouselle, Melissa Pintar-Obenauf, and Pam Lacko-Kelley. Drucilla departed for other pursuits after a few years, but Melissa remained as executive director and Pam as artistic director for the entire three-decade duration of the troupe. The directors were highly qualified in their artistic and intellectual preparation to create a company that could have a wide but unified artistic vision (Lacko-Kelly 2004; Pintar-Obenauf 2004).

Melissa, whose paternal grandparents were from Gorski Kotar, was raised in the world of the fine arts. Her mother was a professional violinist and Melissa learned piano, cello, and violin in addition to tambura. She was formally trained in dance, earning degrees in dance and education at the Ohio State University. Pam, whose maternal grandparents were from Lika, was raised in northwest Indiana, where she obtained grounding in Croatian music and dance in the Indiana Harbor Junior Tamburitzans. She met Melissa at Ohio State, where she also received an education degree; they became lifelong friends and business partners. The aesthetic principles of their troupe were informed by their training at the Summer Folklore School in Croatia, where they became acquainted with Ivan Ivančan and eventually developed a lasting relationship with Lado (ibid.).

Located in the university town of Columbus, they were able to recruit dancers from the OSU dance program, among whom Richard Graber stands out as a professional dancer who proudly cites his years with Živili on his resume. Because Ohio is a state with significant South Slavic communities, notably in cities such as Cleveland, Youngstown, and Columbus itself, Živili was able also to recruit junior tamburitzan alumni.

Živili toured extensively throughout Ohio and all of the nearby states of the Midwest. The troupe performed at the 1982 World's Fair in Knoxville, Tennessee, and was Dance Company in residence at Disney World's EPCOT Center in Florida. They performed in former Yugoslavia, noticing during their 1990 tour the mounting tensions that were about to result in the outbreak of the Homeland War in 1991.

Personally concerned about the plight of war victims in former Yugoslavia, Pam and Melissa engaged in a remarkable artistic collaboration with the renowned experimental modern dance choreographer Mark Morris, an accomplishment unequaled among American Balkan dance companies. On the occasion of Živili's twentieth anniversary, they premiered *The Office*, choreographed by Morris. The *New York Times* dance reviewer Anna Kisselgoff called *The Office* "a highly unusual and haunting work, with implicit reference to the war in Bosnia," praising the choreography's "depth" and "beautiful restraint" (Kisselgoff 1994).

Following the Homeland War, Živili performed in refugee camps and orphanages located in Hungary, Slovenia, Croatia, and Sarajevo, and acted as a key facilitator in Plovdiv, Bulgaria, at a UNESCO-sponsored "Balkan Youth Reconciliation Seminar."

Ending their work in Živili in 2004, Pam and Melissa have thrown their considerable energies into Heart of Croatia, their online gift shop featuring culturally significant Croatian gifts, and as mentioned earlier, bringing their pop-up store to the larger Croatian gatherings such as the CFU tamburitza festivals and the Tamburitza Extravaganza (Lacko-Kelley, 2004; Pintar-Obenauf 2004).

It is in the village dance groups that the authentic folklore notions of the Croatian ethnologists have been most thoroughly realized. The professional groups show an admixture of the Gaj ideology of "ennobling" the folk dances with the aesthetic principles of balance and symmetry. In Europe the ethnologists' influence has been direct and pervasive, but in North America their influence has been indirect and fragmentary. The repertoires of junior tamburitzans and even the Duquesne University Tamburitzans are heterogeneous. Only Živili Kolo had directors fully versed in the ethnographic "canon" and even that group had one of its greatest triumphs by adapting ethnic dance to experimental modern dance.

Conclusion

The tambura, a Middle Eastern long-necked lute, was brought to the Balkan Peninsula by Ottoman invaders nearly seven hundred years ago. It was a basic chordophone, highly portable, and originally made from natural materials. This type of lute has continued to be played in something quite similar to its original form, notably in the variant called *šargija*. Because the Balkan Peninsula is a place where the culture of the Middle East meets the culture of Central Europe, this lute, like everything else in the region's traditions, has been modified by the competing influences of the two spheres. Thus, the Central European musical idea of a string section of various-sized instruments of the same type was applied to these Middle Eastern lutes, and the tamburitza orchestra came into being.

Early on, the tamburitza was a manifestation of the manipulation of folklore for other purposes, termed "folklorism" by scholars. Nineteenth-century musicians using these tamburitzas imbued them with meaning: they were the instruments of Croatians or Serbs in the Austro-Hungarian Empire, the embodiment of their nationality. Promoting tamburitza as a national instrument fit well into the ideology of the Illyrian movement, a Croatian-led movement to unify the South Slavs. Their goal was to ennoble the simple peasant instrument to render it on a par with the violins of classical music. Orchestral forms of the tamburitza were created and music composed for that type of orchestra. The orchestras performed in concerts with the pretensions of classical music.

The players of these improved orchestral *tambure* adapted them to other uses, performing on them in informal bands at weddings and other festivities. In the late nineteenth and early twentieth centuries, South Slavic immigrants carried tamburitzas across the Atlantic to North America. The tamburitza as the national instrument of the South Slavs in Austro-Hungary fit well into the New World setting as it became the national instrument of Croatian and Serbian ethnic communities in the United States and Canada.

According to the Illyrian idea, the tamburitza expressed and validated Slavic culture to the dominant Austrians and Hungarians in Europe and to the dominant Anglo-Saxons and Germanic-heritage nationalities in America. In Europe tamburitza performance was imbedded with the political notion that there should be a South Slavic nation-state. In America it expressed the idea that the Slavs were and are a cultured people, and should not face prejudice or discrimination in American society.

After World War I and the downfall of the Habsburg Empire, a South Slavic state was formed—the kingdom of Yugoslavia. Before long the Croatians of Yugoslavia chafed under the Serbian dynasty's rule. The tamburitza and other folk arts and customs of Croatian villagers were displayed, with the expert guidance of Croatian ethnologists to express Croatian particularity, as distinct from the culture of the Serbian rulers, a reversal from Illyrianism. Their implicit message was to justify Croatian cultural and political autonomy, opposing hegemony from another South Slavic nation.

In America there was no such dramatic change in the aftermath of World War I. The same Illyrian notion that the tamburitza validated South Slavic identity still applied in the United States. Moreover, Serbian and Croatian Americans held the same status in the United States; there were no ethnologists directing cultural activities of the immigrant workers, and the American tamburitza tradition evolved under the influence of American sociocultural conditions.

World War II and the socialist revolution in Yugoslavia did not fundamentally change the meaning of the tamburitza traditions either in Yugoslavia or in North America. Postwar developments, however, eroded the identification of Serbian Americans with the tamburitza tradition. Refugees from regions that did not embrace tamburitza became a significant part of the Serbian ethnic community.

During the disintegration of Yugoslavia at the beginning of the 1990s, the tamburitza, like many other Croatian patriotic symbols, received greater emphasis, and there was an increase in musical activity involving the tamburitza. The overtly Serbian versus Croatian nature of the Homeland War disinclined both nationalities toward each other's national symbols, which hastened the decline of the tamburitza's use among Serbian Americans.

Recently the interactions of *tamburaši* have been facilitated and intensified by the many improved means of communication: the Internet, social networking sites, cell phones, and less expensive international airline flights that bring musicians together. As a result, recent developments in the tamburitza tradition are becoming much more unified with diminishing differences between its European and American manifestations.

Both in Europe and in North America, the tamburitza tradition enjoys the support of institutions to ensure its perpetuation. These institutions are more official in Croatia while in North America they are outgrowths of grassroots community activity. In all cases, the tamburitza tradition has become ingrained in the cultural matrix both of Croatia and of the Croatian American communities. The tamburitza tradition should continue to flourish for a very long time.

Glossary

baglama. The Turkish term for the long-necked, pear-shaped lute generally considered to be the original form of the tamburitza. It is often called by its Persian name *saz* and is played by many peoples of the Middle East, the Mediterranean, and Central Asia.

Ban. The title of the office of governor of the Austro-Hungarian province of Croatia.

bajs. A small bowed string bass, usually used as a rhythm instrument.

basprim. The name for the Srijemski system *tambura* also known as *brač*. This term is commonly used in Vojvodina.

bečar. A young man or bachelor. The term implies merrymaking, drinking, and carousing.

bečarac. A genre of improvised singing, usually during socializing, in the *deseterac dvostih* verse form. The themes are often sexually suggestive.

beglajt. See *bugarija.*

berde. The bass instrument in the tamburitza family of instruments. About the size of a string bass, it has steel wire strings and steel frets.

bisernica. Literal translation "little pearl," this is the term used for the smallest and highest-pitched instrument in the Farkaš system of tamburitza instruments. They are typically shaped like a tiny guitar.

brač. The term for the second-smallest instrument in tamburitza systems. The term is identical to *Bratsch*, the German word for viola, the equivalent instrument in the violin family of instruments, and a lower pitch than the violin.

bugarija. The rhythm instrument in tamburitza systems. It is about the size of a guitar, tuned in an open chord, and normally played by striking chords across all strings of the instrument. Other terms for it are *kontra* and *beglajt.*

čelo brač. The lower-pitched instrument in tamburitza instrumental systems, equivalent to the cello in the violin family. It is typically the size of a guitar.

ćitelija. A small two-stringed tambura.

dangubica. Literal translation "day waster," it is another term for the soloistic tambura most frequently called *samica.*

deseterac. A ten-syllable line verse form that is the most frequent form in Serbian and Croatian folk poetry and singing.

deseterac dvostih. Two-line verses in the *deseterac* meter, usually rhymed. See also *ojkan.*

drmeš. Another prominent Croatian dance form in 2/4 time.

džezvice. Coffee pots in the shape of a truncated cone.

Dinaric. The Dinaric Alps are the mountain range that runs parallel to the western, Adriatic coast of the Balkan peninsula. The term refers to cultural expressions from that geographic area.

Farkaš system. The system of orchestral tamburitza instruments for which the early twentieth-century tamburitza leader Milutin Farkaš wrote an instruction book.

folklorism. The term for folklore that has been changed or put into a changed cultural locus and invested with a self-conscious notion that the expression is a part of one's folklore heritage.

Folklorismus. The German-language term translated as folklorism. Because it was German scholars who developed the concept, the German term is often used instead of folklorism in English writings.

Gaj ideology. Ideology based on the Illyrian movement's founder and key leader, Ljudevit Gaj.

gajde. Bagpipes from the inland areas of the Balkans.

guci. Folk music string ensembles in northern Croatia featuring violins.

gusle. A one-stringed, bowed musical instrument with a leather or skin head played exclusively in the Balkans for the accompaniment of epic songs.

izvorni. The adjectival form of the word *izvor* meaning "wellsprings." Applied to folk cultural forms, its meaning is close to "authentic" in English.

kajkavski. The dialect of Croatian prevalent in the northern sections of the country. It is named for its characteristic word *kaj* meaning "what" in that dialect.

kapele. Hungarian Romani musical ensembles.

kolo. The term applied to a broad range of South Slavic line and circle dances.

kontra. See *bugarija.*

Kordun. A province of western Croatia.

Kordunaši. People from Kordun.

kozarica. See *samica.*

KUD. Kulturno i umjetničko društvo (cultural and artistic society).

kuterevka. See *samica.*

Lika. A province of western Croatia, an important center of *samica* playing. Lika is home to a substantial Serbian population as well as Croatians. Many Serbian Americans are descended from immigrants from Lika.

mih. Bagpipes from the Adriatic coastal area of the Balkans.

mjesna zajednica. Neighborhood council.

mišničar. Bagpiper.

na bas singing. A form of folk singing in harmony, typically ending on the dominant (V.) chord to the tonic.

narodni orkestar. Ensemble that plays *narodnjak.*

narodnjak. Folk-influenced musical genre.

ojkan. A type of folksong common in Lika and Kordun that features two lines of *deseterac,* usually rhymed, ending on a strong, sustained dominant fifth chord. See *deseterac dvostih.*

oro. A type of line dance common in Macedonia.

Pannonia. The central European lowlands of the Danube River basin. The valleys of the Danube tributaries Sava and Drava are important locations of the tamburitza tradition.

pohodi. Traditional outdoor events, such as weddings, holiday concerts, etc.

prelo, or *sijelo.* Communal work bee.

prigorsko nošnje. Zagreb hill country native costumes.

prim or *prima.* The smallest and highest-pitched tamburitza instrument. It normally carries the melodic lead part.

primaš. The player of the *prim* or *prima,* often the lead player who directs and gives cues to the other band members.

Romani. The ethnic group, also called Roma, Romany, or Roms, living mostly in Europe who trace their ancestry to the Indian subcontinent. In English they have been called "Gypsies" but nowadays the term may be considered pejorative. Romani also refers to their language. Many Romani clans have specialized as professional musicians. They have made a great contribution to the tamburitza tradition.

salaš. The term for a farm, used in Vojvodina.

samica/samice (pl.). A soloistic tambura, normally with four strings. The name literally means "little by-itself thing." It is most widespread in the folk traditions of Slavonia, Kordun and Lika.

sastav. A band or ensemble.

saz. A large Middle Eastern long-necked lute, an early form of tambura, that is still actively played in the Middle East, North Africa, and southeastern Europe. See *baglama.*

šargija/šargijaš. A plucked, fretted long-necked lute with four to six strings used in the folk music of various Balkan countries, including Bosnia-Herzegovina, Croatia, Albania, Kosovo, and Serbia.

Seljačka sloga. United Peasants, the cultural wing of the Croatian Peasant Party (HSS).

sevdah. A Turkish word meaning "love," a loan word in South Slavic languages with the connotation of unrequited, unhappy passion. Also the shortened term for *sevdalinka*.

sevdalinka. A very popular and widespread genre of vocal music originating in Bosnia-Herzegovina that has *sevdah* as its key emotive basis.

Slavonia. A province of northeastern Croatia located in the Sava River valley on the Pannonian plains. It is the region of Croatia with the most active tamburitza tradition.

smotra. A Slavic-root word for exhibition that is mostly associated with exhibitions or festivals of folk arts.

srijemski system. The tamburitza instrumental system, also called *sremski* in Serbian, which features strings or courses of strings tuned in the interval of a fourth. The most common tunings are the so-called G–D system and the A–E system.

starogradske pjesme. Literal translation "old town songs," referring to a genre of songs that are about romance, patriotism, or drinking. Although some songs continue to be composed in the genre, the bulk of the repertoire was created in the later nineteenth century and early twentieth century.

štokavski. A dialect of Croatian, Bosnian, and Serbian that is the basis of the literary languages spoken in much of the area of former Yugoslavia. It is named for its characteristic word *što* meaning "what."

tambura. The most general term for the various forms of tamburitza instruments, soloistic and orchestral. It is also used to mean the music played on the instrument.

tambura dvožica. A two-stringed instrument known in the Banija region of central Croatia near the Bosnian border.

tamburaš/tamburaši. The player/s of a tambura.

tamburašica/tamburašice. Female player/s of a tambura.

tamburica. The diminutive version of the word tambura. The diminutive ending implies small size or affection or in this specific case, it is the name most commonly used for the major manifestations of tambura playing.

tamburitza. The anglicized spelling of *tamburica*.

Tamburitzans. The name of the music and dance ensemble based at Duquesne University in Pittsburgh. The term Junior Tamburitzans is applied to most of the youth tamburitza ensembles in North America. Ordinarily a player of a tambura is not called by this term, but rather *tamburaš*.

Vojvodina. The autonomous province in the north of Serbia that is home to a strong and musically sophisticated tamburitza tradition. The Romani *tamburaši* of Vojvodina have been especially influential in shaping the tamburitza tradition of the past half century.

zabavna glazba. Urban popular music.

zbor. A choir, usually of voices, but occasionally it is used to mean an ensemble of instruments.

Essay on Sources

The Tamburitza Tradition is a study of a folk music idiom that has evolved in the context of a cultural and political movement to affirm the national identity and to validate the cultural autonomy and worth of South Slavic peoples, particularly Croatians. The musical tradition is practiced in its original homeland and in Croatian and Serbian ethnic communities around the world. The tamburitza tradition has been a self-conscious expression of national heritage for more than 150 years, and perhaps coincidentally, the efforts of the scholars who established the discipline of folklore studies also occurred during the same historical period.

My scholarship for this study was shaped and informed by my graduate training in the Folklore Institute at Indiana University and especially by my thesis adviser Richard M. Dorson. I began graduate school in 1973 and completed my dissertation in 1983; the scholarly trends that were current at that time in the field of folklore and related disciplines were influential on this work. In updating the work for publication, I had the good fortune to have the assistance of the ethnomusicologist Naila Ceribašić of the Institut za etnologiju i folkloristiku in Zagreb, Croatia, a specialist in closely related topics, who critiqued my work and acquainted me with newer scholarship on the subject matter.

GENERAL ORIENTATION AND METHODOLOGY

Richard Dorson's works shaped my basic concept of folklore itself and of how to do the historically oriented aspect of this study: Richard M. Dorson, "Folklore," in *American Folklore and the Historian*, ed. Richard M. Dorson (Chicago, 1971); and Richard M. Dorson, "Concepts of Folklore and Folklife Studies," in *Folklore and Folklife*, ed. Richard M. Dorson (Chicago, 1972). Moreover, my fieldwork for this study began in team research efforts directed by Dr. Dorson in the Calumet Region of northern Indiana from 1975 to 1977. Dorson's *Land of the Millrats* (Cambridge, MA, 1981) is a compendium of results from that team research effort.

I derived notions of how folklore functions in a culture and society from such works as: William Bascom, "Four Functions of Folklore," in *The Study of Folklore*, ed. Alan Dundes (Englewood Cliffs, NJ, 1965); Warren L. d'Azevedo, ed., *The Traditional Artist in African Society* (Bloomington, IN, 1973); and Linda Degh, *Folktales and Society: Storytelling in a Hungarian Peasant Community* (Bloomington, IN, 1969).

The practice of studying folklore in its performance context began as an innovative approach in the early 1970s. The writings of the performance-oriented scholars influenced my approach to field research. A few influential articles were: Dan Ben-Amos, "Toward a Definition of Folklore in Context," *Journal of American Folklore* 84 (1971); Barbara Kirshenblatt-Gimblett, "A Parable in Context," and Dell Hymes, "Breakthrough into Performance," both in *Folklore: Performance and Communication*, ed. Kenneth Goldstein and Dan Ben-Amos (The Hague, 1975); and Richard Bauman, "Verbal Art as Performance," *American Anthropologist* 77 (1975).

Henry Glassie was another professor whose seminars were crucial to my graduate training. Aside from challenging me to study the theoretical works of scholars like Jean Piaget, Kenneth Burke, Noam Chomsky, Del Hymes, Erving Goffman, and Clifford Geertz, the conceptual aspects of his own works influenced this study: Henry Glassie, *Folk Housing in Middle Virginia: A Structural Analysis of Historic Artifacts* (Knoxville, 1975); and Henry Glassie, *Passing the Time in Ballymenome: Culture and History of an Ulster Community* (Philadelphia, 1982).

I had the opportunity to conduct field and library research in 1977–78, based at the Institut za etnologiju i folkloristiku in Zagreb, Croatia. The institute's scholars were invaluable to furthering my education and helping shape this work. Maja Bošković-Stulli and especially Dunja Rihtman-Auguštin acquainted me with their own and other European scholars' work on folklore, especially on the issue of folklorism or "second-existence" folklore: Maja Bošković-Stulli, "O folklorizmu," *Zbornik za narodni život i običaje* 45 (1971); Maja Bošković-Stulli, "O pojmovima usmena i pučka književnost i njihovim nazivima," *Umjetnost riječi* 17 (1973); Dunja Rihtman-Auguštin, "Pretpostavke suvremenog etnološkog iztrazivanja," *Narodna umjetnost* 15 (1976); and Dunja Rihtman-Auguštin, "Folklor, folklorizam i suvremena publika," *Etnološka tribina* 7–8 (1978).

They encouraged me to read the works of German scholars like Hans Moser and Hermann Bausinger: Hans Moser, "Vom Folklorismus in unserer Zeit,"

Zeitschrift fur Volkskunde 58 (1962); Hermann Bausinger, *Formen der Volkspoesie* (Berlin: 1961); Hermann Bausinger "Zur Kritik der Folklorismus–Kritik," *Populus revisus* (1966); Hermann Bausinger, "Folklorismus in Europa (Eine Umfrage)," *Zeitschrift fur Volkskunde* 65 (1969).

GENERAL HISTORY SOURCES

The politics of the nationalist movements that swept Europe in the nineteenth century had a decisive role in shaping the tamburitza tradition. Even though I certainly am not a historian, I have endeavored to present the historical context in which this musical tradition developed. In graduate school I attended history classes and seminars taught by Charles and Barbara Jelavich, noted scholars of Balkan history. Moreover, Charles Jelavich served on my dissertation committee and reviewed the historical statements in my work for accuracy.

General information on the history of the tamburitza's homeland derived from such sources as: Stephen Clissold, ed., *A Short History of Yugoslavia* (Cambridge, 1966); Charles and Barbara Jelavich, *The Balkans* (Englewood Cliffs, NJ, 1965); Charles and Barbara Jelavich, *The Establishment of the Balkan National States, 1804–1920* (Seattle, 1977); Vjekoslav Klaić, *Povijest Hrvata* (Zagreb, 1972); Noel Malcolm, *Bosnia: A Short History* (New York, 1996); Carlyle A. Macartney, *The Habsburg Empire, 1790–1918* (New York, 1969); and Alan Palmer, *The Lands Between* (London, 1970).

THE ILLYRIAN MOVEMENT

The Illyrian movement that emerged in Croatia in the 1830s and 1840s has been a much discussed topic in Croatian history. The movement not only crystallized the nascent sense of Croatian national identity but also its pan–South Slavic aspirations; it laid a foundation for the Yugoslav idea that ultimately contributed to the formation of the two Yugoslav states that existed from 1918 until 1991. Moreover, Illyrism was midwife to the birth of the modern Croatian literary language. It initiated artistic and cultural endeavors conceived on a national basis, including the beginnings of the tamburitza tradition as a self-conscious expression of nationhood.

Because his life and activities were so central to the movement, biographies of the Illyrian movement's founder and key leader Ljudevit Gaj are essential: Josip Horvat, *Ljudevit Gaj* (Zagreb, 1975); and Elinor Murray Despalatović, *Ljudevit Gaj and the Illyrian Movement* (New York, 1975). Gaj's musical endeavors are treated in Nikša Stančić, *Gajeva "Još Horvatska ni propala" iz 1832–33: Ideologija Ljudevita Gaja u pripremnom razdoblju hrvatskog narodnog preporoda* (Zagreb, 1989). Articles by Elinor Murray Despalatović, "Peasant Culture and National Culture," *Balkanistica* 3 (1976), and Wayne S. Vucinich, "Croatian

Illyrism: Its Background and Genesis," in *Intellectual and Social Developments in the Habsburg Empire from Maria Theresa to World War I*, ed. Stanley B. Winters and Joseph Held (New York, 1975), treat Illyrism with a wider focus. Late in the nineteenth century, Franjo Kuhač had the foresight to conduct oral history research with the surviving Illyrian musicians: Franjo Š. Kuhač, *Ilirski glasbenici* (Zagreb, 1893).

The historical, cultural, and literary developments that preceded Illyrism are well discussed in Zvane Črnja, *Cultural History of Croatia* (Zagreb, 1962); and Antun Barac, *Jugoslavenska književnost* (Zagreb, 1963). Works that explain the influence of South Slavic folk poesy on the development of romantic nationalism include: Alberto Fortis, *Travels into Dalmatia* (New York, 1971); Duncan Wilson, *The Life and Times of Vuk Stefanović Karadžić* (Oxford, 1970); and Jakša Ravlić, introduction to *Razgovor ugodni naroda slovinskoga* by Andrija Kačić-Miošić (Zagreb, 1967).

MUSICOLOGICAL, ETHNOLOGICAL, AND ETHNOMUSICOLOGICAL SOURCES

Descriptions of the original type of tambura may be found in Matija Murko, *Tragom srpsko-hrvatske narodne epike* (Zagreb, 1951); Kosta Hormann, *Narodne pjesme muslimana u Bosni i Hercegovini* (Sarajevo, 1933); Božidar Širola, "Gradnje samica i dangubica u Zagorju," *Zbornik za narodni život i običaje* 38 (1935); Jerko Bezić, "Muzički folklor Sinjske krajine," *Narodna umjetnost* 5–6 (1967–68); and Milovan Gavazzi, *Tradicijska narodna glazbala Jugoslavije* (Zagreb, 1975).

The origins of the tambura and its early development among the South Slavs were topics that were much discussed and sometimes hotly disputed for several decades in the nineteenth and twentieth centuries. Early origin theories that were later rejected were espoused by Franjo Kuhač, "Prilog za povjest glasbe južnoslovjenske: Kulturno-historijska studija," *Rad Jugoslavenske akademije znanosti i umjetnosti* 39 (1877); and Franjo Kuhač, *Turski živalj u pučkoj glazbi Hrvata, Srba i Bugara* (Sarajevo, 1898). An Enlightenment-era treatise that mentions tambura negatively was written in 1762: Matija Antun Reljković and Ivo Bogner, *Satir iliti divji čovik* (Osijek, 1974).

Later studies resulted in the consensus view on origins that prevails today: Josip Andrić, *Tamburaška glazba: Historijski pregled* (Slavonska Požega, 1962): Josip Andrić, "Tamburica," in *Enciklopedija Jugoslavije*, ed. Miroslav Krleža (Zagreb, 1968); Walter W. Kolar, *A History of the Tambura*, vol. 1 (Pittsburgh, 1973); Koraljka Kos, "Muzički instrumenti u srednjovjekovnoj likovnoj umjetnosti Hrvatske," *Rad JAZU* 351 (1969); and Cvjetko Rihtman, "Yugoslav Folk Music Instruments," in *The Folk Arts in Yugoslavia*, ed. Walter W. Kolar (Pittsburgh, 1976).

Musical and musicological developments in the tamburitza tradition's formative era were discussed in Josip Andreis, *Music in Croatia* (Zagreb, 1974); Božidar Širola, *Hrvatska narodna glazba* (Zagreb, 1941); F. Kuhač, "Prilog za povjest glasbe južnoslovjenske," *Rad* 39 (1877); Josip Andrić, "Razvoj tamburaške glazbe," *Tamburaška glazba* 3 (1958); Julije Njikoš, "Značenja Paje Kolarića u tamburaškoj glazbi," *Tamburaška glazba* 2 (1957); Andrija Gojkovič, "Uloga Roma u narodnoj muzici," *Narodno stvaralaštvo* (1972); and Maja Bošković-Stulli, "O folklorizmu," *Zbornik za narodni život i običaje* 45 (1971). The following works are evaluations of the important contributions of Franjo Kuhač, the initiator of ethnomusicology in the Balkans: Branko Rakijaš, *Franjo Kuhač* (Zagreb, 1974); Jerko Bezić, ed., *Zbornik radova sa znanstvenog skupa održanog u povodu 150. obljetnice rođenja Franje Ksavera Kuhača (1834–1911)* (Zagreb, 1984); and Grozdana Marošević, "Kuhačeva etnomuzikološka zadužbina," *Narodna umjetnost* 26 (1989).

The early development of tamburitza ensembles and the changes made to the instruments to render them suitable for ensemble playing are discussed in several articles, mostly written by self-taught musician-scholars. They appeared in *Tamburaška glazba*, a short-lived periodical for tamburitza enthusiasts: Josip Andrić, "Razvoj tamburaške glazbe," *Tamburaška glazba* 3 (1958); Josip Andrić, "Kod nestora tamburaške glazbe," *Tamburaška glazba* 1 (1955); Josip Andrić, "Ivan Zajc i tambure," *Tamburaška glazba* 1 (1955); Petar Z. Ilić, "Iz početnog razdoblja tamburaške glazbe," *Tamburaška glazba* 1 (1955); Milan Stahuljak, "Nepoznate crtice iz života Paje Kolarića," *Tamburaška glazba* 5 (1960); Adolf Grobming, "Tamburaška glazba kod Slovenaca," *Tamburaška glazba* 1 (1955); Sava Vukosavljev, "Marko Nešić," *Tamburaška glazba* 5 (1960); and Franjo Korlović, "Tamburaška glazba u radničkom domu nezavisnih sindikata u Mostaru," *Tamburaška glazba* 4 (1959).

The earliest influential instruction book for orchestral *tambure* was Milutin pl. Farkaš, *Kratka uputa u tamburanje po kajdah* (Zagreb, 1906). Julije Njikoš, an important composer for tamburitza, in addition to his short article about Pajo Kolarić in *Tamburaška glazba* also wrote a more extensive work about the "founder" of tamburitza music: Julije Njikoš, *Pajo Kolarić: Život i rad (1821–1876)* (Osijek, 1995). Extensive data on the early tamburitza orchestras in Croatia is provided in Nada Bezić, "Tamburica: Hrvatski izvozni proizvod na prijelazu od 19. u 20. stoljeće," *Narodna umjetnost* 38.1 (2001). Ruža Bonafačić discussed the interplay of tamburitza and patriotism in more recent years in the following articles: Ruža Bonafačić, "Uloga rodoljubnih pjesama i tamburaške glazbe u Hrvatskoj početkom 1990-ih: Primjer neotradicionalne grupe 'Zlatni dukati,'" *Arti musices* 24 (1993); and Ruža Bonafačić, "Changing of Symbols: The Folk Instrument Tamburica as a Political and Cultural Phenomenon," *Collegium Antropologicum* 19 (1995).

Immigration to America and Americanization

The great wave of immigration to the United States in the late nineteenth and early twentieth centuries, in which the South Slavs took part, has been studied by many influential scholars. I relied on the following works among others: Oscar Handlin, *The Uprooted* (New York, 1951); Leonard Dinnerstein, Roger L. Nichols, and David M. Reimers, *Natives and Strangers: Ethnic Groups and the Building of America* (Oxford, 1979); John Bodnar, *The Transplanted: A History of Immigrants in Urban America* (Bloomington, IN, 1985); John Higham, *Strangers in the Land* (New Brunswick, NJ, 1988); and Emily Green Balch, *Our Slavic Fellow Citizens* (New York, 1910).

Studies focused specifically on South Slavic immigrants include: Većeslav Holjevac, *Hrvati izvan domovine* (Zagreb, 1967); Ivan Čizmić, *Jugoslovenski iseljenički pokret i stvaranje Jugoslavije 1918* (Zagreb, 1974); Ivan Čizmić, *Hrvati u životu Sjedinjenih američkih država* (Zagreb, 1982); George J. Prpić, *The Croatian Immigrants in America* (New York, 1971); and Adam S. Erterovich, *Croatian Pioneers in America, 1685–1900* (San Francisco, 1979).

The development of American leisure and entertainment is discussed in the following works: Robert W. Rydell, *All the World's a Fair* (Chicago, 1984); Roy Rosenzweig, *Eight Hours for What We Will* (New York, 1983); Larry Widen and Judy Anderson, *Silver Screens* (Madison, WI, 2007); Bill C. Malone, *Country Music USA* (Austin, TX, 1968); and Pekka Gronow, "Ethnic Recordings, an Introduction," in *Ethnic Recordings in America: A Neglected Heritage* (Washington, DC, 1982).

How *tamburaši* found a foothold in American entertainment is treated in the following works: Walter W. Kolar, *A History of the Tambura*, vol. 2 (Pittsburgh, 1975); Richard K. Spottswood, *Ethnic Music on Records*, vol. 2 (Chicago, 1990); Milan Opacich, *Tamburitza America* (Tucson, AZ, 2005); Richard March, "The Tamburitza Tradition in the Calumet Region," *Indiana Folklore* 10 (1976); Mark Forry, "Bećar Music in Los Angeles," *Selected Papers in Ethnomusicology* 3 (1977); and Andrei Simic, *The Peasant Urbanites: A Study of Rural-Urban Mobility in Serbia* (Taradale, New Zealand, 1973).

Ethnology, Ethnologists, and Festivals of Croatian Peasant Culture

The founding document of ethnology in Croatia was the all-encompassing questionnaire for researchers of village life by Antun Radić: Antun Radić, "Osnova za sabiranje i proučavanja građe o narodnom životu," *Zbornik za narodni život i običaje južnih slavena* (1897). Examples of data on the tamburitza tradition in village monographs based on Radić's *Osnova* include: Ivan Lovretić, "Otok," *Zbornik za narodni život i običaje južnih slavena* (1897); Milan Lang, "Samobor," *Zbornik za narodni život i običaje južnih slavena* (1911–13);

and Vatroslav Rožić, "Prigorje," *Zbornik za narodni život i običaje južnih slavena* (1907–8). The ethnomusicologist Grozdana Marošević evaluated the music-related data contained in these monographs: Grozdana Marošević, "Podaci o glazbi u monografijama *Zbornik za narodni život i običaje južnih slavena*," *Narodna umjetnost* 34.2 (1997).

Conceptual differences from Radić that emerged with the next generation of Croatian ethnologists is discussed by Jasna Čapo Žmegač: Jasna Čapo Žmegač, "Two Scientific Paradigms in Croatian Ethnology: Antun Radić and Milovan Gavazzi," *Narodna umjetnost* 32.1 (1995). This approach to ethnology became established at Zagreb University and is well documented in the works of Milovan Gavazzi: Milovan Gavazzi, *Vrela i sudbine narodnih tradicija kroz prostore, vremena i ljude* (Zagreb, 1978). Branimir Bratanić delineated the ethnologists' thinking about the role of folklore festivals: Branimir Bratanić, *O smotrama hrvatske seljačke culture* (Zagreb, 1941). Naila Ceribašić prepared an extremely comprehensive and detailed work on the history and ethnography of the public practice of folk music in Croatia: Naila Ceribašić, *Hrvatsko, seljačko, starinsko i domaće: Povijest i etnografija javne prakse narodne glazbe u hrvatskoj* (Zagreb, 2003); and an article focused on the *Međunarodna smotra folklora*: Naila Ceribašić, "Festivalski okviri folklornih tradicija: Primjer *Međunarodne smotre folklora*," in *Predstavljanje tradicijske kulture na sceni i u medijima*, ed. Zorica Vitez and Aleksandra Muraj (Zagreb, 2008).

Bosnian folk music, which originally was frequently performed to the accompaniment of soloistic *tambure*, evolved into a folk-referencing form of popular music in the former Yugoslav countries, especially Bosnia, Serbia, and Croatia. In turn, this music in various stages of its evolution became adapted into the repertoire of tamburitza combos. Vlado Milošević, a music specialist at a regional museum in Bosnia, wrote two useful books on the original folk music: Vlado Milošević, *Bosanske narodne pjesme* (Banja Luka, 1963); and Vlado Milošević, *Sevdalinka* (Banja Luka, 1964); see also Damir Imamović, "Priča o sevdalinci u kontekstu politike kulture i politike identiteta u BiH," in *Na tragu novih politika: Kultura i obrazovanje u Bosni i Hercegovini*, ed. Jasmina Husanović (Tuzla, 2005).

MY FIELDWORK

A great deal of my writing is based on personal communications with scores of people involved in the tamburitza tradition. I conducted structured fieldwork as a trained folklorist as well as having a lifetime immersion in Croatian culture and familiarity with tamburitza music. From 1975 to 1977, I was a research assistant to Dr. Richard M. Dorson in his team fieldwork project in the Calumet Region of Northwest Indiana, which enabled me to meet and interview more than a dozen of the active *tamburaši* from that area. In 1977 I was hired by the

American Folklife Center to conduct fieldwork in a team project in Chicago, which allowed me to contact and interview several key figures there.

From 1977 to 1978 I was based at the Ethnology and Folklore Institute in Zagreb. From there, I made more than a dozen field trips to various locations in Croatia, Bosnia-Herzegovina, and Vojvodina, accompanied on a few of those forays by my Croatian colleagues, Dr. Jerko Bezić, Dr. Zorica Vitez, Krešimir Galin, Vladimir Salopek, and Dr. Stjepan Sremac.

From 1978 until 1983 I lived in Milwaukee, making a sustained effort during those years to observe the tamburitza tradition in that city. From 1979 to 1982 I was hired as a contract fieldworker on projects in Ashland, Wisconsin, in Cleveland, Ohio, and in Nevada, Utah, Idaho, and in the later 1980s and early 1990s in Michigan, which brought me into contact with more *tamburaši*. From 1983 to 2009 I served as Folk Arts Specialist at the Wisconsin Arts Board. In that capacity I had occasional contacts with *tamburaši* in Wisconsin and in neighboring states. Moreover, seldom has a year passed when I failed to attend a Croatian picnic or a tamburitza concert and from 2002 to 2008 I was a member of Graničari, an adult amateur tamburitza orchestra, performing with them in the group's home city of Milwaukee as well as traveling to tamburitza performances and gatherings in Pennsylvania, Ohio, Illinois, and Missouri.

In the section titled "Informants," I have endeavored to make a complete list of the many people whose thoughts and statements have contributed to my knowledge of tamburitza.

Sources

Ahmethodžić-Zečaj, Emina. 1976. Personal communication. Philadelphia, August.

Aman Folk Ensemble. The First 30 Years. http://www.phantomranch.net/folk danc/perform/aman-30.htm.

Andreis, Josip. 1974. *Music in Croatia*. Zagreb.

Andrić, Josip. 1955a. "Ivan Zajc i tambure." *Tamburaška glazba* 1.

———. 1955b. "Kod nestora tamburaške glazbe." *Tamburaška glazba* 1.

———. 1958. "Razvoj tamburaške glazbe." *Tamburaška glazba* 3.

———. 1962. *Tamburaška glazba: Historijski pregled*. Slavonska Požega.

———. 1968. "Tamburica." In *Enciklopedija Jugoslavije*, edited by Miroslav Krleža. Zagreb.

Balch, Emily Green. 1910. *Our Slavic Fellow Citizens*. New York.

Barac, Antun. 1963. *Jugoslavenska književnost*. Zagreb.

Bascom, William. 1965. "Four Functions of Folklore." In *The Study of Folklore*, edited by Alan Dundes. Englewood Cliffs, NJ.

Bauman, Richard. 1975. "Verbal Art as Performance." *American Anthropologist* 77.

Bausinger, Hermann. 1961. *Formen der Volkspoesie*. Berlin.

———. 1966. "Zur Kritik der Folklorismus–Kritik." *Populus revisus*.

———. 1969. "Folklorismus in Europa (Eine Umfrage)." *Zeitschrift für Volkskunde* 65.

Ben-Amos, Dan. 1971. "Toward a Definition of Folklore in Context." *Journal of American Folklore* 84.

Bezić, Jerko. 1967–68. "Muzički folklor Sinjske krajine." *Narodna umjetnost* 5–6.

———. 1978. "Tambure u Hrvatskoj." Text of Radio Zagreb program, January 10.

———, ed. 1984. *Zbornik radova sa znanstvenog skupa održanog u povodu 150. obljetnice rođenja Franje Ksavera Kuhača (1834–1911)*. Zagreb.

———. 1976. "The Tonal Framework of Folk Music in Yugoslavia." In *The Folk Arts in Yugoslavia*, edited by Walter W. Kolar. Pittsburgh.

Bezić, Nada. 2001. "Tamburica—hrvatski izvozni proizvod na prijelazu 19. u 20. stoljeće." *Narodna umjetnost* 38.2.

Bodnar, John. 1985. *The Transplanted: A History of Immigrants in Urban America*. Bloomington, IN.

Bonifačić, Ruža. 1993. "Uloga rodoljubnih pjesama i tamburaške glazbe u Hrvatskoj početkom 1990-ih: Primjer neotradicionalne grupe 'Zlatni dukati.'" *Arti musices* 41.1.

———. 1995. "Changing of Symbols: The Folk Instrument Tamburica as a Political and Cultural Phenomenon." *Collegium Antropologicum* 19.1.

Bonifačić-Rozin, Nikola. 1978. Personal communication. Zagreb, April.

Bošković-Stulli, Maja. 1971. "O folklorizmu." *Zbornik za narodni život i običaje* 45.

———. 1973. "O pojmovima usmena i pučka književnost i njihovim nazivima." *Umjetnost riječi* 17.

Bradić, Željko. 1978. Personal communication. Samobor, May.

Bratanić, Branimir. 1941. *O smotrama hrvatske seljačke culture*. Zagreb.

Ceribašić, Naila. 1998. "Folklorna glazbena praksa i kulturna politika: Paradigma smotri folklora u Hrvatskoj." PhD diss., Zagreb.

———. 2003. *Hrvatsko, seljačko, starinsko i domaće: povijest i etnografija javne prakse narodne glazbe u hrvatskoj*. Zagreb.

———. 2011. Personal communication. Zagreb, March.

Čižmić, Ivan. 1974. *Jugoslovenski iseljenički pokret i stvaranje Jugoslavije 1918*. Zagreb.

———. 1982. *Hrvati u životu Sjedinjenih američkih država*. Zagreb.

Clissold, Stephen. 1966. *A Short History of Yugoslavia*. Cambridge, UK.

Črnja, Zvane. 1962. *Cultural History of Croatia*. Zagreb.

Crnković, Rudolf. 1933. *Sa "Zvonimirom" po Americi: Zapisci 5 godišnjeg tamburaškog putovanja*. Chicago.

Cvitković, Mato. 1979. Personal communication. Cleveland, OH, March.

Daniels, Agnes. 1982. Personal communication. San Pedro, CA, September.

d'Azevedo, Warren L., ed. 1973. *The Traditional Artist in African Society*. Bloomington, IN.

Degh, Linda. 1969. *Folktales and Society: Storytelling in a Hungarian Peasant Community*. Bloomington, IN.

Despalatović, Elinor Murray. 1975. *Ljudevit Gaj and the Illyrian Movement*. New York.

———. 1976. "Peasant Culture and National Culture." *Balkanistica* 3.

Dimter, Vjeko. 2003. Personal communication, Philadelphia, February.

Dinnerstein, Leonard, Roger L. Nichols, and David M. Reimers. 1979. *Natives and Strangers: Ethnic Groups and the Building of America.* Oxford.

Dobro jutro Hrvatska. 2008. Croatian morning television news, December 10. http://www.youtube.com/watch?v=nJfP3gjSmGo.

Dorson, Richard M. 1971. "Folklore." In *American Folklore and the Historian,* edited by Richard M. Dorson. Chicago.

———. 1972. "Concepts of Folklore and Folklife Studies." In *Folklore and Folklife,* edited by Richard M. Dorson. Chicago.

———. 1981. *Land of the Millrats.* Cambridge, MA.

Elias, Charles. 1924. *Škola za tamburaše.* Milwaukee.

Elias, Charles, Jr. 1981. Personal communication. Kenosha, WI.

Erterovich, Adam S. 1979. *Croatian Pioneers in America 1685–1900.* San Francisco.

Farkaš, Milutin pl. 1906. *Kratka uputa u tamburanje po kajdah.* Zagreb.

Ferić, Mihael. 2011. *Hrvatski tamburaški brevijar.* Zagreb.

Forry, Mark Edward. 1977. "Bećar Music in Los Angeles." *Selected Papers in Ethnomusicology* 3.

———. 1990. "The Meditation of 'Tradition' and 'Culture' in the Tamburica Music of Vojvodina Yugoslavia." PhD diss., Los Angeles.

Fortis Alberto. 1971. *Travels into Dalmatia.* New York.

Gavazzi, Milovan. 1972. Lecture notes for the course "Etnografija jugoistočne Evrope." Zagreb University.

———. 1975. *Tradicijska narodna glazbala Jugoslavije.* Zagreb.

———. 1978. *Vrela i sudbine narodnih tradicija kroz prostore, vremena i ljude.* Zagreb.

Gilg, Katarina. 1978. Personal communication. Sisak, April.

Gojković, Andrija. 1972. "Uloga Roma u narodnoj muzici." *Narodno stvaralaštvo.*

Gornick, John. 2004. Personal communication. Chicago, September.

Greverus, Ina Maria. 1976. "How to Decode a 'Folk' Symbol." In *Folklore Today,* edited by Linda Degh, Henry Glassie, and Felix J. Oinas. Bloomington.

Grobming, Adolf. 1955. "Tamburaška glazba kod Slovenaca." *Tamburaška glazba* 1.

Gronow, Pekka. 1982. "Ethnic Recordings, an Introduction." In *Ethnic Recordings in America: A Neglected Heritage.* Washington, DC.

Handlin, Oscar. 1951. *The Uprooted.* New York.

Higham, John. 1988. *Strangers in the Land.* New Brunswick, NJ.

Hlad, Michael. 1977. Personal communication. Chicago.

Hlad, Slavco. 1977. Personal communication. Berwyn, IL.

Holjevac, Većeslav. 1967. *Hrvati izvan domovine.* Zagreb.

Hormann, Kosta. 1933. *Narodne pjesme muslimanske.* Sarajevo.

Horvat, Josip. 1975. *Ljudevit Gaj.* Liber, Zagreb.

Hymes, Dell. 1975. "Breakthrough into Performance." In *Folklore, Performance, and Communication,* edited by Kenneth Goldstein and Dan Ben-Amos. The Hague.

Ilić, Petar Z. 1955. "Iz početnog razdoblja tamburaške glazbe." *Tamburaška glazba* 1.

Imamović, Damir. 2005. "Priča o sevdalinci u kontekstu politike kulture i politike identiteta u BiH." In *Na tragu novih politika: kultura i obrazovanje u Bosni i Hercegovini,* edited by Jasmina Husanović. Tuzla.

Ivančan, Ivan. 1965. "Geografska podjela narodnih plesova u Jugoslaviji." *Narodna umjetnost* 3.

———. 1971. *Folklor i scena.* Zagreb.

———. 1977. Personal communication. Zagreb, November.

Jakelić, Mirjana. 1978. Personal communication. Zagreb, March.

Jeić, Jadran. 2010. "Tvornica tamburica i ostalih glazbala Terrezija Kovačić." *Hrvatska revija* 1.

Jelavich, Charles, and Barbara Jelavich. 1965. *The Balkans.* Englewood Cliffs, NJ.

———. 1977. *The Establishment of the Balkan National States, 1804–1920.* Seattle.

Jergan, Željko. 2004. Personal communication. Pittsburgh, November.

Jones, Peter d'Alroy, and Melvin G. Holli. 1981. *Ethnic Chicago.* Grand Rapids, MI.

Jordanoff, Nicholas. 1987. Personal communication. Lake Nebagamon, WI, July.

Jurčević, Tomo. 1979. Personal communication. Cleveland, March.

Jurisich, Matt. 1976. Personal communication. Gary, IN.

Jurkovich, Michael. 2003. Personal communication. Milwaukee, February.

Kanaletić, Josip. 1972. Personal communication. Nerezine, October.

Kapugi, Martin. Personal communication. Chicago, August.

Katz, Jonathon. 2003. "Birth of a Digital Nation." *Wired* 5. http://www.wired.com/5.04/netizen.html

Kirin, Joe. 2002. "Jokirin Around" (blog). September 30. http://www.tamburaland.com.

———. 2003. "Jokirin Around" (blog). January 22. http://www.tamburaland.com.

Kirshenblatt-Gimblett, Barbara. 1975. "A Parable in Context." In *Folklore, Performance, and Communication,* edited by Kenneth Goldstein and Dan Ben-Amos. The Hague.

———. 1983. "Studying Immigrant and Ethnic Folklore." In *Handbook of American Folklore,* edited by Richard M. Dorson. Bloomington.

Kisselgoff, Anna. 1994. "Review/Dance; Mark Morris's Unlikely Collaboration on Bosnia." *New York Times,* April 25.

Klaić, Vjekoslav. 1972. *Povijest Hrvata.* Zagreb.

Klajić, P. 2004. "Tamburaši se vračaju na Petrovaradinsku tvrđavu." *Dnevnik* (Novi Sad) 30 (June).

Kolar, Walter W. 1973. *A History of the Tambura,* vol. 1. Pittsburgh.

———. 1975. *A History of the Tambura,* vol. 2. Pittsburgh.

———. 1987. Personal communication. Lake Nebagamon, WI, August.

Korlović, Franjo. 1959. "Tamburaška glazba u radničkom domu nezavisnih sindikata u Mostaru." *Tamburaška glazba* 4.

Kos, Koraljka. 1969. "Muzički instrumenti u srednjovjekovnoj likovnoj umjetnosti Hrvatske." *Rad Jugoslavenske akademije znanosti i umjetnosti* 351.

———. 1972. "New Dimensions in Folk Music: A Contribution to the Study of Musical Tastes in Contemporary Yugoslav Society." *International Review of the Aesthetics and Sociology of Music* 3.1.

Kosovec, David. 2004. Personal communication. Pittsburgh, May.

Kosovec, Peter. 2003. Personal communication. St. Louis, November.

Kosovec, Sonya. 2008. Personal communication, Chicago, June.

Kuhač, Franjo Š. 1877. "Prilog za povjest glasbe južnoslovjenske: Kulturno-historijska studija." *Rad Jugoslavenske akademije znanosti i umjetnosti* 39.

———. 1878–89. *Južno-slovjenske narodne popievke* 1 (1878), 2 (1879), 3 (1880), 4 (1881). Zagreb.

———. 1893. *Ilirski glasbenici.* Zagreb.

———. 1897. *Ilirski glasbenici.* Zagreb.

———. 1898. *Turski živalj u pučkoj glazbi Hrvata, Srba i Bugara.* Zagreb.

———. 1909. *Osobine narodne glazbe naročito hrvatske.* Zagreb.

———. 1941. *Južno-slavijenske popijevke* 5 (1941). Božidar Širola and Vladoje Dukat, eds. Zagreb.

Lacko, Tony. 1976. Personal communication. Whiting, IN, April.

Lacko-Kelly, Pam. 2004. Personal communication. Pittsburgh, May.

Lang, Milan. 1911–13. "Samobor." *Zbornik za narodni život i običaje južnih slavena.*

Leopold, Siniša. 1995. *Tambura u Hrvata.* Zagreb.

———. 2011. Personal communication. Zagreb.

Lovretić, Ivan. 1897. "Otok." *Zbornik za narodni život i običaje južnih slavena.*

Luketich, Bernard. 1998. Personal communication. Washington, DC, July.

Macartney, Carlyle A. 1969. *The Habsburg Empire, 1790–1918.* New York.

Malcolm, Noel. 1996. *Bosnia: A Short History.* New York.

Malone, Bill C. 2002. *Country Music USA.* Austin, TX.

March, Richard. 1976. "The Tamburitza Tradition in the Calumet Region." *Indiana Folklore* 10.

———. 1982. "Folklor, tradicionalno ekspresivno ponašanje i tamburaška tradicija." *Narodna umjetnost* 19.

————. 2003. "Globalno selo moje malo: Suvremeno tamburaško glazbovanje u Sjedinjenim Američkim Državama." *Narodna umjetnost* 40.2.

————. 2009. "Tamburaštvo u 20. stoljeću: Glazba i simbolika." In *Hrvatska glazba u XX. Stoljeću.* Zagreb.

March, Tonka. 2009. Personal communication. San Pedro, CA, October.

Marincel, Tom. 1977. Personal communication. Ashland, WI, August.

Marošević, Grozdana. 1986. "Kontinuitet i promjene u glazbenom repertoaru u svadbenim običajima Karlovačkog Pokuplja." In *Zbornik od XXXI kongres na Sojuzot na združenijata na folkloristite na Jugoslavija: Radoviš, 1984.* Skopje.

————. 1989. "Kuhačeva etnomuzikološka zadužbina." *Narodna umjetnost* 26.

————. 1995. "The Influence of Folkloristics on Ethnomusicology in Croatia." *Narodna umjetnost* 32.1.

————. 1997. "Podaci o glazbi u monografijama *Zbornika za narodni život i običaje južnih Slavena*." *Narodna umjetnost* 34.2.

Metiljević, Ćamil. 1976. Personal communication. Philadelphia, August.

Miholić, Irena. 2007. "Folk Music Ensembles of Hrvatsko Zagorje." *Narodna umjetnost* 44.1.

Mikolajek, Lisa V. 2001. "Tamburitzan Musician Plays and Sings His Way to International Acclaim." *Duquesne University Times*, November 5.

Milošević, Vlado. 1963. *Bosanske narodne pjesme.* Banja Luka.

————. 1964. *Sevdalinka.* Banja Luka.

Moser, Hans. 1962. "Vom Folklorismus in unserer Zeit." *Zeitschrift für Volkskunde* 58.

Murko, Matija. 1951. *Tragom srpsko-hrvatske narodne epike.* Zagreb.

Njikoš, Julije. 1957. "Značenja Paje Kolarića u tamburaškoj glazbi." *Tamburaška glazba* 2.

————. 1970a. "Glazbena djelatnost Josipa Andrića." *Sveta Cecilija* 40.1.

————. 1970b. *Slavonijo zemljo plemenita: Narodni običaji, pjesme, kola i poskočice.* Osijek.

————. 1978. Personal communication. Zagreb, May.

————. 1988. *Gori lampa nasrid Vinkovaca: Narodni običaji, kola i poskočice vinkovačkog kraja.* Privlaka.

————. 1995. *Pajo Kolarić: Život i rad (1821–76).* Osijek.

O'Dell, Cary. n.d. "Interview with Rudy Orisek." chicagotelevision Alumni Club. http://chicagotelevision.com/RUDY.htm.

Opacich, Milan. 1975–77. Personal communications. Schererville, IN.

————. 2005. *Tamburitza America.* Tucson, AZ.

Palčok, Zoran. 1978. Personal communication. Gospić, May.

Palmer, Alan. 1970. *The Lands Between.* London.

Panović, Zoran. 2006. "Bački meraklija." *Danas* (Belgrade), May 11.

Pintar-Obenauf, Melissa. 2004. Personal communication. Pittsburgh, May.

Popovich, Adam. 1976. Personal communication. Dolton, IL, April.

Popovich, Todor. 1976. Personal communication. Chicago, April.

Prpić, George J. 1971. *The Croatian Immigrants in America.* New York.

Radić, Antun. 1897. "Osnova za sabiranje i proučavanja građe o narodnom životu." *Zbornik za narodni život i običaje južnih slavena.*

———. 1899. "Kolo." *Zbornik za narodni život i običaje južnih slavena.*

Rajković, Zorica. 1978. Personal communication. Zagreb, June.

Rakijaš, Branko. 1974. *Franjo Kuhač.* Zagreb.

Ravlić, Jakša. 1967. Introduction to Andrija Kačić-Miošić, *Razgovor ugodni naroda slovinskoga.* Zagreb.

Reljković, Matija Antun, and Ivo Bogner. 1974. *Satir iliti divji čovik.* Osijek.

Rihtman, Cvjetko. 1951. "Polifoni oblici u narodnoj muzici BiH." *Bilten Instituta za proučavanje folklora.*

———. 1955. "O ilirskom porijeklu polifonih oblika narodne muzike Bosne i Hercegovine." *Rad Kongresa folklorista Jugoslavije, u Puli 1952 i na Bjelašnici.*

———. 1976. "Yugoslav Folk Music Instruments." In *The Folk Arts of Yugoslavia,* edited by Walter W. Kolar. Pittsburgh.

Rihtman-Auguštin, Dunja. 1976. "Pretpostavke suvremenog etnološkog iztraživanja." *Narodna umjetnost* 15.

———. 1978. "Folklor, folklorizam i suvremena publika." *Etnološka tribina* 7–8.

Rosenzweig, Roy. 1983. *Eight Hours for What We Will.* New York.

Rožić, Vatroslav. 1907–8. "Prigorje." *Zbornik za narodni život i običaje južnih slavena.*

Rukstales Hughes, Julie. 2011. Personal communication. Madison, WI, January.

Rydell, Robert W. 1984. *All the World's a Fair.* Chicago.

Šidak, Jaroslav. 1968. *Povijest hrvatskog naroda g. 1860–1914.* Zagreb.

Simic, Andrei. 1973. *The Peasant Urbanites: A Study of Rural-Urban Mobility in Serbia.* Taradale, New Zealand.

Širola, Božidar. 1935. "Gradnje samica i dangubica u Zagorju." *Zbornik za narodni život i običaje* 38.

———. 1940. "Smotre hrvatske seljačke kulture s osobitim obzirom na njihovo značenje za napredak hrvatske muzikologije." *Zbornik za narodni život i običaje južnih slavena.*

———. 1941. *Hrvatska narodna glazba.* Zagreb.

Skertich, Nick. 1996. Personal communication. Hammond, IN, September.

Spiranović, Mladen. 1998. "Ej salaši: Osvrt na rad Zvonka Bogdana." http://web.vip.hr/hrvoje.ban.vip/zvonko/Zvonko%20Bogdan%20Osvrt%20na%2orad%20-%20A%20short%2oretrospective.htm.

Spitzer, Nick. 1992. Comment on "Folk Masters" radio broadcast.

Sporčić, Pajo. 1978. Personal communication. Kuterevo, April.

Spottswood, Richard K. 1990. *Ethnic Music on Records*, vol. 2. Chicago.

Sremac, Stjepan. 1978. "Smotre folklora u Hrvatskoj nekad i danas." *Narodna umjetnost* 15.

———. 2002. "Hrvati i tambura u Sjedinjenim Drzavama." *Etnološka tribina* 25.32.

Stafura, Paul. 1999. Personal communication. St. Louis, September.

Stahuljak, Milan. 1960. "Nepoznate crtice iz života Paje Kolarića." *Tamburaška glazba* 5.

Stančić, Nikša. 1989. *Gajeva "Još Horvatska ni propala" iz 1832–33: Ideologija Ljudevita Gaja u pripremnom razdoblju hrvatskog narodnog preporoda.* Zagreb.

Stepić, Kata. 2004. Personal communication. Pittsburgh, October.

Stjepušin, Janko. 1914. "Rat." *Tamburica* 7 (Sisak).

Svilar, Michael. 1979. Personal communication. Cleveland, March.

Tamburaška glazba. 1957. 2.3.

Tamburitza Association of America. 1970. Program booklet, Tamburitza Testimonial Dinner, Dolton, IL.

Tarailo, Nick. 1977. Personal communication. Merrillville, IN, February.

Vitez, Zorica. 2011. Personal communication. Zagreb, July.

Vrdoljak, Dražen. 1978. Personal communication. Zagreb, March.

Vučinić, Steve. 1977. Personal communication. Chicago, August.

Vucinich, Wayne S. 1975. "Croatian Illyrism: Its Background and Genesis." In *Intellectual and Social Developments in the Habsburg Empire from Maria Theresa to World War I*, edited by Stanley B. Winters and Joseph Held. New York.

Vukosavljev, Sava. 1960. "Marko Nešić." *Tamburaška glazba* 5.

Werner, Kenn. 1980. Personal communication. Milwaukee, December.

Widen, Larry, and Judy Anderson. 2007. *Silver Screens.* Madison, WI.

Wierichs, Loddie. 2003. Personal communication. Kewaunee, WI, March.

Wilson, Duncan. 1970. *The Life and Times of Vuk Stefanović Karadžić.* Oxford.

Winick, Steve. 1993. "From Limerick Rake to Solid Man: The Musical Life of Mick Moloney." *Dirty Linen* 48.

Žmegač, Jasna Čapo. 1995. "Two Scientific Paradigms in Croatian Ethnology: Antun Radić and Milovan Gavazzi." *Narodna umjetnost* 32.1.

Zulić, Mirsad. 2011. Personal communication. Chicago, February.

Web Sources

Sources of information found on the Internet played an important role in the process of updating this work. Although it was not possible for me to do extensive new fieldwork, musicians, music, and other cultural organizations have placed a wealth of information about themselves and their activities on their web pages. Video clips of performances on various types of tambura are abundant on YouTube. E-mail and Facebook contacts with informants enriched the data for this study.

The websites with information about tamburitza are typically very informal in style. The websites from which I gleaned specific information for this work (some of them no longer functioning) are cited in the text and listed below. In addition, in the Discography/Videography section, I have selected several online videos that are good examples of characteristic performances from various aspects of the tamburitza tradition.

Cognizant of the evanescent nature of information on the Internet, I have provided the URLs. Although items may change or disappear on the Internet, I encourage researchers and music enthusiasts to search for tamburitza-related topics; there you will certainly find much pertinent data and enjoyable material.

Croatian Fraternal Union (CFU). http://www.croatianfraternalunion.org/.
Detroit Tamburitza Orchestra. http://detroittamburitzaorchestra.com/.
Donji Andrijevci. http://ww2.donji-andrijevci.net/.
George Tomov. http://www.phantomranch.net/folkdanc/teachers/tomov_g .htm.
KUD "Dučec" Mraclin, Croatia. http://www.kud-ducec.hr/.
Najbolji hrvatski tamburaši. http://www.najboljihrvatskitamburasi.com/.
Sokačko sijelo. http://www.tz-zupanja.hr/.
Tamburaland. http://www.tamburaland.com.
Tamburitza Association of America, Hall of Fame. http://www.tamburitza.org/ TAA/hof.html.
University of Iowa Libraries, Special Collections and University Archives. Records of the Redpath Chautauqua Collection. http://sdrc.lib.uiowa.edu/ traveling-culture/inventory/MSC150.html.
Županje. http://www.zupanja.hr/.

Discography/Filmography

100 tamburaša. *Hrvatska tamburaška rapsodija*. 2010. DVD. Šokadija-Zagreb.
Antologija BH Sevdalinke 2. 2005. CD and booklet. Muzička Produkcija Javnog Servisa BiH.
Antologija BH Sevdalinke 7. 2006. CD and booklet. Muzička Produkcija Javnog Servisa BiH.
The Balkan Records Singles, vol. 1, *Tamburitza from the 1940s*. ca. 2003. CD. Balkan Records BAL CD501.
Bogdan, Zvonko. *Zlatna Kolekcija*. ca. 2008. 2-CD set. Croatia Records.
Duquesne University Tamburitzans. 2010. *Premier*. DVD 2-disc special edition.
Franjo Knežević i tamburaški sastav Berde Band. *Kućo moja, kućo stara*. 1998. CD. Croatia Records.

Grcevich, Jerry. *Daleko je selo moje*. 2001. CD.

Hrašćanski Čestitari. *Od sela do sela*. 1999. CD. Croatia Records.

Kapugi, Martin, and his Tamburitza Orchestra. *Folk Songs and Dances*. ca. 2005. CD. Balkan Records BAL CD-5003/9.

Kosovec, Peter. *Kuda idu godine*. 2002. CD. Tamburaland Productions.

Kosovec, Sonya, and Jerry Grcevich. *Sonya i Jerry: Kao Nekad*. 2011. CD.

Lado. *Iz hrvatske narodne glazbene riznice*. 2005. DVD. Aquarius Records.

Lubich, Edo. *Volume 1*. 2007. CD. Balkan Records BAL CCD-1045.

Mostar Sevdah Reunion. *Mostar Sevdah Reunion*. 2000. CD and booklet. World Connection B.V.

Otrov. *Otrov*. 2005. CD. Udri me letvom productions.

Požega 2000 glazbeni festival "Zlatne Žice Slavonije." *Tamburaske pjesme*. 2000. Croatia Records.

Slabinac, Krunoslav Kičo. *Zlatna Kolekcija*. ca. 2008. 2-CD set. Croatia Records.

Slavonske Lole. *Zlatna Kolekcija*. ca. 2008. 2-CD set. Croatia Records.

Skertich Brothers Best. ca. 2005. CD. Balkan Records BAL CCD-1017.

Tambura Hitova 20 u 10 Godina, vol. 3. 2000. CD. Orfej d.o.o. CD ORF 207.

Tamburaški orkestar Mileta Nikolića. *U Novom Sadu . . .* 2004. CD.

Tamburaški Spomenar. 2010. 6-CD box set. Croatia Records.

Tamburitza from the Balkans to America: 1910–1950. Chris Strachwitz, ed. 2007. 2-CD set. Arhoolie Productions.

Tamburitza Rroma. *Ciganski Poso: Way of the Romani*. ca. 2003. CD.

Vaudeville Comes to Hunkytown: Croatian and Serbian-American Humor from the 1920s. 2003. CD. Balkan Records BAL CCD-1012.

Verni, Milan. *The Music of Milan Verni*, vol. 1. ca. 2005. CD. Balkan Records BAL CCD-1023.

Zlatni Dukati. *Zlatna Kolekcija*. 2008. 2-CD set. Croatia Records.

ONLINE VIDEO RECOMMENDATIONS

100 tamburaša Budimpešta 6. veljača. 2011. VTV. http://www.youtube.com/watch?v=cxqsUOUIIeA.

Ansambl LADO—Slavonija 1 deo/Ensemble LADO—Slavonia dance part 1. http://www.youtube.com/watch?v=ZDAdSlJZQRg&feature=related.

Braća Domić-Bosanac sam rodom od glave do pete. http://www.youtube.com/watch?v=QZ002GGVvaE&feature=related.

Detroit Tamburitza Orchestra—4. http://www.youtube.com/watch?v=nHl-Ao2HStM.

Emina Zecaj-Pita Fata Halil mejhandziju. http://www.youtube.com/watch?v=2LJVyc7MEZQ.

garavuse u Lijepom našom. http://www.youtube.com/watch?v=HXrijLVL9rk.

Krunoslav Kico Slabinac—Becarci. http://www.youtube.com/watch?v=uqdta
    2tKplk&feature=related.
Janka Balaz I Zvonko Bogdan—Osam Tamburasa. http://www.youtube.com/
    watch?v=zqDzpiq-DpA&feature=related.
Lowell Folk Festival Jerry Grcevich 1 Kraj Jezera and Nema Ljepse Djevoke.
    http://www.youtube.com/watch?v=U4UASURbr8E&NR=1.
Otrov—Pozega. http://www.youtube.com/watch?v=H9_0FGAT7dw&NR=1.
Pete Tomicic 85 Birthday Party TAA Extravaganza 2009 Chicago Video 1.
    http://www.youtube.com/watch?v=MnS6v_OqqoA&feature=related.
The Popovich Brothers of South Chicago. http://www.folkstreams.net/film,40.
Sevdah uz saz—Mirsad Zulic—Selam alejk kozarcanko. http://www.youtube
    .com/watch?v=0wwZzXGW1lk.

INFORMANTS

Over the years I have had conversations with many participants in tamburitza
and related musical traditions. The following are those who contributed to my
understanding and knowledge of the subject:

Roko Abramovich
Emina Ahmethodžić-Zečaj
Damir Bačić
Drucilla Badurina-Rouselle
Janika Balaž
Darlene Balog
Jerry Banina
Dario Barišić
Zvonko Bogdan
Željko Bradić
Mark Brajak
Mickey Crnoevich
Bill Cvetnich
Agnes Daniels
Vjeko Dimter
Marko Dreher
John Filcich
Ljubica "Libby" Fill
Mark Forry
Andrija Frani
Katarina Gilg
Tom Glibota
Joe Gornick

John Gornick
Jerry Grcevich
Eli Grubor
George Halaschak
Ken Herak
Mike Hlad
Slavco Hlad
Rose Husnick
George Ivancevich
Nicholas Jordanoff
Dražen Jozić
Michael Jurkovich
Steve Jurkovich
Martin Kapugi
Marinko Katulić
John Kezele
Joe Kirin
Steve Kirin
David Kolar
Walter Kolar
David Kosovec
Dennis Kosovec
Ken Kosovec

Ludwig Kosovec

Peter Kosovec

Sonya Kosovec-Sestili

Mark Kramarich

Richard Krilich

Ivo Kučan

Joan Kutz

Tony Lacko

Pam Lacko-Kelly

Siniša Leopold

Patsy Lucas

Paul Lucas

Walter Mahovlich

Tonka March

Tom Marincel

Tony Markolin

Margy McLain

George Medakovich

Joe Mesich

John Mesich

Ćamil Metiljević

Nikola Miković

Joe Modrich

Walter Naglich

Momčilo Nikolić

Annette Nikoloff

Julije Njikoš

Mike Orlich

Dan Ovanin

Steve Ovanin

Steve Paulich

Steve Petrovich

Melissa Pintar-Obenauf

Jerry Poborsky

Adam Popovich

Eli Popovich

Todor Popovich

Davor Požgaj

Joseph Požgaj

Nancy Požgaj

Stephanie Požgaj

Dawn Radicevich

Mike Radicevich

Hasan Redžović

Mark Richards

Zulfeta Rizvić

Julie Rukstales-Hughes

Frank Sepich

Frank Sepich Jr.

Robert Sestili

Robi Sestili

Leo Sharko

Sharon Sharko

Tim Sharko

Linda Sharko Baker

Paul Stafura

Mike Stosic

Vera Svoboda

Bronko Tarailo

Nick Tarailo

Jack Tomlin

Gordana Trbuhovich-Grasa

Mickey Trivanovich-Arangelovich

Honey Trivanovich-Zimmerman

Frank Valentich

Dražen Vrdoljak

Steve Vucinic

Stefanija Vuljanić-Lemke

Kenn Werner

Michael Werner

Russ Werner

Ryan Werner

Ken Zivic

Peter Zugcic

Index

accordions, 212, 233, 235, 255; in American combos, 167, 179, 180, 181; in *narodni orkestri*, 200, 222; played by Tom Marincel, 147–48; in *sevdalinka*, 151, 157, 158; *smotra* policy on, 106, 110; Yankovic style, 132

adult tamburitza orchestras, 247–51

amateur performers, 5, 75, 252; in Europe, 226, 227, 228, 229, 232–36, 256–58, 262, in nineteenth-century Croatia, 59–61; in post-war Yugoslavia, 107; social status of, 53; in the United States, 119, 141, 170, 214, 218, 221, 239, 245–47

Andreis, Josip, 59

Andrić, Josip, 14, 61; on the origins of tambura, 20, 24–26, 52, 71, 73–75, 81

Bačka, 24, 72, 75, 82, 211; early development of tambura in, 26, 30, 33, 51, 52, 69, 76; groups at *smotra*, 95, 100; influence on

American *tamburaši*, 124, 131, 133; three-toned *tambure* in, 81

bagpipes, 9, 71, 72, 93, 253, 255. See also *gajde; mih*

Bahr, Caroline, 245

Balaž, Janika, 176, 201–2, 203, 204, 221, 229; influence on Jerry Grcevich, 219, 220

Banat, 95, 131, 133, 207, 211; early tambura in, 69, 76, 82; influence on American *tamburaši*, 122, 123, 124

Banat Tamburitza Orchestra, 122–23, 124, 127

Banija, 16, 17, 85, 95, 185, 211; early *tamburaši* in, 69, 70; *samica* playing in, 148, 149; two-stringed tambura of, 32, 33

Barišić, Dario, 207, 266

bećar, bećari, bećarac, 14, 140, 195, 238; as a term for American combo musicians, 170, 176–78

Bećari tamburitza band, 180–81

Belgrade, 72, 101, 104, 202, 207, 229